FALCON FEVER

BOOKS BY TIM GALLAGHER

The Grail Bird
Falcon Fever

FALCON FEVER

A Falconer in the Twenty-first Century

Tim Gallagher

HOUGHTON MIFFLIN COMPANY

BOSTON NEW YORK 2008

www.houghtonmifflinbooks.com

Library of Congress Cataloging-in-Publication Data

Gallagher, Tim.
Falcon fever : a falconer in the twenty-first
century / Tim Gallagher.
p. cm.
ISBN-13: 978-0-618-80575-4
ISBN-10: 0-618-80575-3
1. Gallagher, Tim. 2. Falconers — United States —
Biography. 3. Falconry — United States — Anecdotes.
4. Falconry — Italy — Anecdotes. I. Title.
SK17.G2G35 2008
799.2′32—dc22 2007043923

DESIGN BY DEDE CUMMINGS & CAROLYN KASPER / DCDESIGN

Printed in the United States of America
MP 10 9 8 7 6 5 4 3 2 1

To protect the privacy of individuals, the following names appearing in chapters
8 and 9 are pseudonyms: Andy, Wayne, Eldon, and Cruz.

For Frederick II and all who follow him

The falconer must be diligent and persevering, so much so that as old age approaches he will still pursue the sport out of pure love of it. For, as the cultivation of an art is long and new methods are constantly introduced, a man should never desist in his efforts but persist in its practice while he lives, so that he may bring the art itself nearer to perfection.

— Frederick II of Hohenstaufen

CONTENTS

INTRODUCTION

"YOU'RE NOTHING BUT a falconry bum, and I never want to see you again," she said, slamming the telephone down. By then it was almost midnight. I was supposed to have had dinner with her at seven o'clock and meet her parents for the first time. We'd been planning the dinner for almost a month. Instead, I was huddled shivering in a phone booth beside a field, covered in mud and swamp water from searching all day for my lost falcon.

That was almost forty years ago, when I was seventeen. The sad thing is, I never got the falcon back — or the girlfriend. And this was not the first (or last) time something like that happened to me. For many years, this was the story of my life — a person who lived and breathed to hunt game with trained hawks and falcons.

I've been a falconer for a very long time. I can't say why exactly, but something about falconry completely captured my passion and spirit as a twelve-year-old and has held me enthralled ever since. I think about what drew me to falconry more and more as I get older. As a kid, I always loved nature, and I'd been training and handling various animals — dogs, parakeets, frogs, toads, snakes, lizards, pigeons, sparrows — since early childhood, but for me, from the time I first put a falcon on my fist, no other interest ever came close to competing with falconry. Even when I quit flying birds of prey for a few years at one point in my life, falconry was always there, lying just below the surface like an incurable affliction temporarily in remission.

Why is that? What is it about my personality that makes me so susceptible to this kind of obsession — an addiction really? And what is it about falconry that seems to attract such over-the-top devotees? An entire subculture exists outside the mainstream of American society consisting of people like me who still use the ancient training techniques and language of falconry. I suspect almost any of us could communicate effectively with most medieval falconers if we happened to be dropped somehow into a twelfth-century hawking establishment. But we are not some kind of creative anachronism society. We borrow freely from both ancient and modern techniques, equipment, and medical expertise to train and care for our birds. We just love raptors and thrill to see them hunt game. There aren't many of us — just a few thousand in the United States — but I can't think of any group as enthusiastic about their endeavor as falconers.

I'm sure psychologists would have a field day examining our addiction. I'm still trying to puzzle it out myself. Of course, the birds are beautiful. To my mind, nothing else in nature rivals the power and elegance of a raptor in flight. Most people who see a wild falcon dive at prey remember the sight for the rest of their lives — the sheer speed, the roar of the wind through the bird's flight feathers, the frightening violence. I'm sure that's all part of the lure of these birds for me, but there is so much more. I've never been the kind of person who takes the killing of an animal lightly. I love animals. I'm fascinated by everything about them, and I've spent much of my life observing and photographing nature — a passive witness to its wondrous spectacle. But when I'm flying a raptor, I'm a different animal, as fierce and determined as a rampaging wolverine to flush game for my bird. If falconry didn't exist, I would probably never have become a hunter. That's but one of the many paradoxes in my life I'm still working out.

The magical, intuitive bond that develops between a falconer and a trained raptor is a great attraction for me and is one of the things that keeps me getting up before dawn, day after day, on workdays and weekends, through autumn and early winter, trudging through the fields in all kinds of weather to fly my eight-year-old peregrine falcon, Macduff. I named him after the Shakespearian character who killed Macbeth in a ferocious fight at the end of the play. "Lay on, Macduff," says Macbeth in his famous last words. "Damned be he who first cries, 'Hold. Enough.'"

That's just the way I feel about it. As long as Macduff is willing to keep flying hard, soaring high above me and hammering game in blistering vertical power dives, I'll be damned if I quit hunting with him.

As I step into his flight chamber to pick him up on this blustery December morning in 2005, he flaps his wings powerfully, eager to fly. I lift him quickly onto my gauntleted fist, slip a leather hood on his head to keep him calm, and carry him out to my car. While most of my neighbors still lie sleeping, I load up my gear and drive away in search of game.

This morning is more special than most. Exactly 755 years earlier, on December 13, 1250, Frederick II of Hohenstaufen, Holy Roman Emperor and King of Sicily and Jerusalem, departed this life. I'm sure few took time to note this anniversary, besides a handful of eccentric falconers like me, who feel a bond with Frederick that has endured through the centuries. You see, Frederick II is like the patron saint of falconry — although the Catholic Church is unlikely to grant him sainthood any time soon; he spent most of his life at odds with a succession of popes and was excommunicated twice. He was a lifelong falconer as well as a scientist, scholar, poet, and architect, and he authored a massive tome on falconry, *De Arte Venandi cum Avibus* (*On the Art of Hunting with Birds*), that is still a useful guide for training falcons. You could say I've been obsessed with Frederick II for most of my life — really for as long as I've been a falconer.

I consider Frederick to be the spiritual forebear of all falconry bums. He lived the life of a transient monarch, with no single city to call his home: just a series of castles and hunting lodges he visited to go hawking. It's a telling fact that he suffered the worst defeat of his entire reign when he went off hawking during the siege of Parma, leaving his camp lightly defended. The people of the besieged city stormed the camp, slaughtering Frederick's soldiers, burning everything to the ground, and stealing his entire treasury — a staggering defeat that he never really got over. It sounds like something I might have done.

⁓

IT IS A chilly morning and several inches of snow lie on the ground as I drive through the low wooded hills and farmland surrounding Ithaca, New York, making my usual game-hawking circuit, checking ponds and small creeks for ducks. Frederick called hunting ducks with a falcon "hawking at the brook." His falconry treatise — a classic medieval illuminated manuscript — has a beautiful hand-painted illustration of a medieval falconer who has stripped naked and is swimming across a lake to get to his peregrine, sitting on a duck kill on the other side of the water. I'm hoping I won't have to do that today in the subfreezing weather, but you never know.

Some of the ponds I visit are already frozen, but I know of a few spring-fed ponds and running creeks that usually have open water well into winter. At the first pond, in a vast open field surrounded by woodlands, I spot at least two mallards, though it's difficult to see most of the pond because of its high banks and the trees and shrubs along the sides.

A mallard is big for Macduff to tackle, weighing more than twice as much as he does. A female peregrine would be more appropriate for mallard hawking. As with most hawks and falcons, male peregrines are about one third smaller than female peregrines and better suited for catching smaller quarry. (The correct term for a male falcon is tiercel, which comes from the French word *tierce*, meaning "third.") But Macduff has taken many mallards over the years, and I'm sure he'll put on a good effort whether he catches a duck or not.

Parking my car behind the trees, I walk quietly down a path through the woods. It's quiet. The only sound is the breeze whistling through the canopy of the trees and the high-pitched tinkle of the brass bells on Macduff's legs. Falconers have used bells like these for centuries to help locate their birds whether they are flying high above or sitting in cover on a kill. Macduff also wears a tiny radio transmitter, which is like a high-tech bell I can use to track him down from several miles away with a telemetry receiver.

When I reach the edge of the field, I slip off Macduff's hood and hold him into the wind. He shakes his feathers, looks quickly around in all directions as he flaps his wings, and explodes powerfully from my fist. He flies straight away from me for nearly a hundred yards, then starts circling upward, pumping his wings hard to gain altitude as quickly as possible. If the ducks or other game spot a falcon before it has gained enough altitude to make an effective stoop (or power dive), they sometimes flush prematurely and slip away to safety. That won't happen today. He's already high enough to keep them sitting tightly in the water.

I take a moment to evaluate the situation — to figure out the direction and strength of the wind and which angle of attack would make the most sense. Should I flush from the east side of the pond or the west? Which would give my bird the best chance to catch a duck? A falcon has to know that its trainer is an effective tactician in the field. If I'm always flushing game at the wrong time or in a bad situation — or failing to find game at all — a falcon will quickly lose respect for my abilities and go off hunting for itself. What would Frederick have done in this situation? I opt to approach the pond from the east side, giving my bird a downwind stoop on the mallards.

By this time, Macduff is so high I have a hard time spotting him as he flies in broad circles that are more than a hundred yards wide. I finally see him, a tiny speck right above me, breasting the wind like a gull. I break for the pond, sprinting as fast as I can in my neoprene chest waders. I keep low to the ground, bent over to stay out of sight below the raised bank of the pond. Taking a last look at Macduff to make sure he's in a good position, I charge the pond, leaping over the side and plunging up to my waist in the icy water with a great splash. A dozen mallards — far more than I had seen — burst from the other side of the pond. I know this will be good.

Macduff is still circling, almost like the ducks aren't there. But it's just a tactical maneuver; he doesn't want to commit to a stoop if there's a chance the birds will drop back into the safety of the pond. (Once ducks do that, it's difficult to flush them again.) The ducks make three or four circles, seventy feet above the pond, and then break away across the open field, headed for a nearby river.

I lose sight of Macduff as he folds up and turns downward, going into a powerful stoop. A second later, I spot him again with my ten-power binoculars as he plummets earthward, and I hear the amazing whistle of wind blowing through his flight feathers. When he hits the duck — a huge drake mallard — with his feet, it sounds like the crack of a Major League batter hitting a home run. The duck does three or four somersaults and slams into the ground, while my falcon pulls up from the dive, swooping up perhaps two or three hundred feet with his wings held back, then drops down onto the duck.

I run to him as fast as I can, in case I need to help out. But it's all over; Macduff is biting the back of the duck's neck, severing its spinal cord with his powerful bill.

It's a nice moment sitting on the ground beside a falcon on a kill. To me, it's one of the wonders of falconry that a bird this innately wild would accept my presence so completely. I reach over and help hold the dead mallard as he plucks its feathers. A few minutes later, I slip my fingers inside the duck's chest cavity and pull out its heart, which falcons relish, holding it out for him to eat, steaming in the frosty morning air. After letting him feed on the duck for a short time, I lift him onto my fist with a piece of meat I had in my game bag, while hiding the duck carcass from view. Using a falconer's sleight of hand, I accomplish this without Macduff suspecting for an instant that he's been robbed. I intend to take the rest home for a duck dinner with my family.

It's only eight A.M., and I've already had a great flight to start my day. In another half hour, I'll be back to everyday life, driving to work, and Macduff will be sitting puffed up on his perch, well fed and contented. It sounds easy, but not every day goes like this. Far more often, I come home with an empty game bag. Hundreds of things can go wrong in falconry. But catching a lot of game is not the reason I fly hawks. "The falconer's primary aspiration should be to possess hunting birds that he has trained through his own ingenuity to capture the quarry he desires in the manner he prefers," wrote Frederick II. "The actual taking of prey should be a secondary consideration." These are words I live by. If I wanted to kill a lot of ducks, I'd get a shotgun. New York State's bag limit for mallards is currently four per day, a number that can easily be reached with a firearm. With a falcon, I'm happy if I take one. For me, seeing a great flight is everything, whether the falcon catches its quarry or not.

Some people say it's unfair and cruel to attack poor, defenseless waterfowl with a trained falcon. Ducks are anything but defenseless — especially when pitted against a predator like a falcon with which they've evolved side by side for countless millennia. All of the world's wild animals are hard-wired with strategies for survival. Mallards are big and fast and tough. They can take a hard pounding and escape unscathed. It's an enormous challenge for Macduff to tackle and hold a mallard. Smaller ducks have different strategies. Green-winged teal are quick and slippery; they can turn on a dime and will throw themselves hard onto the ground and come out flying in the opposite direction, leaving a falcon baffled. Pintails are intelligent and spooky, making them more difficult to approach. I'm endlessly fascinated by what animals will do to escape a predator; it is in those situations that you see them at their best. I rarely have any regrets when a duck or other prey eludes my falcon.

To me, falconry at its highest level is an art form in which the canvas is the entire sky. For my part as a falconer, I set everything up and let the falcon complete the work of art. I'm not the first person to describe falconry as an art. Again, that would be Frederick II, who considered falconry the noblest of arts. When I first became interested in falconry as a twelve-year-old in the early 1960s, the only book on the subject I could find at the local library was a 1943 edition of Frederick's book, which translators Casey A. Wood and F. Marjorie Fyfe titled *The Art of Falconry*. It took months, but I read it from cover to cover and then went back to study the sections that interested me most. What an amazing piece of literature. It covers much more than falconry — it is a scientific work of the first order and one of the first works of ornithology, looking at the behavior, anatomy, and physiology of birds.

I view Frederick as an old friend. Through his book, written in the thirteenth century, he taught me how to train falcons. I made my first jesses (the thin leather straps put on a falcon's legs) from his patterns. I took my first game with a falcon using his carefully written advice. But more than that, I think Frederick II — and the sport of falconry he championed — helped me through some of the most trying times in my life. I believe if it were not for falconry I would not be alive today.

As I sat in the field with Macduff on the anniversary of Frederick's death, I was fifty-five years old — the same age as Frederick when he passed away. Besides being a sobering reminder of my own mortality, it made me think there would never be a better time to take stock of who I am and to examine the central role falconry has played through most of my life. Did I have an innate affinity with birds of prey that made it inevitable for me to become a falconer? I used to think so. Or was falconry just a way for me to escape a brutal, depressing childhood — a way to create my own private world, forging deep relationships with the wildest, freest creatures in nature?

I didn't know the answers to any of these questions, but I wanted badly to find out. At that moment an idea started taking shape in my mind. I would begin a personal quest, examining experiences in my life that I'd blocked from my mind for decades. I would spend a year on a journey of self-discovery, using falconry and Frederick II as keys to my psyche. To accomplish this, I knew I would first have to trace my earliest memories as a boy in England and relive my many personal trials and tragedies. It would not be easy — at times it would be harrowing — but I knew it was the only way I would ever come to a full understanding of who I am and why.

A lot of people will be surprised by the revelations I unveil in this book — especially those who didn't know me when I was growing up and got into serious trouble with the law. I have since become what most would consider a model citizen, working at a respected university and raising my family in an idyllic farm village in upstate New York. It wasn't always like that.

During my year of personal exploration, I decided I would immerse myself in falconry in a way I had not done since my teens and twenties. I saw it all taking shape in my imagination. I would travel to Wyoming and watch falconers hunt hard-flying winter sage grouse — perhaps the pinnacle of the sport in modern times. I would visit the heather-covered Highlands of Scotland and see trained peregrine falcons stoop from the clouds at red grouse as my falconry forebears had done for ages. I would go crow hawking on horseback in northern England, watching the dark birds circle up into the sky with a falcon in pursuit. I would attend the annual field meet of the North American Falconers' Association as I had done as a sixteen-year-old some forty years earlier. And I would finish by traveling through the fertile lands of southern Italy that Frederick adored, visiting the place where he was born, the place he died, the amazing castles he built, and finally the red porphyry sarcophagus that holds his earthly remains to gain a fuller understanding of what falconry and Frederick II mean to me.

This would be my Frederick II year, an exploration of the inner workings of my own mind and spirit and the nature of the art that Frederick and I share. Why was I drawn to predatory birds at such an early age? Why did they become such an overwhelming passion, eclipsing everything else in my life? What was it that made me want to join falcons in the chase — to hunt other animals with them? I can't explain it, but I know Frederick felt the same sense of awe and mystery about falconry as I; I'm only following in his footsteps.

PART I

MY BACK
PAGES

1

THE FALCON DREAMER

MY DAD WAS one of those people with so much charisma and such a gift as a storyteller that everywhere he went people seemed to gather around him and hang on his every word. That's how my mother got hooked. It was during World War II, and she was volunteering at a dinner for servicemen on leave from the war. She saw my dad dressed in his Royal Navy uniform, surrounded by a group of Boy Scouts sitting in rapt attention, listening to his tales of great sea battles with colossal explosions and sinking ships and dying men — the best and the worst of the human experience.

Dad really knew how to spin a story, drawing his listeners slowly in, painting vivid images with his words, providing harrowing details of the most trying events imaginable. Then his blue eyes would glisten and he'd flash the most engaging smile, launching into a self-deprecating side story, relieving the tension of the moment as everyone burst out laughing. Then he'd start again on another incredible story plucked from his wartime naval experience. And to look at his face as he spoke, there was no question of his honesty and authority — everyone knew in their hearts that everything he said was true.

At the age of twenty-four, he was already a veteran of so many all-out naval battles, he didn't have to tell tall tales; the truth was enough. He was at the servicemen's dinner only because his ship had just been sunk, and he had been given a two-week survivor's leave. It's funny to think that the only reason my sisters and I are here is because his ship went down. And this was not the only time this happened to him. During the course of the war, he was sunk three times, twice through enemy action and once because the ship's engine exploded.

My mother was drawn in as she was walking past, carrying some plates of food, and she paused to listen. My dad caught sight of her and said, "I'll see you after," then went back to his storytelling. They got together at the end of the evening. He spent the rest of his leave with her, and they were married soon after. Everything happened fast during the war. And my mother was particularly vulnerable to his charms. She had already lost her father — who had been a wartime reserve policeman, taking on the job so younger policemen could enter the military and fight, and who had been killed in a Luftwaffe bombing raid — and her eldest brother, Frank, a sailor who was missing in action after his ship was sunk by a German U-boat.

But Dad had problems. I guess he would have been diagnosed as manic-depressive or bipolar — if he had ever gone to a psychiatrist. Or maybe he was suffering from some kind of battle stress. What those fighting men of his generation went through is barely imaginable. We talk about the psychological problems faced by men who served a few months in Vietnam or, more recently, in Iraq. But for my father and the other Royal Navy sailors, the war began in September 1939 and lasted all the way to V.E. Day in 1945. And they were always on the frontlines — strafed by Luftwaffe planes as they were running convoys through the frigid northern seas to supply Leningrad, or blockading Axis ports for months in the Atlantic and the Mediterranean — always in the thick of it, always surrounded by imminent death and destruction.

My father had run away and joined the Royal Navy when he was fifteen years old, in the mid-1930s. Of course, the timing of his enlistment couldn't have been worse. The Royal Navy was on the frontlines immediately when war was declared in 1939, long before the Royal Air Force got into the fray in the Battle of Britain. Really the only reason the Germans needed to launch an air war against England was because the Royal Navy was such a formidable obstacle to invasion. So the ships my dad served on were rushed here and there, wherever a convoy needed protection, wherever a port needed to be blockaded. One time he was manning a naval artillery piece when a German plane came in low across the sea, heading straight for him firing its guns. Bullets ricocheted all around him, making flaming sparks as they slammed into the armor plating. Miraculously, he was untouched — but dead sailors lay all around him, including his best friend who sat beside him at the same gun, a bullet hole in his forehead and a serene smile on his face: an image my father would carry for the rest of his life. Dad had been at Omaha Beach on D-day, ferrying American troops ashore under the raking fire of German artillery, offering each man a sip of rum, then saying, "Let's go, Yank," and sending them wading into the living hell onshore. He was struck in the back by shrapnel that day.

So perhaps my father's psychological problems were understandable, but it didn't make it any easier to live with him. Dad was the kind of person who for weeks or even months on end could be so bright and optimistic and full of energy, it seemed he could do anything. And then his mood would change as quickly as a cloud passing over the sun, and he'd become dark and brutal. My sisters and I learned to read his face instantly, even at a distance, and to avoid him when the pendulum of his spirit swung downward. But sometimes there was no escape; sometimes his mood became so black he would turn to his navy fix-all, a bottle of rum or whiskey or gin — it didn't matter which — and he would obliterate his mind. At that point, he might do anything. Turn into a raging beast, throwing the television through the window; pulling over the refrigerator so it landed on the kitchen floor in a great clatter of broken ketchup bottles, spilt milk, and shattered eggs; smashing, ripping, or cutting clothing, furniture, pictures on the walls, or anything in sight; slapping my mother across the face and breaking her eyeglasses; or staggering around the living room holding a huge butcher knife against his chest and threatening to kill himself as my sisters and I lay huddled and trembling in a corner.

After one of these episodes, we often found ourselves moving — to another house, to another city, sometimes to another country — to get some new neighbors, to get a new job, to start a new life. And after the boil was lanced, after his fury was spent, Dad was all contrition. Let's forgive and forget. Let's start anew. Life will be great. We can do anything. And the cycle would begin again. Sometimes his explosions were so horrendous that the family broke up for a time. But then he'd throw on a charm offensive and before long we'd be back together again.

It is perhaps telling that one of my earliest memories of my father was when I was three or four years old and was living with my mother and my older sister Maureen at my grandmother's house in England. This was apparently one of those times when my parents were separated. My dad came over sullen and unshaven, probably drunk. I remember he was wearing a long tan overcoat, and he and my mother were arguing loudly in front of the house. My grandmother, who was in her seventies, tried to intervene, and he shoved her so hard she fell to the ground. Then we all yelled at him to go — even me — and he strode off down the street.

The next we heard, my father had moved to Canada. This was in the mid-1950s, when Canada was eagerly courting potential immigrants. He began writing to my mother saying how great things were going to be. He had a good job and an apartment in Toronto. Things were starting to boom in Canada; opportunities abounded. He would soon be able to afford a house. Why not come with the kids and join him?

After leaving the navy he had worked in a variety of sales jobs, and he excelled at them. With his charm and his gift for gab he could sell anything to anyone. And even working for straight commission, he usually made a good salary.

It wasn't long before Maureen and I found ourselves on a train one night with our mother headed for Southampton, where we would board a ship bound for Montreal. My mother was cutting herself off with three thousand miles of ocean from anyone who could help us if my father blew up again. And it was inevitable that it would happen again . . . and again.

My younger sister, Janet, was born in Ajax, a small town in Ontario, less than a year after we rejoined my father. We lived there somewhat peacefully for a few years. I really liked it there. We lived near the woods, and my friends and I would spend hours running wild, climbing trees, searching for unusual animals, and exploring new places. But after a couple of scuffles that cost him the respect of his coworkers and neighbors, my dad wanted to move again — this time either to San Diego or Mexico City. He had visited San Diego as a young sailor before the war, and it had seemed like paradise to him. I'm not sure what the attraction was with Mexico City, but after the U.S. Immigration Service gave us the nod a few months later, we headed for California, all of us — two adults and three children — packed into a tiny Renault Dauphine with a roof rack strapped to the top piled high with our belongings.

But my dad's mental condition only got worse: he was drinking more than ever and becoming ever more abusive. We left him for a couple of weeks one time when we lived in San Diego. My mother had been working part time in an office, and the family of one of her friends there, who knew about my father, let us stay with them. But it didn't last long. And when we went back with my father, he made my mother quit her job. A short time later, we left San Diego entirely, moving north to the Long Beach area.

My parents broke up a couple of more times there. On one of the times we were apart, my father invited my mother to his apartment and then brandished a loaded rifle in her face, saying he was going to kill her. It was a World War II Italian carbine, exactly like the one Lee Harvey Oswald later supposedly used to assassinate John F. Kennedy. She told him to go ahead and shoot her, which he ultimately decided not to do. After he moved back in with us, he kept the rifle and a pack of ammunition in the bedroom closet.

One night a couple of years later as he was on another rampage, I quietly got the gun and took it to my room. My plan was to shoot him fatally and then turn the gun on myself, ridding my family of this terrible burden. But I wasn't sure I could go through with it cold, so I brought the gun to my room to practice.

As my father walked drunkenly around the house, cursing and throwing dishes at the wall and breaking furniture, I was working the bolt action on the unloaded rifle, releasing the safety catch, holding the barrel to my forehead, and pulling the trigger. I repeated the whole process again and again and again — just to get used to the idea of it, just to somehow get myself on autopilot so I could go through with it.

By the time I felt ready, it was well past midnight, and I could still hear my dad laughing wildly and muttering to himself, though he wasn't breaking things anymore. I took a deep breath and let it out slowly. Then I put a clip with five cartridges into the rifle and worked the bolt action once, shoving a cartridge firmly into the chamber. I pushed against the safety catch with my thumb. It was a spring-loaded safety catch on the side of the bolt, and it always took all my might to budge it, pushing hard against the knurled metal, but this time it was harder than ever. I felt so weak — so detached from everything in life and yet also so determined. I finally got it to move to the off position.

I could feel my heart pounding in my brain and my ears were ringing. I closed my eyes and took two more deep breaths then stood up and walked out of my room. Nothing could stop me now.

As I walked into the living room, my father was slumped in an easy chair, muttering to himself and laughing, holding a whiskey bottle in his hand. He didn't see me as I stood there five feet in front of him. I raised the rifle to my shoulder and sighted down the barrel at his forehead. He still didn't see me. Then he chuckled for an instant and passed out, his head slumping to the side. The bottle crashed loudly to the floor, breaking my trance, and I felt all the energy, all the resolve, drain instantly from me. I could barely hold the rifle. I walked slowly back to my room and slid the gun under my bed. I was drenched in a cold sweat with my teeth chattering as I crawled under the covers and fell into a nightmarish sleep.

But I'm getting ahead of myself. This would happen later, at the ripe age of thirteen. I'm so glad I didn't go through with it — not just for my own sake but because I know it would have destroyed my family, not saved it, as I had hoped. It all seems like a distant dream now. I wish it were a dream.

❧

IN SIXTH GRADE, my friend Roger and I were obsessed with pigeons. Although we lived in an apartment block in Lakewood, near Long Beach, we secretly built a pigeon coop on top of the building. We would climb on top of the second-floor railing of the apartment, grab onto the edge of the roof, and haul ourselves up. Getting back down safely was even harder. We got several young pigeons from Roger's friends in North Long Beach, where Roger used to live. When the birds got older, we would swap them with his friends for birds that they had raised. Because pigeons always return to the loft where they were raised, we were able to send messages to his friends, and they could reply using the pigeons we raised. But after several months of this, the apartment superintendent discovered the pigeon coop and tore it down. Our birds kept returning to the spot where it had stood and would hang around the top of the building. They seemed lost. We kept feeding them, but we were never able to build a loft again; the superintendent was watching too closely.

Roger and I would walk miles on most Saturdays to get to the Dominguez Hills, which, at that time, seemed spectacularly remote and wild, with rabbits, foxes, birds, and other wildlife. It wasn't quite as good as the area where I had lived near San Diego — and nowhere near as good as my old woods in Canada — but a nice place for a pair of budding young naturalists to hang out.

Roger had a brother who was a couple of years older and couldn't have been more different. While Roger spent all his time communing with nature or playing with his pets, Gary hung around with a crowd of young toughs, cruising through the bad parts of town in a lowered Chevy sedan, drinking, popping pills, and picking fights. Roger's hair was dark, unruly, and rarely combed. Gary's was light brown and slicked back, except for the front, which rose up in a pompadour.

I don't know what Roger's father did for a living: maybe nothing. He was always hanging around like Ozzie Nelson gone to seed — a gray presence with a pencil-thin mustache and red capillaries showing in his face from years of hard drinking. He usually wore an old fedora and a gray suit, and he seemed like someone from a faded black-and-white 1940s movie.

Roger's mother was a hard worker. She waited tables six days a week at a restaurant at the edge of Lakewood Plaza and still found time to cook meals, clean house, and take care of everyone. I liked her. She was just like Roger, with the same dark hair, brown eyes, and amiable nature. She was one of the nicest parents I knew. But sometimes I noticed she had a busted lip or a bruise on her face. No one ever mentioned it.

Roger was my best friend — maybe one of the best friends I've ever had. We were inseparable. But my family moved to Orange County, about twenty miles away, shortly after I started seventh grade. My dad still worked selling appliances at a department store in Lakewood Plaza, so on Saturdays I would hitch a ride with him so I could get together with Roger. He and I would go to the restaurant where his mother worked and get ice cream or a coke. Sometimes we'd go to a movie. This went on for two or three months, until one day Roger didn't show up where I was supposed to meet him. His mother wasn't at the restaurant that day, so I walked the mile or so to his apartment. I knocked on the door for several minutes and then tried to look through the window. I couldn't see anything; the Venetian blinds were closed. I was just about to go when the door opened a few inches and Roger's dad called out. "What is it? What do you want?"

"I was supposed to meet Roger today," I said.

"Well, he's not here," he said, slamming the door.

It was dark inside. Roger's dad looked like he hadn't shaved or gotten dressed in days. I didn't want to say anything to my dad about it, so I started walking to kill time. I have no idea how far I walked, but at least eight hours had passed by the time I met my dad and went home.

I came back the following Saturday, pretending that nothing had happened and I was going to meet Roger again. I stopped at the restaurant, but the manager told me Roger's mother didn't work there anymore. When I went to his apartment, the door was unlocked, so I peeked inside. All the furniture was gone. I never saw Roger again.

Although we never flew hawks together, in some ways I consider Roger one of my earliest falconry friends. We had both seen a movie on Walt Disney Presents a couple of years before we met. It was called *Rusty and the Falcon* and told the story of a twelve-year-old boy who lives in a mining community out West. With few other people his own age to hang around with, he spends hours by himself, often playing in an abandoned mineshaft, his own private place in the world. One day he finds an injured peregrine falcon. He befriends the bird and eventually trains it to be his hunting companion.

Roger and I had talked about the movie a few times and wondered what it would be like to train a hunting falcon. In some ways, it seemed like a natural progression for us. We both loved to train animals and had been doing it most of our lives. I had gotten a parakeet for my sixth birthday, and spent most of my spare time in first grade working with my bird, named Billy, getting him accustomed to me and teaching him to ride around on my shoulder or sit on my finger. And I'd had a couple of dogs in the past. Roger and I sometimes raised young house sparrows that had fallen from nests in front of our apartment. And then the pigeons. Falcons were just the next step. I didn't realize that for me they would be the last step.

As I was later training my first hawks, I often thought how great it would be to run into Roger again and bring him up to date on everything that had happened since the last time I saw him. I could tell him all about falconry and take him to see my falcon hunt. I even imagined he might have started flying hawks, too, and that maybe we'd see each other at a falconry meet someday, but it didn't happen.

℮

THE ONE GOOD thing about moving to Orange County was that we had a big brand-new tract house, which had a huge wedge-shaped backyard because it was at the end of a cul-de-sac. And it was completely fenced in. Right away we bought two dogs from the SPCA in Laguna Beach. The first was a beautiful one-year-old husky named King; the second a goofy three-month-old pup we named Rex — so both dogs basically had the same name, one in English, the other in Latin. Rex was golden red with a white patch on his chest and three white paws. He obviously had a lot of golden retriever in him, but was more sleek and agile. He grew up to be beautiful. King was shy at first, but quickly got used to us. He had an endearing habit of sticking his nose under my elbow and throwing my arm up around his head so I'd pet him. But his time with us was too short. He became ill with distemper just a couple of weeks after we got him and died pitifully. I worried for weeks that the pup would catch this awful disease. I repeatedly scrubbed the areas where King had been with cleanser and, thankfully, Rex stayed healthy.

I also had some pet guinea pigs and a rabbit that I'd had in Lake-wood, and we soon added a few more creatures. A friend in Long Beach gave me a huge desert tortoise that he'd had for a few years, and a while later someone else gave me another one. And our parents gave us a couple of ducklings for Easter that soon grew up into big spooky white things that ran amok in the yard. I don't know if it was the size of the yard or what, but we quickly started filling it up with livestock like a farmyard.

I made a new friend named Jerry during my first couple of months at my new school. A tall, stocky kid with dark straight hair and blue-green eyes, Jerry lived with his parents and two older sisters in a tract house five or six miles away in Stanton. We would ride bikes together and go exploring in local fields. (At that time, there was still a lot of open land in the area, which is now wall-to-wall houses and strip malls.)

Like Roger, Jerry enjoyed animals and the natural world but there the similarities ended. He had a way of teasing people endlessly and was constantly playing tricks or practical jokes on his friends. Jerry had a young hoodlum side. He would sometimes steal cash from his mother's purse and also engage in pointless acts of vandalism, blasting streetlights late at night with a .22 rifle. He shot out all of the Christmas lights on the eaves of his parents' house with a BB gun, hitting them one by one from his bedroom window.

Jerry also had a habit of picking trouble with authority figures. Once when we were riding our bikes together and saw a police car drive by with its windows down, Jerry shouted, "Dirty Fuzz!" The policemen immediately turned their squad car around and flipped on the red lights. (I guess it was a slow crime day in Buena Park.) They hauled us both to the police station and made our parents pick us up, which did not endear Jerry to my father.

Jerry was already getting interested in falconry when I met him. He'd had an unusual encounter a few months earlier with a semitame male kestrel that had started hanging around his neighborhood. A kestrel is the smallest North American falcon and one of the prettiest, with dark intense eyes and long, beautiful pointed wings. Although the bird did not have jesses on his legs or other signs that it had been a falconry bird, someone had obviously raised it from a nestling. It had little fear of humans and would catch small pieces of raw steak in midair as Jerry tossed them up. The bird hung around for a few weeks.

Jerry desperately wanted to capture the kestrel and train it to fly back to him on command. One day, he saw it go to roost on top of a small light fixture above a neighbor's back door and figured this was his big chance. He thought he could sneak up to the corner of the house then reach around with a long-handled fishing net and snag it. If he were quick and accurate, he'd soon have the bird.

Jerry waited until the neighbors had gone to sleep and then sneaked into their yard, staying close to the wall as he made his way to the corner of the house. He took a peek around the corner and could make out the bird's shape, barely four feet away, with its head tucked in, sleeping soundly. Jerry could feel his heart pounding wildly. He took a deep breath and let it out slowly and quietly, trying to calm down. Finally he was ready. The time had come. He swung the net around the side of the house, lunging as far as he could to get it dead center over the small lamp where the kestrel sat. And it worked. He had the kestrel firmly in the net and was trying to lift the whole thing away from the light fixture, without letting the kestrel slip away.

And then everything fell apart. The scared kestrel dug his talons into Jerry's bare hands, causing him to cry out in pain. Then the kestrel began screaming loudly in an incessant high-pitched distress call — *kle-kle-kle-kle-kle-kle*. Dogs barked. Lights went on all through the neighborhood. In the middle of all this, the kestrel slipped away and flew off over the rooftops, never to be seen again. But this was enough to hook Jerry on falconry.

The two of us started neglecting our classes. All we wanted to do was search through books for pictures of hawks so we could sketch them and learn as much as possible about how they lived and how to train them. We didn't find much at first. Few falconry books were available at that time, but I finally found a copy of Frederick II's book in the public library. It was just what I was looking for, and I checked it out immediately. I kept renewing it every two weeks for months. The librarian became annoyed, because she thought someone else might want to read it. But I explained that it was such a long, detailed book, it would take me months to absorb it all. And besides, the library had owned the book for several years, and no one else had ever checked it out. She finally made a special exception for me and said I could keep it until someone requested it. So began my in-depth study of falconry and of Frederick II.

The English translation of *De Arte Venandi cum Avibus* included additional material about Frederick II and pictures of some of his castles in Italy, which got me interested in him as a man and not just as a falconer. Frederick was great. He did many things that made the religious establishment furious, because he was such a freethinker. And he didn't care. He always did what he felt was right, and to hell with the consequences.

Frederick was the consummate scientist. At a time when many people believed that birds disappeared into earthen burrows and hibernated for the winter, Frederick postulated that birds migrate south to warmer climes when the weather turns cold. He insisted that science should be based on solid, verifiable observations, not speculation or hearsay, and he took Aristotle to task for many of the misstatements in his great natural history work, *Liber Animalium* (*Book of Animals*). "We find [in Aristotle's book] many quotations from other authors whose statements he did not verify and who, in their turn, were not speaking from experience," wrote Frederick II. "Entire conviction of the truth never follows mere hearsay."

Frederick also pointed out that because Aristotle did not have the benefit of being a falconer, perhaps his lack of a basic understanding of natural history was not surprising. Of course, insisting on having empirical evidence for every phenomenon did not endear him to the medieval church and may have been the root cause of many of his problems with a series of popes.

I started reading anything I could get my hands on about Frederick II — books, scholarly articles. The local libraries were woefully inadequate for this research, but I started requesting interlibrary loans. Frederick's story was endlessly fascinating to me. I especially liked reading about his boyhood. Orphaned at the age of three, he lived the life of a waif for several years, wandering the streets and wharves of Palermo without escort or protection. Sometimes local people took pity on him and would give him food. He was a beautiful child, with bright blue eyes and thick golden blond hair.

Frederick saw an amazing variety of people in his ramblings. The island of Sicily was at the cultural crossroads of the medieval world. Jewish temples and Islamic mosques with tall minarets stood side by side with Norman churches and elaborate Byzantine cathedrals adorned with golden mosaics. Greeks, Jews, Italians, Normans, and Saracens — he knew them all, and they each played a part in developing his worldview. He learned their customs, their speech, and their culture. Not only could he speak their languages with complete fluency, he could do so with wit and charm. The street smarts and skills he picked up on his own would serve him throughout his reign in accurately reading people and potentially dangerous situations.

Frederick's story was a compelling one, and I couldn't get enough of it. I read about Frederick at every opportunity. Sometimes I tried to combine it with my schoolwork, writing a book report on a biography of Frederick II for my English class and later presenting an oral report on him. But for the most part, my research on Frederick got in the way of my regular studies. And I really had no one to talk to about Frederick. Whenever I started babbling to Jerry about Frederick, he'd say: "So what?" That always shut me up, but I continued to read about him and to study his book on falconry.

Frederick encouraged a kind of stoicism that appealed to me, and I strove constantly to develop physical toughness and an acceptance of hardship and discomfort. He set high standards for the physical, mental, and emotional qualities and character traits an aspiring falconer should strive toward. "He must be alert and agile in his movements, that there may be no delay in assisting his falcons when the necessity arises." He must have a "daring spirit and not be afraid to cross rough and broken ground" or to swim across "unfordable water and follow his bird when she has flown over and requires assistance." He must be diligent and persevering, resourceful, naturally ingenious, and have good eyesight and acute hearing so that he can "readily hear and identify the call notes of birds he is looking for . . . and the tones of the bells on his own hawk." And he must be able to "rise early, often before daylight" (no problem for me). Frederick also provided a list of character traits to avoid: bad temper, gluttony, laziness, drunkenness, and absent-mindedness. When a person finally meets the grade in every way and becomes proficient in all aspects of falcon handling, "only then can he be regarded a worthy member of the guild and deserve to be called by the name of falconer." Frederick's teachings became a touchstone for me and helped me to get through some personal tragedies. But that came with a price as I tried to insulate myself from my feelings.

In addition to my Frederick II readings, I also discovered several articles on falconry in some old copies of *National Geographic*. This was a major find for me, because for the first time I was reading about falconry in the twentieth century instead of the thirteenth. And these articles completely captured Jerry's interest. Our junior high school library had bound copies of every issue of *National Geographic* ever published, and they were thoroughly indexed, so it was easy to look up falconry. The earliest was a 1920 article entitled "Falconry, the Sport of Kings," written and illustrated by famed bird artist Louis Agassiz Fuertes. (Fuertes was a native of Ithaca, New York, near where I live now, and many of his original paintings adorn the walls of the Cornell Laboratory of Ornithology, where I work.)

This article was just a teaser. It had beautiful paintings of trained falcons, but there wasn't enough information in the text to be useful to Jerry and me. But a couple of later articles by twin brothers Frank and John Craighead were great. If we had been wavering at all in our budding interest in falconry, their 1937 article, "Adventures with Birds of Prey," cemented our attraction to the sport.

The Craighead brothers were amazing. They had grown up in Washington, D.C., and were students at the University of Pennsylvania when they submitted their manuscript and a stack of black-and-white 8 × 10 glossy photographs to *National Geographic*. They personally carried their submission into the headquarters of the society and handed it to the editor — and he loved it. The article detailed their early efforts in falconry as well as nature photography. There were pictures of them climbing mammoth trees to photograph a bald eagle nest or rappelling down treacherous cliffs to get a look at peregrine falcon chicks. And their photographs were fabulous. Most of them had been taken with big, heavy press cameras using 4 × 5 sheet film. They'd build blinds from boards and burlap and hang them precariously on the sides of cliffs or in trees so the birds couldn't see them as they were taking pictures. And the stories of training their wild-eyed Cooper's hawks and their spectacular peregrine falcon to hunt were mesmerizing.

These were the kinds of adventures any red-blooded boy in America wanted to have. Jerry and I certainly did. We'd look at the group shot of the Craigheads and their buddies, each of them holding a hawk or falcon on his fist, and we wanted to be there; we wanted to be part of that group.

After this first triumph at *National Geographic*, the twins expanded the topic of their article into a full-length book, *Hawks in the Hand: Adventures in Photography and Falconry*, published by Houghton Mifflin in 1939. I still have a signed copy of the first edition on my bookshelf.

But the Craigheads' greatest adventure had not yet begun. An Indian prince, R. S. Dharmakumarsinjhi, who had read of their exploits in *National Geographic*, wrote to them and invited Frank and John to visit him in India to experience his country's falconry, which had been going on uninterrupted for perhaps three thousand years or more. The twins approached *National Geographic* to fund the trip, so they could write an article about it, and quickly got a thumbs-up from the editor. I'm sure Frank and John saw this as the opportunity of a lifetime, but they could not have known that they would bear witness to the final glorious days of the Indian Raj.

The Craigheads steamed away in 1940, just as World War II was getting under way in Europe — a war that would change everything. For nearly a year, the two lived like princes themselves. Everything was opulence and spectacle. Riding on the backs of elephants, they escorted falconers on hunts, flying falcons in much the same way as they had been flown through the millennia, chasing herons, ibises, cranes, and other large quarry, flying in great circles high in the sky. They saw trained cheetahs (with leather masks covering their faces so they couldn't see the game until the right moment) carried on oxen-drawn wagons. The Craigheads documented their stay in "Life with an Indian Prince," a 1941 *National Geographic* article. (In 2001, the Archives of Falconry published the Craigheads' complete diary of their India trip in a book of the same title.)

I started getting library passes from my English teacher almost every day, just so I could read and reread these articles and look in field guides and other bird books. I became a voracious reader of anything having to do with birds of prey or wildlife photography. I started daydreaming about someday writing books about hawks, illustrated with my photographs, just as the Craigheads had done.

My English teacher started getting suspicious about my motives in getting so many library passes, and before long I was called into the vice principal's office. He wanted to know where I was really going when I was away from English class. I told him all about the Craighead articles, describing in minute detail everything I'd read. He took a few notes, then said: "OK, we're going to the library to check on this — unless you want to tell me the truth right now."

"That's fine," I said. "Let's go."

We both stood up for a moment, then he sat down. "That's OK," he said. "I believe you."

☙

IF I WAS the scholar, Jerry was the craftsman, always designing and building the equipment we would use with our falcons. He had an amazing talent for any kind of construction. He could make almost anything, from an exquisite piece of furniture to a minibike — or even a tiny zip gun that shot .22 caliber bullets.

Jerry started designing elaborate block perches for the falcons we dreamed of having someday. He would glue together two-inch-thick boards of ash and walnut, alternating the light and dark wood, forming a square post measuring about eight inches across and twelve inches tall. Then he would turn it on a lathe in the school's wood shop, peeling off long strips of wood shavings and eventually producing a work of art. He would then bore a hole precisely in the center of the bottom of the block and insert a long metal spike he made in metal shop, complete with a metal ring on which to tie a falcon's leash. After putting a shiny finish on the wood, he would glue a thin piece of cork on top of the block to protect a falcon's feet from the hardness of the wood.

But we were still just falconers in desire only and had not yet figured out how to move to the next step: actually flying falcons. We hoped to accomplish that soon.

2

REX AND ROWDY

IT WAS ABOUT this time that I finally encountered a person who actually owned a hawk. For some time, I had been visiting a place in Stanton called Hobby City — a collection of several small houses, each dedicated to a particular hobby, such as rocks and minerals or coins and stamps. My favorite was the Indian Store, which I often visited to buy leather to make equipment for the falcons I didn't even have yet. One day I was speaking with the elderly woman who ran the shop, and I told her about my interest in falconry. She told me I wasn't the only one around here who liked hawks. There was a high school student in Buena Park named Keith who had a trained hawk, and he sometimes bought leather at her shop. She gave me his phone number, and I couldn't wait to get home and call him.

It turned out Keith was sick with the flu, but I decided to visit him anyway. He lived in a housing tract on the other side of the Buena Park Shopping Center, about eight miles from my house. I jumped right on my bike and took off. His mother let me in and escorted me to his tiny bedroom at the back of the house. I glanced in the room and was taken aback. A beautiful male Harris's hawk named Yankee sat calmly on the headboard of his bed, keeping Keith company.

Keith was two or three years older than me and attended Savanna High School in Anaheim. The school, which I later attended during eleventh grade, had a Confederate theme. The students were called the "Rebels," and the school mascots were a boy dressed in a Confederate uniform and a girl dressed as a Southern belle. They would parade around during assemblies and games to rev up the school spirit. This, of course, was in the days before political correctness. The school banner — which flew daily on a flagpole alongside the flags of the United States and California — was that favorite symbol of rednecks and neo-Nazis, the Confederate battle flag.

I asked Keith why he called his hawk Yankee, since he was a student at Savanna. He explained that his friend Dave had bought a Swainson's hawk the same day Keith got a Harris's hawk, and he had immediately named it Rebel. Not to be outdone, Keith dubbed his hawk Yankee. This was years before falconers discovered the potential of the Harris's hawk, which now is one of the most popular raptors flown in America. Many people in Europe and other places also love the species, because it adapts so well to falconry and is so easy to train and maintain.

Yankee was an amazing bird. Completely tame, he would fly around the neighborhood like a mischievous crow, sometimes teasing neighborhood cats and dogs, other times landing in peoples' backyards to see what they were up to. He seemed well adapted to the presence of humans — perhaps too well. One day he flew home clutching an entire freshly cooked barbecued chicken, still warm to the touch. Keith never found out where it came from. I can just imagine a family sitting down at their backyard picnic table, eagerly awaiting the chance to dig into this mouthwatering chicken, when a hawk dashes in, snatches it away, and flies off over the rooftops. Who would ever believe them?

Yankee would often fly down to the next-door neighbors' swimming pool and stand at the edge of the ramp, dipping his beak into the water, then raising his head to let the water run down his gullet. Other times he would plunge right into the pool, spreading his wings out to stay afloat and using them as oars, pulling back with them repeatedly to scoot around.

I don't know if you could say that Yankee was a trained hawk, but he was completely workable in the field. He would follow Keith around and occasionally plunge down on an unsuspecting rodent or other prey in the field behind his house. I'm sure he would have been an excellent rabbit hawk if he'd had the opportunity to hunt them.

KEITH AND HIS friends Kenneth and Dave were avid about falconry. They got into the sport through the backdoor, really, obtaining hawks before they knew much about training them. Kenneth had a part-time job at a local dairy that had a small zoo the owner had built to attract customers. He received a small wage for stopping by every day after school and feeding the lynx, the skunks, the hawks and owls and vultures, and all the other exotic creatures. And he needed the money; his family was nowhere near as well off as Keith's or Dave's. But Kenneth loved the animals and would spend lots of time with them above and beyond the basic maintenance for which he was paid. The animals looked forward to seeing him. One caracara — a large hawk-like raptor that lives in Florida, Texas, and Mexico — had the endearing habit of running up to the wire at the front of the cage whenever he saw Kenneth and putting his head down to be scratched. The zoo also had a pair of Harris's hawks, like Yankee, and two Swainson's hawks — large, pretty soaring hawks with cream-white breasts with a chestnut band across the top and dark backs, somewhat similar to red-tailed hawks.

Kenneth, Keith, and Dave thought how wonderful it would be to have hawks of their own and to train them for falconry. They found out who the dairy owner was buying his animals from — a man with the great name Jack Wilder. (In those days, the early 1960s, it was fairly easy to import animals into the United States legally.) The three of them went to see Wilder at his home in Riverside. He had recently brought some Swainson's hawks and a couple of Harris's hawks from Mexico. Kenneth couldn't afford to buy anything but went along for the ride. Dave saw a beautiful young Swainson's hawk the minute he stepped into Wilder's garage and said he wanted to buy it. He paid thirty dollars. Keith was coy. He kept looking around and evaluating the remaining hawks. There was one young male Harris's hawk he was interested in, but it had scraped off most of the feathers on its head rubbing against the cage, so it had an unfortunate turkey vulture look. Wilder finally said he'd let Keith have the bird for twenty bucks — a great bargain; Yankee's feathers grew back in a couple of weeks.

ℯↄ

ONE DAY, A few weeks after I met Keith, Jerry and I were riding our bikes past an open field not far from Keith's house. A huge date palm and a couple of pepper trees stood above the dry, knee-length grass in the field. At the side of the road, we noticed a two-by-two cardboard box, with a square hole about four inches by four inches cut in the front and covered by a piece of wire screen. I looked at it for a minute with my binoculars and thought I saw something moving inside. We raced over to see what it was.

Suddenly we heard a disembodied voice calling from the box: "Stop! Go away! Get out of here!" We looked at each other blankly, then back at the box. "Please! Get out of here!"

A second later, Kenneth came skidding up on his bike, looking furious. "He's gone. They scared him away," he said.

We still had no idea what was going on. Then Kenneth reached down and picked up the box, revealing Keith, buried up to his neck in dirt with only his head showing. He was beet-red and angry as he sat up, dirt falling away everywhere. They had been trying to trap a wild kestrel, and we unwittingly scared it away. The two of them had gone to the trouble of digging a six-foot-long trench, about two feet deep, and putting an old sleeping bag in the bottom. After Keith slipped inside the bag, Kenneth buried him, leaving only his head uncovered, then put the cardboard box over that, so the box was the only thing visible and looked like an innocuous piece of garbage in the field. Keith had a live mouse tied to his hand with a piece of string. Apparently, he had been there for hours in the blazing sun, hoping the kestrel that lived in the field would eventually try to attack the mouse, and Keith could grab it by the legs. Just before we pulled up on our bikes, the kestrel had finally landed in the pepper tree right beside Keith.

Jerry started laughing. "Hey, you should thank us," he said. "We probably saved your life. A box on the shoulder of the road is just the kind of thing people like to hit with a car. If I had a car, I would've run you over." We finally all started laughing and then went to Keith's house to let Yankee out and watch him fly around the neighborhood.

❧

BY THIS TIME, Rex had grown into a beautiful young dog and accompanied me everywhere I went around the local farms and fields. He had a great disposition and loved to run across the fields with me as I looked for birds and other interesting things. I got into the habit of waking up at 4:00 A.M., even on school days, and sneaking out to the field to explore with Rex, letting him chase jackrabbits and sniff around for game birds in the cover along fences. This really bugged my dad, and whenever he heard my alarm clock go off in the predawn hours, he'd come charging into my room and forbid me to leave the house. I'd lie awake for a while, and then, if it sounded like he went back to sleep, I'd slip quietly out and get Rex. Eventually I started automatically waking up a minute or two before the alarm rang — something I still do. We would silently walk out the gate and sneak away. As soon as we were far enough from the house, we'd run the rest of the way to the field — and we rarely stopped running the entire time we were there, because I had to get back home before my father woke up.

With all that exercise, I became a fast runner, with boundless endurance. (A year or so later I took part in an open track meet and slaughtered the school's best runners in a 660-yard race. The kid in the lead didn't even see me coming until midstretch, when I blew past him, then we fought hard all the way to the finish line. I held on for first place, to the astonishment of almost everyone present, especially the track coach, which later turned out not to be such a good thing.)

One day Rex and I took a longer run than usual, to a distant corner of the field we rarely visited, where two incredibly tall but skinny palm trees towered above us, swaying to and fro in the wind. This was in spring, and I had already been out looking for hawk nests, riding my bike to check likely looking trees. Of course, since I'd never found a hawk nest before, I wasn't exactly sure what constituted a likely looking tree. But that morning, Rex and I got lucky — or did we? We certainly found a nest. I saw a male kestrel flying around with a mouse in his feet. His mate came out to greet him and took the mouse in a midair swap, returning to the nest with it, obviously to feed their young.

So I had overcome the first obstacle — I had found a falcon nest. Unfortunately, the nest was located in the ruff of dead palm fronds hanging down from the tip-top of the tallest palm tree. Just looking up at the tree, swaying wildly in the slightest breeze, gave me chills and made me feel nauseous. But I was determined to climb it. At that point in my life, I was convinced that all someone needed to accomplish anything was simply enough courage and drive. I'd already gone to a secondhand store and bought a battered old pair of climbing spurs — the kind used by telephone linemen — and had practiced with them on a telephone pole and a couple of trees. I felt I was ready for anything. Still, as I sat daydreaming in my classes at school, the thought of that palm tree made me break out in a cold sweat.

The day I chose to take a young falcon was about a week after I found the nest. I did it on a Saturday, so that I wouldn't have to race back home to get ready for school. I slipped out of the house with Rex, carrying a brown canvas Boy Scout backpack with my climbing spurs protruding from the top. When I got to the bottom of the tree, I pulled out the climbing spurs, which looked like some kind of orthopedic braces, with a flat metal shaft that lay along the inside of my leg from just below the knee down to my foot, attached with leather straps. A small, sharp spike, pointing at an outward angle, comes out at the arch, which a climber jams into a tree trunk or telephone pole in order to "walk" up it — at least that's the theory. It is much more difficult in practice.

After strapping the climbing spurs securely to my legs, I stepped up to the tree and jammed the spur on my right foot into the trunk of the palm tree and hoisted myself up. But as I tried to repeat the process with my left foot, I lost my hold with my right foot and dropped back to the ground. The palm trunk was harder to work with than I expected. I tried again, and this time got up about seven feet before losing my hold and having to jump back and fall to the ground. I stood there trying to concentrate for a few minutes and figure out what I was doing wrong. I realized that the spurs were not as sharp as they should have been — I really should have bought a file and worked on their points, but there was nothing I could do about that now. I did have a thick piece of rope, several feet long, that I could put around the tree and then tie around my back so that I could lean against it. This would give my spikes a better angle of attack, driving them deeper into the trunk instead of allowing them to slip out and slide down the palm without getting an adequate bite.

I decided to tie Rex to the other palm tree before I started climbing. He had been jumping up against the trunk and barking as I tried to climb earlier, and I was afraid something might drop on him if he were right there. This only made him wilder. As I dug my spurs into the palm trunk again and worked my way up, ten feet, twenty feet, he barked loudly and jumped against his leash, sometimes flipping himself over onto his back. I ignored him and continued upward. It was working much better now. When I got up about forty feet, the kestrels took notice of me and started screaming — *kle-kle-kle-kle-kle-kle* — and diving, putting in pretty vertical stoops, sometimes coming within a foot or two of my head. By this time, it felt like I was already very high, but when I looked up, I was nowhere near even a third of the way up. I felt sick, but I shook it off and continued up — fifty feet, sixty feet. Still I was nowhere. "I can do this, I can do this," I whispered to myself and pushed on.

The tree already seemed so narrow. I started to have doubts. What would I do when I got all the way to the top? How could I get into that scruff of palm branches and find the nest? The tree was already swaying wildly. What would it be like up there? But I forced myself to stop thinking about it. All I could do was keep going up. That was the only thing that mattered now. Rex seemed miles away as he barked and howled far below.

Then suddenly one of the kestrels came very close to me, with a *whoosh* I could feel against my face, and it startled me enough to make me pull in toward the trunk for a second, and the spurs instantly lost their grip. Then I panicked and hugged the tree tightly — and began my long, agonizing slide to the ground. There was nothing I could do to stop it. Occasionally the rope would get stuck, and I would hang there tight against trunk, barely able to breathe. And I'd have to pull myself up a few inches to get it to break loose again. Finally, when I was about twelve feet from the ground, I got jammed again and decided to pull out my pocketknife and cut the rope. The instant I did that, I fell free the rest of the way to the ground, throwing my knife far from me so I wouldn't land on it.

I lay on the ground trembling for fifteen or twenty minutes and then threw up. I was a mess. Luckily I had worn an old jacket and jeans, but they were almost entirely shredded, as was some of the skin on my arms, chest, and legs. I untied Rex and we walked to a ditch beside a massive pump with ice-cold water gushing out to irrigate the nearby agricultural fields. I took my shirt off and washed the blood from my arms and my chest. Then I sneaked back home and slipped into the bathroom. I took a long soak in a tub, cleaning my wounds as well as I could, then I spread ointment on them and wrapped them in gauze. I was in a lot of pain, but I didn't want my dad or anyone else in the family to know what had happened. I wore long-sleeved shirts for the next few weeks, like a junky trying to hide his needle marks.

A FEW DAYS later, I told Keith what had happened. He was amazed and said that he and Kenneth had found another kestrel nest that was much easier to reach, and he would be happy to show it to me. The following weekend, I rode my bike to his house, and together we visited the nest. It was in a billboard along Interstate 5, with freeway traffic blasting constantly past below — the least likely place I could ever have imagined for a falcon nest. They had only checked it out because they had seen kestrels perched there a few times. The billboard advertised the Carnation products sold at Disneyland and had large three-dimensional letters along the top spelling out the company's name. But a small square metal plate at the back of the first "A" in "Carnation" was missing. This was an access plate an electrician would remove to repair the wiring or replace a light fixture, and the kestrels were using it to get in and out. It was probably a perfect place for a nest — completely protected from the elements and perhaps warm enough inside to incubate the eggs even without the adult sitting on them. And who would ever think to look there?

Just in case someone did climb up the sign, Keith wrote "Danger, High Voltage" next to the access hole with a black marker, hoping to discourage someone from reaching a hand into the nest. (The funny part was, this nest inspired Keith and his friends to climb up other billboards along the local freeways and remove the electrical access plates from any that had similar three-dimensional letters. And the following season, one of the signs they tampered with did have a kestrel nest.)

The day I climbed up the billboard with Keith, the young were just hatching, so the parents were quite aggressive. One of them actually struck me lightly on the back as I looked into the nest hole. The nest had five young, and Keith had no objections to my taking one, although it was obviously too early that day. Falconers had traditionally always taken young falcons as close as possible to fledging, thus avoiding some of the problems that can arise with birds that imprint on humans, such as incessantly screaming for food and other bad habits. (This was years before some falconers started deliberately raising imprinted raptors, using special techniques to help minimize these negative qualities.) Keith said he would keep an eye on the nest and let me know when the birds were ready.

It was less than three weeks later when Keith called me and said I'd better take a kestrel soon, because they were getting pretty old. This was late in the day, and I wouldn't be able to ride my bike there before it got dark. I talked with my dad about it, and he said he would drive me there. I remember it was on May 16, my father's forty-fourth birthday. When we got there, he was a little surprised to see me scramble up the billboard and stick my hand into the back of the letter as the parent kestrels flew around above me scolding. I had a square leather camera bag I often carried binoculars and other equipment in when I tramped around the hills, and I used this to put my kestrel in. It was stiff sided and large enough to easily accommodate the bird, and I had put a clean white rag in the bottom for him to sit on.

When I reached into the nest, all the young kestrels pushed themselves into the back of the letter, a couple of them flipping onto their backs and holding their feet out. A feisty male sunk his talons into my hands, which hurt, but actually made it easy to get him out. I put him into my camera bag and quickly detached his claws. I showed him to my dad briefly after I climbed down from the sign. He seemed dubious that I would be able to care for a wild bird like that, but he thought he was beautiful. We stopped at a market on the way home, and I bought some raw beef heart to feed him.

When I got home, I cut the meat into bite-sized pieces, then got the kestrel out and perched him on the back of a dining room chair. He sat there calmly enough and when I offered him a piece of raw meat, he took it without hesitation, closing his eyes as he wolfed it down. Before I was finished, he had a bulging crop full of meat. "He'll be OK," my dad said.

I named my new kestrel Rowdy, after the Clint Eastwood character Rowdy Yates in the television show *Rawhide*. I had watched it every week for years. Rowdy settled down quickly. I cut out jesses for him from some split-cowhide leather I'd bought at the Indian Store, and I adapted a pattern from Frederick II's book. I greased the leather strips with Vaseline and then had to wrap a T-shirt lightly over Rowdy and hold him as I attached a jess to each of his legs. He didn't like the process but was forgiving, afterward jumping onto my fist and shaking his feathers — a sure sign of contentment in any raptor. His stubby tail was always bobbing up and down as he eagerly surveyed his surroundings, sometimes turning his head upside-down to get a better look.

I started getting other, more natural foods to feed Rowdy. I put a mousetrap in our backyard and managed to catch a few field mice, and I also shot some house sparrows with my BB gun. It's important for growing young falcons to get essential nutrients and calcium from the kinds of food they would eat in the wild. Eating bones, fur, and feathers is also good for them, because they form tight pellets (traditionally called castings by falconers) out of all the indigestible material they ingest and cough them up later. This cleans out their crop.

Rowdy and Rex got along well. Sometimes Rex would put his nose right up to Rowdy to sniff, and Rowdy would reach over and nip Rex just to establish boundaries, but there was never any fear or anger on either side.

The early part of training went extremely well. I gave Rowdy a tiny morsel of meat every time he came to my fist, and he quickly started flying any distance inside the house. In the backyard, I tied a woven nylon line called a creance to his jesses as a precaution during the training exercises and continued calling him to the fist. He did just as well outside as he did inside the house, so one day I took him to the field and flew him free. It was great. I would cast him high into the air and start running with Rex. Rowdy would fly around above us like a real trained falcon.

Then something started going terribly wrong. He became less and less interested in flying — almost lazy — but it was intermittent. Sometimes he would still fly well, but other times as soon as I cast him off he would fly straight to the nearest fence post or even just straight down to the ground, and he wouldn't fly to my fist at all, even if I tempted him with a huge chunk of meat from only three or four feet away.

What was going on? I knew I wasn't feeding him too much, and yet, according to my scale, he was gaining an enormous amount of weight. (Weight regulation is an important part of falconry, especially in the early training, and I was very careful always to feed him the proper amount of food.) And there was another mystery. Often when I went to pick him up from his perch in the morning, I would find a chunk of uneaten meat under it. I was completely puzzled. I always fed him his entire ration on my fist. I never left him eating meat on the perch. So where did the meat come from? Could he possibly be throwing it up after I fed him? No, because he always ripped his meat into bite-sized chunks before swallowing it. The pieces I found below his perch were much too large for that. And besides, if he were coughing up that much meat, why wasn't his weight dropping? I weighed him two or three times a day on a little postal scale, and he was gaining weight. It just didn't make sense.

Then disaster struck. One day I took Rowdy flying in the field but instead of just landing somewhere and refusing to fly to my fist, he took off, circling higher and higher above me, finally disappearing in the distance. I spent days trudging up and down the local roads, going from field to field, blowing my whistle and swinging my lure until I could barely raise my arm. But I never saw Rowdy again.

I was heartbroken. I talked about it with my mother a couple of times, and she finally admitted that my father had been secretly feeding Rowdy at night after I went to bed. She tried to talk him out of it, but he insisted he knew what was best for the falcon. No wonder I'd been having such a hard time with him. He was eating twice the amount of food he should have. I never understood why my father did that. Maybe he didn't think I knew enough to care for a bird like that — although I'd always been responsible with my animals, and there had been many over the years. Or maybe he identified with Rowdy in some way, because I took him from his nest on my father's birthday, and he had driven me there to get him. I suppose I'll never know why.

I made some flyers with my phone number and information about my lost kestrel and pinned them on bulletin boards at various feed stores, pet shops, and laundromats in the area. A woman responded who, by a lucky coincidence, had found a young female kestrel that had fallen from a nest in a palm tree in Stanton. She was happy to give the bird to me, even though it wasn't the one I had lost. I named her Banshee after the scary Irish spirit women who come for people when it's their time to die. It wasn't that I thought my kestrel was dark and frightening, I just thought the name had a nice sound to it.

To prevent a repeat of what happened with Rowdy, I built a hawk house (or "mews") out of two-by-fours, plywood, and split-bamboo fencing and put a padlock securely on the door. I went to work right away training her, and in a couple of weeks she was flying free. I started stooping her to the lure — a small stuffed leather pouch with meat attached to it that is swung around on the end of a piece of line to call a falcon back. To stoop a bird to the lure, a falconer twitches the lure away at the last instant, just before the falcon is about to grab it, and the bird ends up diving at it again and again until the trainer lets her catch it. It was great fun and made her as fit as any wild falcon.

About this time, I had a visit from a state game warden. I did not have a falconry license — or even realize that one was required — and someone had turned me in. (I always suspected it was Jerry, because we'd had a falling out.) He looked at Banshee and the hawk house where I kept her, and he could see she was well taken care of. He decided not to confiscate her but said I would have to get a license. This was before would-be falconers had to pass a test and serve an apprenticeship for at least a couple of years under a sponsor who was already licensed. People just had to fill out an application and pay fifteen dollars a year. But I was not legally old enough to be a licensed falconer. To solve the problem, the game warden let me use my mother's name on the application, so for my first couple of years as a licensed falconer, my name was Daphne.

3

THE BIKER

JIMMIE WHITE WAS a biker. Or really I should say he used to be a biker. I never actually saw him ride a motorcycle, and he didn't own one when I knew him. (Maybe he was in remission; like falconers, motorcyclists rarely give up their obsession.) He was thirty-five years old when I met him — stocky and muscular with thinning reddish-blond hair, a ruddy complexion, and a broad Texas drawl. He ran a grass-cutting service and had recently married a divorcée named Mary, who had three school-age children — a thirteen-year-old daughter, an eleven-year-old son, and a five-year-old son. Jimmie also had several dogs, some hawks and owls, and a bunch of mice and rats he raised to feed them.

That's how I met him. I was at the feed store in Stanton buying alfalfa pellets for my pet rabbit and my guinea pigs, and I started talking with the owner about my kestrel, Rowdy, which I had lost a few days earlier. The storeowner told me about Jimmie, who bought all of his rat and mouse food at the store. And it turned out Jimmie lived only a couple of miles from me in a big tract house in Cypress with a county flood-control channel behind it. The man at the feed store gave me his phone number, and I called him up as soon as I got home.

Jimmie was a remarkable character. For several years he had owned a huge female golden eagle and hunted jackrabbits with her. She died at some point before I knew him, though he never told me how. She was obviously a favorite bird of his, and he spoke of her often. He never stopped praising that eagle — her raw intelligence, her speed and resourcefulness in the field.

He also recognized her potential to be dangerous. He would often carry her on a big curved T-perch, which was strapped to his body in such a way that the eagle sat with her feet at Jimmie's eye level, just a couple of feet away from his face. (This contraption helped reduce the fatigue that carrying a fourteen-pound bird on your arm would cause.) One day as she sat on her T-perch, Jimmie was blowing a referee's whistle and feeding her tiny tidbits of meat, trying to develop a Pavlovian association between the sound of the whistle and the food. Annoyed, she suddenly snatched the whistle right out of his mouth with her massive foot — so deftly and quickly that he was still blowing air out of his mouth for a couple of seconds after the whistle vanished. She could just as easily have taken his whole head in her foot and brought him thrashing to the ground, squealing like a dying rabbit. (Years after she had died, Jimmie still had her feet. They stood stiff and dry as jerky on a bookcase in his living room, and they were as big as my hands.)

Jimmie had pictures of himself with his eagle. One of my favorites was an 8 × 10 black-and-white glossy print of him riding a big Harley-Davidson, clad in a black leather jacket and wearing a Harley hat like the one Marlon Brando wore in *The Wild One*. His eagle stood proudly on the handlebars in front of him as he rode. I heard he once attended a biker funeral with his eagle onboard the motorcycle, leading the procession as a hundred Harleys and a three-wheel-motorcycle-drawn casket rumbled along behind.

But when I knew Jimmie, he drove an aging blue Chevy pickup with a huge self-propelled lawnmower, a couple of gas-powered edgers, and some hoses and shovels stuck in the back. "I may not run the best gardening service around," he told me once, "but it is the fastest."

He would get up at dawn each day and drive to Long Beach, where he had numerous lawn-cutting clients scattered throughout the city and its suburbs. He and his helper would attack each place with blitzkrieg intensity — rolling the powerful mowing machine down the planks they had pulled from the rear of the truck and racing back and forth over the grass while his assistant ran along the sidewalk with a power edger, making a perfectly straight margin along the sides of the lawn. They finished by blasting the sidewalks clean with a power nozzle on the hose. Then they raced off to the next stop. He went through several assistants — including me — during the time I knew him.

Jimmie wanted to get home while there was still plenty of daylight left so that he could fly his birds. Each afternoon, he would load up the truck with his hawks and owls and dog, plus a couple of his kids, and head to a nearby field. I started going along with them to help. He had a tame barn owl that would come screeching any distance to his son's fist when he whistled but then seemed too nearsighted to find the tidbit of raw meat on his glove. The bird would grope around endlessly before finding it and then choke down the tiny morsel, squinting its eyes with delight. His great horned owl was even worse. This bird seemed just plain stupid. No matter how hard she tried, she couldn't seem to make the connection between flying to the fist and receiving a piece of meat.

I had my female kestrel, Banshee, and would take her to the field with them. She usually flew around nicely, making pretty dives at the lure. Jimmie was impressed the first time I flew her for him. He sometimes presented informal shows at parks and other places, flying the birds for anyone who showed up. Banshee was a great addition, sometimes flying right over the audience in the bleachers and stooping repeatedly at my lure as I swung it around in a circle, twitching it away at the crucial instant as she was about to catch it.

I never caught any game with Banshee, but she was a holy terror whenever a wild kestrel tried to drive her away. She'd end up turning the tables, binding to the other falcon in the air and carrying it to the ground. I would have to run up as fast as I could to rescue the wild kestrel. She caught four or five of them that way — although I didn't count them as game. Fortunately, neither she nor any of the kestrels she caught were injured. Of course, these kinds of tussles happen all the time in the wild. This is how territories are established and defended among birds.

Jimmie had a big hawk house that took up half his backyard. Built with a framework of two-by-four studs with split-bamboo fencing for the outer walls and plywood dividing the chambers, he had room for about half a dozen raptors plus an antechamber for his rats and mice. But he soon began a massive new construction project that would more than double the amount of space in his hawk house, and I became one of his main helpers. His idea was to start breeding hawks in captivity, which had really never been done before — except for one young peregrine born to a captive pair in Germany during World War II.

Jimmie began his project at least a couple of years before falconers became aware that the peregrine falcon might be headed for extinction and began trying to develop captive-propagation techniques. No one knew whether it would even be possible to raise falcons in adequate numbers to augment their wild population. It wasn't until the early 1970s that the captive breeding of falcons got fully underway at Cornell University's Peregrine Fund facility. Jimmie just thought it would be an interesting challenge. He had three kestrels — a male and a female in one chamber and a lone male in another. I ended up giving Banshee to Jimmie at the end of the summer to pair up with this male instead of releasing her. A couple of years later, she actually did produce young, one of the earliest successes in breeding raptors in captivity.

Jimmie also may well have been the first person to breed captive Harris's hawks, although I'm sure few people are aware of that. He managed to obtain two pairs of these strikingly colored black, reddish brown, and white southwestern hawks, and together we built a huge addition to the hawk house to accommodate them.

It was amazing that no neighbors complained and no building inspectors tried to shut down the project. It became an enormous plywood structure, standing higher than the house, and was painted with redwood stain. Anyone driving past who happened to look up the flood-control channel couldn't miss it, an enormous red eyesore looming above the row of tidy suburban yards.

Toward the end of summer that year, my father drove my mother, my two sisters, and me all the way to Portland, Oregon, for a vacation. I was never sure why we took trips like that. Although I've always enjoyed seeing new places and had never before visited the Pacific Northwest, when we traveled with my dad, we never got to do any of the usual tourist things — such as sightseeing or exploring the places particular areas are famous for. He would drive frantically for hours, check into a motel long after dark, and then leave us to go looking for a place to get a drink.

Jimmie had previously lived near Portland, and he gave me the name and phone number of Larry Schramm, a local falconer who had several falcons, including a shaheen and a pair of Peale's falcons — the dark, northwest coastal race of peregrine. I called Larry one day while we were sitting around the motel room in Portland and had a nice talk with him. He invited me to visit and gave me directions to his house, which was not far away. I asked my dad if he would drive me there, but he refused. When I called Larry back, he said he would be happy to pick me up at the hotel and bring me back. My father still wouldn't hear of it, so I ended up sitting in the room, watching him drink Scotch all afternoon and evening. It was a shame I didn't get to meet Larry, because a few years later, in 1968, his pair of Peale's falcons became the first peregrines in America ever to reproduce in captivity.

ONE OF THE great things about meeting Jimmie White was getting to read his books. He had one of the most extensive personal collections of falconry books I've ever seen. He not only let me come over and spend hours sitting in his living room reading the books but eventually started lending them to me one at a time to read at home. This certainly didn't help my schoolwork any. Reading these books was the only academic exercise that interested me. I got to read first editions of the classic works of the sport, such as *Falconry in the British Isles* — an exquisite 1856 treatise by Francis Henry Salvin and William Broderick, bound in elegant calf-skin with gold-leaf lettering on the spine and hand-colored illustrations of hawks and falcons inside, each illustration with a protective tissue cover. And this was but one of the books; there were many more. These books were a treasure to me, and I read them all. They gave me an early intellectual basis in the theory of falconry, which I'm sure played a major role in my development as a game hawker in my teens.

ONE OF THE birds Jimmie had in his hawk house when I first met him was a male Swainson's hawk. I'm not sure how he ended up with the bird. No one had ever handled him, and he was unapproachable. He sat alone in his flight chamber and went berserk if anyone stepped inside. That autumn, just as school was beginning, Jimmie asked me if I'd like to train him. The answer was never in doubt. I was craving the chance to fly a big hawk. And he was beautiful — if you could look beyond the beat-up tail and flight feathers and his awful disposition. He had a cream-colored breast speckled with splotches of dark brown, forming a bib on his upper chest, and gleaming, tan-colored eyes, which were filled with hatred toward people. I named him Krag. I don't remember how I came up with the name, but somehow it fit.

I went into his flight chamber one night and grabbed him in the dark. It was not fun. Krag managed to latch onto both of my hands with his feet and clamp down, driving his talons deep into my flesh. You learn early as a falconer to be stoic about pain and discomfort, but this really hurt. Jimmie put new jesses on Krag as I stood there handcuffed by the hawk, bleeding profusely from the talon holes in my skin. Then I carried Krag outside and Jimmie tied his leash securely to a bowperch in the backyard. When I let go of Krag, he released his grip on me and flew to the end of his leash. He kept bating (a falconry term for when a hawk attempts to fly away from the fist or perch but is restrained by the jesses), flapping his wings against the ground, until I walked into the house to clean the wounds in my hands.

Krag was the most difficult bird I've ever tamed. Buteos (the large, common soaring hawks) are generally not so hard to work with — some red-tailed hawks can be as easygoing as a Labrador retriever — but this bird had been ruined. He was fat and ill tempered. He would bate from my fist again and again and again until he was too exhausted to move, and would then hang down with his beak agape. But I followed Emperor Frederick's advice closely and stuck with it, never showing any emotion or fatigue. I never looked at him except in my peripheral vision, because raptors fear being stared at. They know that the fixed stare of a predator usually precedes an attack. In Frederick's time, falconers would go through an elaborate taming process called "manning," which involves holding a newly trapped hawk on the fist for hours at a time while pacing back and forth, getting the hawk used to the trainer's presence and the way he moves. The idea is to inure the hawk to the falconer, to make it accept him in every way. And the bird must never experience anything but kindness and endless patience from the trainer.

Most of the raptors traditionally used in falconry are not social animals — they are largely solitary creatures, coming together in spring as a pair to breed and raise young — so they have no concept of dominance and submission and cannot be coerced with punishment. Pack animals such as wolves have evolved elaborate social hierarchies in which the strongest animals can bend the other members of their group to their will through force and intimidation. That's why punishment can be effective for certain kinds of training with dogs and other social animals. But a hawk would only go berserk and become completely unmanageable if a falconer tried using physical punishment to train it. I'm always amazed to think that falconers were able to come up with such an elaborate system of training, relying solely upon positive reinforcement, centuries or even millennia before the birth of psychology.

While training a raptor, you must become totally passive, putting your own needs and desires out of your mind and doing everything for the benefit of the bird. It is the most amazing exercise in patience and self-control imaginable. No matter what the hawk does — ripping into your fingers, grabbing your hand with its talons — you have to face it stoically, without showing any fear, pain, resentment — or especially anger. They are sensitive creatures and will pick up on any change in attitude or mood. A falconer must show a completely blank visage and do only good for the hawk, offering it fresh bits of meat, picking the meat up for the thousandth time after it knocks it down, and gently setting the hawk back on the fist every time it bates away and hangs by the jesses.

The most extreme form of manning used in the medieval ages was called "waking" and involved carrying a hawk for several days, in which time neither the falconer nor his hawk were able to sleep. I'm sure fatigue has an almost narcotic effect that makes the bird easier to work with, but it also creates an extremely strong bond between a falconer and his hawk. It's almost as though the bird can't remember ever not being with the falconer. This technique is rarely used today but as a follower of Frederick

II, of course, I embraced it fully, and I carried Krag constantly from Friday afternoon through Sunday afternoon — and yes, this included eating, tying my shoes, and going to the bathroom.

I would keep lifting Krag back up until he became so tired he would lay balanced on top of my glove with his wings drooped. And I was in no better shape myself. I got hit in the eye with those jagged flight feathers so often I got a sty in my eye, and the muscles in my back had an excruciating knot in them from the strain of carrying him for hours as I walked around and around in my backyard with him. I consulted Frederick's book many times as I stayed awake in my room. I even used candlelight at the beginning, as his book had advised, though I had problems with it: Frederick didn't explain how to keep the flame from getting blown out when the bird flapped his wings.

Eventually, during this weekend of self-abuse, Krag started slowly coming around, and a week or so later he became quite tame. Training him then became easy. I would tie a creance to his jesses and call him to the fist at ever-increasing distances, giving him a tiny tidbit of meat each time. After a few days, I dispensed with the creance and flew him free. It was a great feeling. I would set him on a fence post in the field and take off running at full speed until I was a hundred yards away, then toot the whistle, and he'd be on his way to me.

&

IT WAS AT about this time that I started being pressured by the track coach at school to join the team. He had seen me annihilate his best runners in an open track meet a few months earlier, and he wanted me to compete for the school. Although I liked running and thought track was a great sport, I couldn't afford to spend every day after school running with the team. It would have made it impossible for me to do justice to Krag. It usually got dark by five in the afternoon, so I had to go straight home, pick up my hawk, and get to the field as fast as I could to fly him.

I didn't want to tell the coach that I couldn't join the team because of my hawk. I tended to keep my falconry activities a secret from most people at school. (I've always disliked the idea of people using captive hawks to show off.) I said I was too busy.

"What are you, a businessman or something?" he said, seething with rage. I just shrugged.

Before long, many of the school athletes started picking on me at lunchtime and in the halls between classes, no doubt at the coach's request. Finally one day I was sitting in the bleachers, watching a game, when Bob, the biggest, toughest kid at school and the top football player, sat down behind me and started spitting on the back of my shirt. After he did this three or four times I turned without thinking and spit right in his face. He instantly punched me hard in the face, sending me tumbling down the bleachers, stunned and bleeding. One of the coaches heard the clatter and came running over to see what happened. I said I had slipped and fallen on my face on the bleachers. It all turned out well ultimately. Bob later apologized and, after that, he wouldn't let anyone else pick on me.

✑

I STARTED TRYING to hunt with Krag. I would walk through an overgrown field, kicking tumbleweeds and bushes and occasionally flushing a rabbit. He didn't seem interested in them. Sometimes I'd throw him off as they flushed, and he would fly in their general direction, but that was about as well as he did.

I began leaving Krag on a fence post, walking a long way off, and seeing if he would hunt by himself. And he did come crashing down after mice a few times — which shouldn't have surprised me: wild Swainson's hawks eat mostly small rodents and insects.

Krag became so tame I often let him sit with me in my bedroom. I had an old hide-a-bed couch along one wall, and I would let him perch on the back of it. I sometimes found it difficult to believe he was the same raging monster I'd held on my arm for that sleepless weekend when I first brought him home.

At the end of the season, Jimmie wanted him back, so once again I was without a hawk. But it was great to have had Krag at this point in my development as a falconer. He put me through the toughest test a person could face training a hawk, and I came out the other side of the process successful and eager to train more birds. It was the kind of acid test that would have flushed me out of the sport if I hadn't had what it takes to be a falconer.

e⌐

THE NEXT BIRD I trained was a tiny tiercel kestrel like Rowdy, with bright blue wings and dark eyes and a tail he would bob constantly whenever he landed. He had been part of a nest-full of young kestrels — five in all — displaced when a farmer moved the huge stack of hay bales where their parents had foolishly decided to nest. Somehow, Jimmie White had ended up with the whole brood, and he asked me if I wanted one. When I looked in on them, they fled to the back of the open-topped cardboard box they were in, cringing in fear and hissing — all except one, the smallest male, which attacked my hand, digging his talons deep and drawing blood. I knew right then I had to have him.

I called him Merlin, and by God, in my imagination, that's exactly what he was. Merlins — the real species, that is — had been flown for centuries and had always been considered a serious falcon, one a person could really take game with, even though they aren't much larger than an American kestrel. In medieval times, they were usually flown by high-born ladies and were thought to be like a miniature gyrfalcon. Instead of being flown at herons as the larger falcons often were at that time, merlins chased skylarks high into the air in beautiful ringing (circling) flights every bit as spectacular as flights with peregrines and gyrfalcons.

I had gotten hooked on the idea of flying merlins after reading *The Art and Practice of Hawking*, published in 1900. Jimmie had a first-edition copy of the book, and I read it from cover to cover twice, then bought a reprint from a used-book store in Long Beach. Although the book covered virtually every branch of falconry practiced in nineteenth-century Britain, it was easy to see that the author, E. B. Michell (pronounced Mitchell), was a confirmed merlin man. He even had a chapter titled "Anecdotes and Adventures," which was devoted entirely to descriptions of some of the best flights he'd experienced over the years with merlins.

Michell was a remarkable man. A superb athlete, he was a first-rate boxer and won three English championship titles: lightweight, middleweight, and heavyweight. In the Badminton Library — an extensive collection of sporting volumes written in the nineteenth century — Michell wrote the section devoted to boxing. He had fought at the height of the bare-knuckle days, and he lamented the fact that people had started using gloves in boxing matches. "Here it should be remarked that the only true and correct style of modern boxing is that in which the bare fists are used," he wrote. "All the rest are mere imitations — mere travesties of the original." He also once reportedly said that a boxing match with gloves was like a cockfight without metal spurs.

And Michell was not afraid to use his fists outside the ring. Two soldiers walking across the moor once came upon one of Michell's merlins right after she had caught a lark, and they started tossing stones at her. Michell was in a fiery rage when he came running up a few minutes later and punched out both soldiers, leaving them unconscious on the ground as he strode away, feeding his merlin.

Another time, he was riding in a train compartment with two merlins perched on the seat across from him. Two drunken men stumbled into the compartment and passed out on the seats across from Michell, right beside the merlins. A while later one of them woke up and noticed the birds. He poked at one of them with his finger and started laughing loudly and trying to wake up his friend. This was more than Michell could take, so he promptly decked the man with a straight left. Later, when the man came to, he was sure his friend had punched him, so he attacked him. Michell picked up his merlins and moved to another compartment, while the sound of a huge brawl raged behind him, finally spilling onto the station platform.

Michell was also a great oarsman who competed solo several times in the famed Henley Royal Regatta, winning the Diamond Challenge Sculls twice and coming in second once. He scandalized the newspaper reporters of the day by racing without a shirt — a habit they surmised may have come about because he was a boxer. A dedicated sportsman, it was also reportedly Michell who bought Wimbledon for the Lawn Tennis Association.

It was Michell's book I dedicated myself to reading after I finished Frederick II's treatise. And I trained Merlin using exactly the same techniques that Michell used in training a real merlin. It should be noted that at the time I was training Merlin, kestrels were not considered serious hunting hawks. They were seen as insect-eaters and mouse-catchers at best, and beginning falconers only used them to learn the ropes of caring for a raptor before moving on to a real hunting hawk. I had nothing to use as an example or an inspiration besides *The Art and Practice of Hawking.* Of course, I had already flown two other kestrels but had not taken any game with them. I was determined it would be different with Merlin. I think Merlin became a great game hawk only because I took him seriously and gave him every opportunity to excel. He never let me down.

Michell would have liked Merlin's first kill. He had been chasing sparrows unsuccessfully for a few days. I was walking across a turnip field with him sitting on my fist when a small sparrow with a streaked breast burst from the ankle-high crop and started going almost straight up. I'm not sure what kind of sparrow it was or why it flew like that, but Merlin went right up after it, snagging the bird nearly eighty feet in the air, then circled the field a couple of times before landing. That was the first real head of game I'd ever taken with a trained hawk, and it meant a lot to me. Although Banshee had been a real scrapper and brought down a few wild kestrels that I had to rescue, I did not consider them game and was not happy when she caught them.

Merlin had a tendency to want to carry the things he caught, so I had to approach him carefully on a kill, slithering toward him on the ground like a snake while holding out a large piece of meat in my gloved hand. I would freeze every time he looked up from the bird he was eating and not resume my movements until he started eating again. Eventually he would drag the bird he caught to my fist and start feeding on the meat. He'd gotten this habit of carrying because my little sister, Janet, had spooked him one day when she was in the field with me and he was feeding on the lure. He took off and managed to take a good-sized chunk of meat with him, so the seeds of the habit were sown.

Michell would have completely understood this. Merlins were notorious carriers, sometimes flying away in the distance with a skylark. Michell had all kinds of ideas about how to cope with the problem. Later, flying real merlins, I developed a few techniques of my own.

Merlin caught three more birds that week, all house sparrows, though none was taken in a spectacular aerial style like the first one. He started hunting birds more in the manner of a Cooper's hawk or sharp-shinned hawk, making long, low-level sneak attacks down crop rows. I often flew him in a nearby rhubarb patch, where the plants grew knee-deep or higher in rows with two-foot-wide spaces between them. The sparrows would sometimes be clustered on the plants a good football-field-length or farther away, and he would drop from my fist and make a beeline toward them, flying only a couple of inches above the ground. The sparrows would flush in a big panic as he swooped through them, often plucking one easily from the flock. They'd still be chattering away as I got there and began carefully approaching him on the kill — called "making in" by falconers.

It was fine sport, and I doubt whether any bird since has given me more pleasure than Merlin. On my proudest day with him, he went flying off in the same way down an open row in the rhubarb patch, but all I saw in the distance through my binoculars was a flock of black-birds. Surely there must be some house sparrows mixed in with them, I thought. He can't really be going after the blackbirds. But he was. The blackbirds burst up from the rhubarb just like a flock of sparrows would, and he shot through them in a blur. Unlike sparrows, though, the flock suddenly turned in the air and all the birds flew down right where Merlin had taken the blackbird. I ran there as fast as I could, using all the speed and endurance I'd built up running in the field with Rex early each morning. When I got there, it was like a scene from Hitchcock's movie *The Birds*, with blackbirds hovering all around me as I shouted at them and swung my hawking bag around trying to swat them away.

When I finally got a chance to look down at Merlin, he was trying awkwardly to walk away into the rhubarb, clutching the blackbird by its neck with one foot while the blackbird grasped him tightly with both feet at the base of his tail. It was quite a job untangling the two of them.

At the time I flew Merlin, I was completely committed to releasing my birds at the end of the season. And, of course, this is what E. B. Michell had always done with his merlins. He would fly them all summer at skylarks then release them in September so they could join the migration.

Just before the new school year started, I gorged Merlin for several days to fatten him up, then rode with him on the handlebars of my bike to the huge fenced-in fields of the Naval Weapons Station. I cut off his jesses and let him go. I loved watching him zip away into the distance like a wild falcon, but I also felt sick. I missed him.

4

BLOW UP

JUDY WAS A young female red-tailed hawk — not a huge one, but the biggest hawk I'd ever flown at that time. You could say she was waiting in the wings the entire time I flew Merlin. Before Jimmie gave Merlin to me, I had spent every weekend that spring riding my bike far into the hills alone, searching for nests. Sometimes I went to the areas past Yorba Linda. I would hide my bike in the bushes just off the road and walk for miles up and down steep hills, sometimes having to make my way through herds of bellowing beef cattle to get to the small stands of eucalyptus trees, sycamores, or cottonwoods that looked like they might harbor a red-tail nest. I also sometimes rode all the way to Irvine Park and even once to O'Neill Park, which involved going up a hill so steep I had to get off my bike and walk for a couple of miles. I found several nests, including one with two young golden eagles. I climbed all the way up the tree to the massive stick nest one day and snapped pictures of the eaglets as they bent toward me hissing and trying to strike me with their wings.

But the most interesting thing I found was a pair of red-tails nesting on a big sandstone cliff. Most red-tails nest in trees, so this one seemed special, and I really wanted to take an eyas (a falconry term meaning a young hawk taken from a nest). But Jimmie gave Merlin to me a few days after I found the red-tail nest, so I didn't take one that spring. I decided to concentrate on training Merlin to be a great game hawk.

But Keith's friend Dave was eager to fly a young red-tail, and I agreed to help him get one. I took him to my cliff nest, carrying a pathetic (and dangerous) hundred-foot length of manila rope. The idea was that Dave would tie the rope to his waist and sit at the top of the cliff as I rappelled to the nest and got a young red-tail — then I'd have to climb hand over hand back up the cliff, because the rope wasn't long enough to reach the ground. We had a gunnysack to put the young hawk in. But we were crazy. Neither of us knew anything about rock climbing. We had studied a few outdated paragraphs about climbing in the Craigheads' old book, *Hawks in the Hand*, but we didn't even have a safety line, as they suggested. I was just going to back over the edge and climb down the rope with no helmet, carabiners, breaker bars, harnesses, or anything to make the task safer.

I think I really lucked out. I guess after the hell I went through trying to climb the palm tree to the kestrel nest the year before, I deserved a break (but not of the fractured bone or broken neck kind). The minute we tossed the rope over the side and it dangled in front of the nest, a young female red-tail leapt from the ledge and flew clumsily across the canyon, finally crashing down into the sage. I made a mental note of where she went down, and we clambered there as fast as possible. We had to climb all the way down into a deep gully and up the other side into nearly shoulder-high sagebrush. And even though we had seen approximately where she went, the bird was difficult to find. We finally spotted her crouched beneath the sagebrush with her bill agape. She tried to grab me with her feet as I got hold of her, carefully folding in her wings and placing her gently into the gunnysack.

I felt an instant twinge of regret that she was not mine. She was beautiful: perfect in every way. An untouched, unspoiled hawk that would be a joy to work with — nothing like old Krag had been. But she was Dave's, and there was nothing I could do about it. When we got back home, I gave him some red-tail jesses I had made earlier, and together we attached them to her legs then connected her leash and swivel. She was quite a bird. She had a stubby, half-grown tail, and the feathers had not filled in around her neck, which gave her an unfortunate chickenlike look. Still, she was great, and I would love to have had her.

Everything seemed fine with the bird, which Dave named Judy. She was eating well and her feathers were quickly growing. She would be ready to start training as soon as her feathers were "hard-penned" — when the blood inside them dried up and the quills hardened. But then a curious thing happened. Dave went to a recruiter and enlisted in the Marine Corps. He would soon be heading for basic training and eventually to Vietnam, and he suddenly had no interest in training a hawk. He dropped her off at Jimmie White's house one day, and that's the last we ever saw of Dave.

Jimmie didn't have time to work with the young red-tail, but he thought perhaps his daughter might train her. His daughter did take Judy to the field a couple of times but soon lost interest. Judy sat on a perch in the backyard, and there she remained until early September, when I released Merlin back to the wild. A few days later, I brought Judy home, and what a great joy she was to work with. She was so eager to fly, so enthusiastic to be out in the field. I had her flying free in just a few days and started flushing rabbits for her right away. What a shock — she went right after them, crashing into cover as she tried to snatch them. But there was only one small area in the field near my house that had cottontails, and it was thick, brushy, and surrounded by fences. Out in the open, there were only jackrabbits, and they were huge. My hawk weighed just over two pounds, whereas jackrabbits sometimes run five or six pounds or more, and they are all muscle and sinew — long-distance runners with huge back legs, perfect for kicking inexperienced predators.

At first she didn't show much interest in the jackrabbits, but eventually she began flying after them tentatively, not really trying to grab them. Then one day I flew Judy in a golf course in Lakewood, right beside the Douglas Aircraft plant. The place was full of jackrabbits, which lived with impunity there, because no one could shoot in the city limits. The man who managed the golf course was happy to have someone go after the jackrabbits. Jimmie and a new friend, Steve, a blond surfer kid from Seal Beach, came along with us as we walked across the greens, poking around in the shrubbery looking for game. It was almost dusk and my bird was feeling especially hungry — raptors don't like the idea of going to sleep on an empty stomach.

A big jackrabbit suddenly burst into view, running across the green, and Judy went right after it. What a flight. She zigzagged left and right and left with the rabbit, shadowing its every move as she closed the gap, then she latched firmly onto its back. The flight instantly became like a bull-ride at the rodeo, the jackrabbit leaping and bucking high in the air with my hawk holding on with all her might. Steve was closest to the action, and as I ran toward them I shouted to him to try to grab the rabbit. He made a lunge for it and missed, which only made the jackrabbit more determined to escape. With one final twisting leap, it flung my bird to the ground and peeled off across the vast lawn. Something about the way it would stop occasionally in the distance, stand up on its hind legs, and look tauntingly back at us reminded me of Br'er Rabbit: "Born and bred in the briar patch!"

Judy sat there uselessly on the grass, clutching tufts of rabbit fur in her pale yellow feet. I picked her up and gave her a good feed, hoping she wouldn't get discouraged after making such a valiant, all-out effort in vain.

I was now all the more determined to fly her at game as often as possible. Every day after school I would ride my bike several miles to a field, holding Judy on my left hand as I steered with my right. Sometimes, riding home at dusk after flying her, she would fall asleep on my fist, standing on one leg with her head tucked behind her shoulder. She must have been quite a sight to the people driving past. On the weekends, I hitchhiked miles with her to reach better fields, but it was hard. She wasn't trained to the hood, and she sometimes became restless in cars.

Judy had a few more tussles with jackrabbits and then made an amazing mental leap and figured out how to hold them long enough so that I could help out. She wasn't really big enough to kill jackrabbits easily by herself and if they were standing up she had no way to control the power of their legs. But one day while chasing a jackrabbit she swung to the left just before she caught up with it, then turned hard right, grabbing the rabbit's back in passing and bowling it off its feet. She then laid flat on her chest with the rabbit on its side behind her, kicking its legs ineffectually into the air until I got there and killed it. I gave her a huge gorge on the rabbit as a reward. This quickly became her trademark technique, and she caught many jackrabbits that way. She also caught cottontails, which were much easier to handle.

ONE DAY AS I was walking home with Judy, a middle-aged woman stopped her car and asked me about my hawk. She told me her son had always been interested in falconry. He was a year older than I was and lived in Long Beach. Rich and I got together soon after, and he started taking me to new hunting areas. He drove a '49 Chevy and seemed a little like one of the young hoods in *Rebel Without a Cause*, which was fine with me. It was great to have some help getting to good places to fly my hawk. Sometimes, though, he'd come over in his dad's tiny red '57 Austin Healey, and we'd go driving on the freeway with my huge, restless red-tail flapping her wings and trying to get out, often blocking Rich's view of the road. Although she always rode well on my bicycle without a hood, the Austin Healey was cramped and noisy, with wind blowing through constantly, so she never felt comfortable.

THAT AUTUMN, AS things were going better and better with my hawk, other aspects of my life were falling apart. As we approached the holidays, my father started drinking more and more after work and on the weekends. It was a familiar pattern. We all could tell he was headed for a major blowup, and there was nothing we could do about it. Two years earlier, though, when I had come close to using his rifle against him, I made a pledge to myself that the next time we left him, I would never go back. It didn't matter what my mother chose to do. Although I was only fifteen years old, I was ready to run away or even to be sent to juvenile hall. And ever since I had made that pledge, I saved every penny I'd been given for lunch money — fifty cents a day — so we would have enough money to get an apartment. I'd become rail thin doing it, but I had saved up nearly three hundred dollars.

The big explosion came on New Year's Eve. My dad had been away at a bar or a party and came back blind drunk, wearing a bent party hat. I don't know how he even drove home. He fell in the driveway getting out of his car then struggled to his feet and staggered into the house yelling

"Happy New Year!" Once inside, he began one of his rants, with eyes agleam, cursing everyone and everything. We went into a back room, sitting in the dark, and listened as he smashed various things around the house. Then he went to my mother's closet and ripped up her clothes.

He finally passed out in an easy chair. I didn't know what to do next, but I called Jimmie White and told him what had happened. He was aware of how things were with my father, and he had offered to help if things got too bad. He said we could stay with them for a few days. We didn't take anything with us. We just jumped into my sister Maureen's little gray Simca and drove to Jimmie's house. Luckily, I already had my hawk there, but we had to leave Rex behind. I put him in the garage with the back door open so he could get into the backyard. And I left some dry food in his bowl and a dish of water. Still, it was hard going away without him.

Jimmie's wife, Mary, was slim with short dark hair, brown eyes, and a distinctive Chicago accent. She took us in and made us welcome. It would have been easy for us to be embarrassed and ashamed in our situation, but she made us feel like family. She cooked a fabulous breakfast the next morning with bacon, sausage, eggs, biscuits, and wonderful flour gravy. My little sister, Janet, who was ten years old, had a great time playing with Mary's kids. And I helped out with feeding the hawks and rats and mice out back.

We ended up ditching school the first couple of days after the Christmas break, to try to get situated. I gave the money I'd saved to my mother, and my sister Maureen also had some money she had made working part-time at a department store. We pooled it together and went looking for apartments. We found a perfect one in Buena Park on the first day. It was right in our price range and allowed pets. We gave the manager the first month's rent and a deposit and started moving in immediately.

Jimmie drove his big blue pickup to our house so we could get some of our things. My dad had obviously cleaned himself up and gone back to work. He was always good at that — coming down off a drunk and looking great the next day in his suit and tie. So we took the opportunity to go to our house when he wasn't there. Rex was running around the yard and seemed wild-eyed and scared. It was great that we'd be able to take him with us to the new apartment, which had a small fenced yard with a patio and some grass where I could perch my hawk. I also planned to build a hawk house soon.

As I walked into our house, I was hit by an overpowering sooty stench, as though something had burned up inside — and it had. I opened the door to my bedroom and saw that my bed was a charred ruin, sodden with water, which was pooled an inch deep on the floor. Soot covered the formerly white walls all the way to the ceiling. Everything I owned, all of my most cherished possessions including my books were inundated with water. The sight knocked me back, and I choked up. I had to walk outside and sit with my dog.

I never knew what happened. Maybe he was mad at me and torched my room. Or maybe he just happened to fall asleep on my bed, smoking a cigarette, and the whole place went up: more likely the latter, knowing my dad.

We didn't take much — mostly some clothes and personal belongings and the bed Maureen and Janet slept in. The first few days, our apartment was pretty empty. I slept on the floor of my room in a sleeping bag. But my mother got a job as a medical transcriber at a hospital in Bellflower and as soon as she got credit at a local department store, we bought a couch, a table and chair set, and a bed for my room. It was a two-bedroom apartment. My sisters shared one room, I had the other, and my mother slept on the couch in the living room.

At that point, we were hiding out, not sure how long it would take my dad to track us down. We knew he would find us sooner or later, but we had no idea what he would do to us. We were only about three weeks into our great escape when he finally showed up at our apartment one night. We pretended not to be home. He tried the front door and then went through the back gate and tried to open the picture window as we huddled in the dark in the bathroom, pretending no one was home.

After he left, we sat there for a good forty-five minutes before venturing out. I went outside and looked around, then walked back to the carport. It was empty. Maureen's car was gone. That was the one thing we needed to make this work, to be independent. My mother's job was almost twenty miles away. It was much too far to walk. My dad had an extra key to Maureen's car. It never occurred to us that he might take it away like that.

I was furious; we all were. The next day we walked to the Buena Park Shopping Center, where he worked in a department store, selling appliances, and we marched right in, demanding he give back the car. You could see he was horrified. People were staring at us, including some of the people he worked with. He asked us to go outside with him and talk. We followed him to a huge concrete patio area with a couple of planters beside the store. He told us it was his car, and he was taking it back.

I got so mad as he babbled on and on that I couldn't speak. I suddenly picked up a red brick from the side of the planter and raised my arm back to heave it at him. He cringed in terror with his eyes wide, holding his arm in front of his head. "I never hurt you, boy," he said. And I paused there, with the brick in my hand, and it was the best feeling. He was beaten. He said he would bring the car back after work, and he did.

He came to our apartment drunk a few weeks later and walked in the door. But I wrestled him and pushed him outside, and we rolled around on the grass hitting each other and shouting. No one took notice. It was par for the course in the working-class apartments where we lived.

Dad didn't come around after that. We went through a divorce settlement in which he refused to pay alimony, and although he was ordered by the court to pay child support for Maureen, Janet, and me, he never paid a cent. We didn't care. We were just glad to be free.

In those days after the divorce, I would go on long walks after school, searching under playground equipment in parks and strolling along the curb, peering constantly in the gutter, hoping to find some lost pocket change. I was good at it, and I did find a lot of money that way, but not enough. So as we became more and more hungry, I started stealing food from a local market. Just small stuff — a twenty-five-cent can of potted meat here, a packet of cheese slices there, an occasional can of dog food for Rex.

I kept a detailed record of everything I took, and a year or so later when I was working evenings as a dishwasher at a local cafe, I sent an anonymous letter to the store manager saying this was in payment for all of the food I borrowed during the previous several months. Inside the envelope, I had the entire amount in cash, down to the last penny (including some coins I taped to a piece of card). I can't imagine what the manager thought of this. Maybe he just put the money in his pocket and forgot about it. As for my mother, she never had a clue about any of this. Years later she would often tell people how lucky I was and how much money I'd found as a kid, walking along with my nose to the ground.

IT WAS AN amazing season for me, a time when I blossomed as a falconer. One evening I went to Santa Ana with Jimmie to attend a meeting of a newly formed club, the Santa Ana Valley Falconers' Association. I met several new people and got to hear stories about all the hawks they were flying — many of which were species I dreamed of having someday: peregrines, goshawks, prairie falcons. Some people brought their hawks with them.

Jeff Sipple — an artist in his midtwenties whom I had met a couple of times before — held his male Cooper's hawk on his bare hand for most of the evening, and it seemed very tame and well adjusted. (Cooper's hawks and other accipiters are famously spooky and wild.) Kurt Stensrude had a beautiful adult female peregrine, which he had trapped the year before as a juvenile. I couldn't help staring at the beautiful blue color of her back as she sat bareheaded on his gauntlet, sometimes pumping her wings powerfully. Another man, Bob Martin, who lived somewhere on the other side of Los Angeles, had brought a juvenile male peregrine he had trapped just a couple of weeks earlier on an island in the Gulf of Mexico. He took the bird's hood off a couple of times, and the bird looked around, bright-eyed and alert but calm. I was in awe. I had never seen any captive peregrines before — and I had only seen a couple in the wild.

The club met at the home of Jack Hagan — a divorced bachelor who shared the house with a friend. Jack was a professional photographer and also a collector of various reptiles and amphibians. I remember the rattlesnakes he kept in aquariums in his garage and the rare tropical turtles he had in his bathtub. He often kept the temperature and humidity high in the house to accommodate these turtles. Jack had taken some great photographs in the late 1940s of a peregrine falcon nest in

Laguna Canyon. When he came back from the Korean War, though, the nest was empty, and the peregrines never nested there again. This was but one of the California peregrine nests he knew of that was abandoned in the DDT era.

Jack was in his midthirties when the club formed, with thinning dark-brown hair and a pipe he puffed on constantly. He had the calmest, most unflappable nature of anyone I've ever met. The younger guys in the club called him the "old man," which always made him smile. He had certain catch phrases he would use a lot in conversation. If you asked him a complex question, he would puff thoughtfully on his pipe and say, "This I do not know," but would then go on to expound in detail his theory on the topic at hand. Jack drove a classic Mercedes 300 SL sports car with gull-wing doors and usually flew goshawks. He would later become the first president of the California Hawking Club, which, in some ways, sprang from the ashes of the Santa Ana Valley group, using the same logo, which Jeff Sipple designed. Jack had an even more extensive collection of old falconry books than Jimmie White, as well as some beautiful framed falconry prints on the walls of his house. He told me I was welcome to come over any time and read his books.

I was wide-eyed the entire evening and spent the ride home with Jimmie babbling about all the great things I'd seen and heard at the meeting. He was quiet, which I was too enthusiastic to notice. I asked him later if he was planning to go to the club's next meeting, and he told me no. He wasn't that impressed with the people in the club and didn't think there was anything to learn from them. I was surprised but didn't say anything. A couple of weeks later, I talked Rich into driving me to the meeting.

I got to know Jeff Sipple a lot better at this time. He had recently moved to Cypress and lived a few streets away from Jimmie White, in a tract house with a yard that backed up against an elementary school playing field. He had a wife and two young sons. I sometimes stopped by his house to visit. Jeff had recently gotten a tiercel prairie falcon, and he let me take some pictures of it for my high school photography class. I lugged over a big old-fashioned press camera that used 4 × 5 sheet film (just like the one the Craighead brothers had used) and put it on a tripod a few feet from his falcon. When the bird would open his wings or flap them, I'd snap a quick picture then go through the hassle of taking out the sheet-film holder and turning it around to the unexposed side. It was nothing like a modern motor-drive 35 mm or digital single-lens-reflex camera, which allow you to hold down the shutter release and blast a bunch of pictures in a row. But it made me slow down and really think about a picture before I took it: not a bad thing for a photographer.

I'd also sometimes run into Jeff in the field when I was flying my hawk. I would watch him fly his tiercel prairie and help flush game, and then he would walk the field with me, trying to find a jackrabbit for Judy. I started closely watching Jeff's training techniques with his bird and thinking about what I would do when I got a large falcon of my own.

Jeff started hosting most of the club meetings at his house, which was great for me — it was much closer than Santa Ana. I could actually ride my bike or even walk the four or five miles if Rich didn't go. The club got together every Wednesday night, and it was the most fun I had all week. Some of the club members — especially Mick St. John — were so funny they could have been stand-up comics.

I felt I was learning useful things every time I went. One night, Jeff did a hood-making workshop, showing how to make a hood quickly, using contact cement on the seams instead of a needle and thread, then wetting the whole thing and shaping the leather with a spoon as a hair-dryer blew against it, evaporating the water and stiffening the leather. Another night, Monte McAndrews demonstrated his attempts to make better brass falcon bells. It was an active, exciting group.

I could see Jimmie was not happy about my going to the meetings and hanging around with the other falconers. He would occasionally say things about some of them — that they were pet keepers who didn't really catch any game. I knew this was not true, because I had gone hunting with several of them. Eventually, I stopped mentioning the club to him, but I still kept going every week. Then one day he had a long talk with me and said he really didn't appreciate my going to the falconry club meetings. "These people are my enemies," he told me. I was stunned. *Why are they his enemies?* I thought. *Most of them don't even know him.*

I didn't say one way or the other what I was going to do, but I had no intention of giving up the club. I had really come to love falconry, and what I was doing with the club seemed like a natural progression to me. I didn't want to spend the rest of my life flying red-tailed hawks at rabbits. I wanted to move on to new challenges: prairie falcons, peregrines, Cooper's hawks, merlins. They were all out there waiting for me. Perhaps I could even accomplish things in falconry that no one had ever done before. I wanted to — as Frederick II had written centuries earlier — help "bring the art itself nearer to perfection."

None of this sat well with Jimmie. One night, he came to our apartment and asked to speak with my mother. The three of us sat together in the living room, but he looked at my mother the entire time he spoke, as though I wasn't there. He told her that I was disloyal and dishonest, and he didn't want me coming to his house anymore. But she was still welcome, he said. My mother said she didn't understand what had come between us and was sorry about it, but she didn't see how she could continue a friendship with someone who had forbidden one of her children from ever visiting him. Jimmie reiterated that she and her daughters would always be welcome, but not her son. He left a few minutes later.

A few days later, a mutual friend of ours asked Jimmie if he would talk to me if he ever happened to run into me in a field or someplace, and he said no. To him, I no longer existed. I saw Jimmie briefly again much later, when I was a senior in high school. I was walking with a friend to the hamburger stand beside the school, and I spotted him on the other side of the street, mowing the front lawn of a house. I noticed he had grown a goatee. I don't know if he saw me. He just kept going back and forth across the yard with his lawnmower, his eyes focused straight in front. That was the last time I saw him.

☙

I RELEASED JUDY that spring, shortly before she would have started molting into her adult plumage with a brilliant brick-red tail. Rich and I drove her in his dad's Austin Healey all the way to O'Neill Park. We crossed a fence and walked a mile or so up and down hills across private land. It was wild in there, with lots of things for her to catch. After gorging her on beef heart, I cut off her jesses and set her in a low tree. Rich and I spent the rest of the day hiking through the hills and gullies, looking for hawk nests. When I came back, she was still perched in the same spot. I picked her up and held her on my glove for a few minutes, then threw her off toward a large tree. She landed in it and started working her way higher, hopping from branch to branch. It was sad. I knew I'd never see her again. It seemed harder than it had been with my other birds. I'd flown her for months. We had become so close. I tried to be hard-nosed about it. *At least she had gotten through the difficult first year when most hawks die*, I reasoned. *Now it's up to her.* But down deep, I really wanted nothing more than to pick her up and take her back home with me. I wanted to fly her forever. I took one last look at her in the tree and trudged back over the hills to the car.

5

FLYING FREE

A FEW WEEKS after releasing Judy, Rich and I drove to a place we had found in a faraway section of Riverside County. It was a large, mixed stand of trees — mostly cottonwoods with a scattering of large eucalyptus and pepper trees — surrounded by an endless expanse of open fields and agricultural land. We called it Kestrel Glen, because it had such an amazing concentration of the tiny falcons nesting there. I decided to take a young female kestrel from an early nest, and I named her Gina. She was already hard-penned and flying free before my school year ended in mid-June. But I had a mishap late one afternoon while I was flying her. A flock of crows flew in and mobbed her, chasing her away in the distance shortly before dark, and I couldn't find her.

I spent several days searching unsuccessfully for Gina, before and after school. That Saturday, I walked farther away, checking every field, large and small, anywhere within three or four miles of home. In one of the fields, I spotted a red-haired boy named Terry flying a young red-shouldered hawk to the fist on a creance. He was a couple of years younger than me and attended La Palma Junior High School, near where I lived. I asked him if he'd seen a female kestrel, and he said yes. It turned out that the morning after I lost her, Gina had shown up at his school, hunting grasshoppers from a backstop in the baseball field. He and his friends had gone back after school and trapped her, and now another person, Mac, had her. We went to his house right away, and he gave her back to me.

Mac and I quickly became good friends. He was the same age as me but went to a different school because he lived on the other side of the district boundary. He had a brother named Willy who was four years older and had a car, so we started going to the hills on weekends to look for hawks, sometimes driving two hours or more each way. We would also often hook up with the other teenagers on the street, all of whom were excited about falconry. Robert, who lived across the street from Mac, and his older brother Philo usually went along (Robert even had a copy of Frederick II's treatise and several other falconry books). And Terry and his brother Marshall would also come sometimes.

It was great meeting those guys. They had an entire little falconry enclave, less than two miles from where I lived, and I hadn't even known about them. Before I met them, I didn't realize how much I had missed during the previous couple of years. I really didn't have any friends my own age anymore, with the possible exception of Rich, who was only a year older, but he and I were mostly just acquaintances. He came over to see my bird fly once a week or so but had a whole set of friends at home that I never met. The younger falconers I had known, like Jerry, Keith, Kenneth, Dave, and a few other people had all drifted away from the sport as they grew older and started dating. Most of the people I knew at that point were members of the Santa Ana Valley Falconers' Association and were much older than me. I'd call them up frequently to talk about hawks — and also because I was so desperately lonely.

Shortly after I met Mac and the others, we drove into the hills of Orange County and made a long hike to a golden eagle nest they had found on a cliff. Their climbing techniques and equipment were not much better than mine, except that they used two pieces of cheap manila rope instead of one, in case the main rope broke. I was the first to climb to the eagle nest. Mac was always a great one for making up imaginary newspaper headlines. Just as I started backing off the edge of the cliff, he said: "BOY, 15, FALLS TO HIS DEATH AT EAGLE NEST."

I went over anyway and saw two beautiful young eaglets, still covered in whitish natal down. Mac was eager to get a look at the birds and snap some pictures, so he went next. As he backed off the cliff, I said: "YOUNG ROCK CLIMBER KILLED AFTER FRIEND CUTS ROPE."

Mac was an athlete at school, though you would never have known it. He didn't wear a letterman's jacket like all the other jocks. He just took the varsity letter and various pins and stuck them away in a drawer in his bedroom. He was a swimmer, a diver, and a water polo player, and he set many records at his school that stood for years. His mother always dreamed of his competing in the Olympics someday — and he may well have been good enough — but he didn't want any part of it. He just loved to swim and to roughhouse during water polo games. Although Mac was two or three inches shorter than me, he was broad-shouldered and muscular from all of his swimming. But I could run rings around him.

One day that summer, Mac and I decided to hitchhike to Riverside to visit Henry Swain, a falconer who had traveled to Britain and Ireland a number of times and met some of the famous falconers there. Jack Hagan had given me his phone number, so I called him up one day and arranged to visit. I was especially excited because he had two young Irish merlins, which had been given to him by the legendary British falconer and author Ronald Stevens.

We first had to walk a couple of miles to the freeway, because no one volunteered to drop us off at the on-ramp. We held up a piece of cardboard with "Riverside" written on it, just as we'd seen other hitchhikers do, and stood there waiting eagerly for a ride. It was against the law to hitchhike on the freeway in California, so we could only stand at the on-ramp with the sign, sticking up our thumbs to get attention. Amazingly, we were there for only ten minutes when a man in a pickup truck stopped for us, and he was going all the way to Riverside. Mac jumped in front, while I stepped over the side rail into the bed of the truck.

After we were dropped off, we still had quite a way to go, but we walked along, sticking our thumbs out at passing cars and eventually got another ride that took us close to Swain's home in the suburbs. When we got there, he was sitting in his backyard in a beach chair, in the blazing sun, dressed only in some baggy swim trunks. Swain was probably in his late forties and skinny, but what seemed most remarkable to us were the rows of thick round scabs all over the top of his head. I'm sure he'd probably had a hair transplant, but Mac was convinced it was something more exotic. Swain was such a world traveler, Mac reasoned that he had probably gone through some kind of tribal initiation ritual in Africa or some other exotic locale.

Swain's falcons were perched nearby: the two merlins and a nice tiercel peregrine. Henry was eating a huge Dagwood sandwich — which instantly reminded us how hungry we were and that we hadn't brought any money. (Who thinks of such things when you're a kid?) We sat there staring at the sandwich, and probably drooling, as we spoke with him, but he never offered us any food. He was friendly, and we stayed for hours, listening to his stories of grouse hawking in Scotland with the likes of Geoffrey Pollard and other great falconers we had heard about. But I was most fascinated by his stories about Ronald Stevens — the grand old man of British falconry. He had some pictures of himself sitting beside a cottage in Ireland, having tea with Ronald and a few other guests. It was all very proper and dignified, and I wanted desperately to be there.

Ronald Stevens was a remarkable character. Born into a wealthy family, he inherited a lavish manor house and a Rolls Royce when he turned twenty-one. He was one of the most innovative figures in twentieth-century falconry and a fabulous writer to boot. When war broke out in Europe in 1939, he came up with the remarkable idea of creating a falconry squad, whose task it would be to attempt to catch German carrier pigeons with trained peregrines. At the time, there was a great fear — not unfounded — that enemy spies would use pigeons to carry secret information to their cohorts back in Germany.

The British military fully bought into the idea. This had to be the dream job of the entire war for a falconer. Stevens even got to choose the people he wanted in his squad. They spent the wartime years on an offshore island, trapping and training peregrines and having them wait on for hours at a time, patrolling high above the coastline, in search of passing pigeons. They did catch a number of pigeons, though, unfortunately, none was carrying an enemy message.

Stevens wrote several wonderful books, including one of my favorites, *The Taming of Genghis*, about a difficult male gyrfalcon (or "gerkin") that he had trained. I had borrowed a first-edition copy of the book from Jimmie White while I was training Krag, and it inspired me to keep going through the toughest part of the manning process. Stevens had taken Genghis from an eyrie in a remote part of northeastern Iceland. Years later, I took part in a gyrfalcon research expedition with the Icelandic ornithologist Olafur Nielsen, and he took me to the very nest cliff where Stevens had gotten Genghis. It was a beautiful spot, far up a steep canyon that seemed like a Scottish glen.

Ronald Stevens also wrote a short, influential book titled *Observations on Modern Falconry*. He originally self-published a tiny number of them in a plain paper cover for his friends, but the book has subsequently been reprinted several times in hardback. In the book, Stevens questioned a number of centuries-old concepts about falconry. For example, he came out against stooping falcons to the lure if they were intended for waiting-on flights. But more radical were his ideas about teaching falcons to home to his cottage if they were lost. (Of course, it helps if you live on an enormous estate adjoining your hawking areas.) The book caused a great deal of rethinking among falconers, which was greatly beneficial to the sport.

After several hours of visiting, we left Henry Swain in the late afternoon and began walking to the closest freeway on-ramp. We were in high spirits and couldn't wait to tell our friends everything about Swain and the British falconers he knew. We assumed our journey home would be similar to our hitchhiking experience earlier in the day. It was not. We waited for hours without having anyone stop to ask us where we were going. It was well after dark when a car with four Native Americans finally let us squeeze into the back seat. As we were driving down the freeway, one of the men pulled out a bottle of whiskey, took a long swig, and passed it behind him to the man who sat next to me. After he took a drink, he held the bottle to me.

"No thanks," I said.

"Dreenk!" he said, annoyed.

I took a short swig, which burned my throat, and passed the bottle to Mac. Although we tried to take only small sips of whiskey, by the time they dropped us off in Buena Park, we were both tipsy. The two of us staggered home, trying to hide in the shadows when cars passed, hoping to avoid being seen by any policemen who might happen by. I slipped into my room and went to bed as soon as I got home. It was already past midnight.

This was not the only time Mac and I had problems hitchhiking. Another time we went to O'Neill Park in the hills of Orange County and got stranded when the sun went down. All the day visitors at the park had already gone home, so there was no one to beg a ride from. We had worn only T-shirts that day and, as it got later, we were freezing. We ended up spending the night in the bathroom at the campground. It was large and out of the wind, but neither of us slept all night. We were starving the next day on our hitchhike home.

MAC AND I both took young Cooper's hawks to fly that summer. We went to a late nest he and his brother had found near Fallbrook. A couple of the young jumped from the nest and glided to the ground as we were climbing the tree. They were wild-eyed hawks, tall and skinny with long legs — custom-made for catching birds. We shot sparrows with BB guns to feed to our hawks, and they grew up quickly, strong and healthy.

That was a wonderful summer of hawking. I still flew often with Jeff Sipple, usually in the late afternoon when he got home from work. He had a new tiercel prairie falcon he had taken from a nest, and it was full of promise. I studied his training techniques closely as he worked on his bird's pitch, encouraging him to fly ever higher in circles above him. I tried to emulate what he was doing and was very successful with my kestrel, Gina. She waited on well and would dive at sparrows I flushed while running across a field. She became an excellent game hawk, flying in a completely different style than Merlin. Sometimes instead of circling she would hover eighty feet or so above a place where she knew there were birds for me to flush. Hovering is the classic hunting technique of wild kestrels, and it was amazingly effective. One morning she caught three house sparrows, one right after another. I let her eat just the head of each one, then put her right back in the air to hunt again, and she didn't hesitate. It was exciting sport.

Jeff was a pioneer in hawking mourning doves with large falcons, and his tiercel came to excel at the flight. He would put in blistering vertical stoops as we flushed dove flocks in the stubble fields, and if he connected, the dove would go down in an explosion of feathers. I always loved to go along and flush game, running through the field and clapping my hands. On the flush we would shout loudly then watch his tiercel fold up and plummet down. I became excellent at finding his bird when we lost him on a kill. (This was long before telemetry had been developed for falcons, so we had only the sound of a hawk's bells to help us detect it in cover on a kill.) I would often look in the less-likely places. This meant that I found his bird less often, but when I did locate him, everyone was amazed and thought how brilliant I was to have ever looked in the place where I found him.

But one day, we couldn't find his prairie falcon at all. He had put in a beautiful stoop across the sky, but our vision had been blocked by a row of trees, and we didn't see where the flight ended. We still hadn't found him when it got dark a short time later. Jeff was going to search briefly before work the next morning, but he didn't have much hope of finding him then. He had to be at work only forty-five minutes after dawn. By the time he got off work at the end of the day, his bird might well have flown away and be lost forever. Without telling Jeff, I decided to ride my bike there the next morning and look for his bird. I thought his tiercel had probably gorged on the dove he caught and would relax in a roost tree most of the morning. I figured if I was out there swinging a lure when he finally popped up, I might be able to call him down and return him to Jeff (and be a hero). But there was a problem: the only lure I had was one I made for my kestrel. It was tiny — not even as big as my wallet.

Jeff's prairie falcon appeared just as I'd thought, around ten-thirty, as the day was starting to warm up. I spotted him waiting on high above the field and was tempted to run through the field and flush some doves. Instead, I pulled out my puny kestrel lure and started swinging it and blowing my whistle. Miraculously, the tiercel turned in the air and folded into a long horizontal stoop, pumping his wings as he blasted toward me, the wind whistling loudly through his feathers. I twitched the lure out of his path at the last instant and he rocketed past, swinging up high from his stoop and looking back over his shoulder.

I stooped him several more times, hoping he would lose some of his momentum. He was flying many times faster than any kestrel. The roar of the wind as he shot past in a blur was like the sound of a howitzer shell whizzing through — both exhilarating and terrifying. I felt almost like a matador sidestepping a charging bull. I finally tossed my little lure to the ground, and he landed on it, looking eagerly around for the meat he thought would be attached to it. Unfortunately, I hadn't brought anything to feed him, but I managed to get hold of his jesses and pick him up before he could fly away.

I quickly attached a leash and swivel to his jesses and held him on my gloved fist. But I didn't have a hood, which was a big problem. Although he was tame, this bird was accustomed to being hooded before and after flying, when he was driven to and from the field. He wasn't used to being carried for miles on the fist along a roadway. And that's what I would have to do. Of course, I couldn't use my bike. That would only frighten him, so I left it there and started walking to Jeff's house, several miles away. The tiercel soon became restless, spreading his wings out, looking for a place to fly to, and bating frequently. And the day was getting hot. I stopped in the shade of any tree I could find along the way and let him cool off. At one point, I saw a garden sprinkler hose — the kind with dozens of tiny holes pierced in it to create a fine spray of water — and I stood in the middle of it, letting the mist gently wet both of us. He seemed to enjoy that, and it cooled him down. He sat on my fist with his wings spread and his damp feathers fluffed out for most of the rest of the way to Jeff's house, letting his feathers dry out completely in the warm summer air.

I finally reached Jeff's house and knocked on the door. His wife, Diana, was amazed to see that I had his bird. She let me into the yard and I tied the falcon to his perch and put a pan of bathwater beside him, which he leapt into. Then I left and walked all the way back to my bike and rode it home. It was dark by the time I got there, and my face and arms were bright red with sunburn.

Jeff drove over later that night to thank me. He handed me a five-dollar bill. I told him he didn't need to give me that; I was happy to help him get his falcon back, because I enjoyed seeing him fly so much. But he insisted. "I know you worked hard today, and I appreciate it," he said. "I really want you to have this."

⁓

MY MALE COOPER'S hawk, Pedro, was a joy to fly, a master of the sneak attack. Some of his flights were similar to Merlin's, slipping down low to the ground and flying fast, using the cover of foliage or the topography of the land to hide himself from the quarry he was attacking. And he was deadly efficient. I never put any bells on him, so there was nothing to give away his presence. Amazingly, I always found him on his kills. He took sparrows in all the local fields and sometimes in the park across from my house, which made him easy to fly, because he didn't need the space a high-flying falcon required. But my favorite place to fly him was in the Bastanchury Hills area near Fullerton. They were rolling hills with good cover and a scattering of pepper trees here and there. And they were full of California quail, my favorite quarry to catch with a Cooper's hawk.

The place I flew was owned by an oil company and had a number of wells here and there constantly pumping oil. But none of the oil company employees ever complained about my being there. Sometimes one or two of them would get out of their pickup truck and help me flush game for my bird. He was an adept quail catcher, and the flights were always exciting. I would walk up and down the hills searching until I heard a covey of quail chittering up ahead in dense cover, then I would try to set up a good flush for Pedro. It always made my heart beat fast as I walked slowly and carefully closer and closer, knowing that any second the quail would explode in front of me with my hawk right behind them. And Pedro was even more excited than I was. I'd occasionally sneak a glance at him, and he would be standing straight and tall, his eyes bugging out in anticipation.

Those were my favorite flights, right off the fist at a rising covey of quail. With an explosive burst of speed, he sometimes flew right up after a quail, snatching it deftly from the air. But other times it was far more difficult. I remember once seeing him flying around and around, in and out of a pepper tree, half running, half flying, chasing a quail, which he ultimately caught. Another time he crashed into a group of quail standing in sparse cover, and I saw them all running around in a panic like a bunch of roly-poly toys, bumping into each other as my hawk ran in the middle of them. (Cooper's hawks are amazingly fast and agile on their feet and are excellent at hunting in cover.) A few of the quail finally flushed, with him right behind them, and he grabbed one from below and carried it back down to the ground.

Pedro became good at following me around the field, flying from tree to tree as I walked down a canyon, poking around with a hiking stick, trying to flush game. He made many great sneak attacks on quail, some of which I flushed for him, others he spotted himself from the trees. He was so good at exploiting the hunting opportunities in those hills that I decided to release him there at the end of the season. I had released Gina much closer to home, at a dairy where I knew the owner. I had often hunted sparrows with my hawks there — or with a BB gun to get food for my hawks — and I knew she would do well. I had decided to fly another red-tail that fall and was already planning to go trapping in the high desert of Antelope Valley, a couple of hours' drive away.

6

CENTERVILLE DAYS

THAT FALL, IN 1966, I experienced one of the high points of my early falconry years, when Rich and I drove all the way to South Dakota to attend the fifth annual field meet of the North American Falconers' Association. Our trip took place just a few months after my parents split up. I was amazed that my mother let me go — even though I'd be gone for almost two weeks and would miss Thanksgiving and several days of school. I think she was trying to let me have more freedom (I didn't have much when my dad lived with us) and for that, I'll always be grateful.

I had one disappointment, though. Rich didn't want me to bring my new hawk to the meet. He thought she would be too much trouble. Although I had released my excellent eyas red-tail Judy in the spring, I had a wild-trapped red-tail that was coming along nicely and chasing cottontails. I know she would have blossomed at the meet, and at that time, few falconers knew what a good falconry bird a red-tail could be. My mother took care of my hawk for me while I was gone.

I had to sell some of my most prized possessions to scrounge together enough money for gas. The hardest thing was taking my buffalo nickel collection to a coin shop. The shop owner gave me barely anything more than the face value of the coins. I really loved those nickels, with their exquisite Indian head on one side and a buffalo on the other. I had collected them for years as a kid. I would go through a checkout line at a grocery store and ask to have a dollar changed into nickels. I would quickly go through them looking for buffalo nickels, then go to another checkout line and get the nickels changed back into a dollar bill. I repeated this endlessly some days, going to several different stores to try to get more of the coins. After all that work, it was hard to part with them, and I still miss those old coins, which have since completely vanished from circulation. But I was determined to go to the falconry meet. I think even at the age of sixteen, I knew this would be a watershed time in my life, when I crossed over some imaginary line and became a serious falconer.

A few days after I sold my nickels we were on our way, put-putting and grinding our way south — yes, south; we were trying to bypass as much as possible of the cold weather and high mountains we would have faced on the northern route. We chose to travel the soft underbelly of America, Route 66, through Arizona, New Mexico, and part of Texas, then due north through Oklahoma, Kansas, Nebraska, and on into South Dakota to a small town named Centerville.

It was a different world back then, cruising along the old Route 66: the Whiting Brothers gas stations gleaming like oases in the desert bleakness; the weird roadside attractions advertised on tiny signs for a couple of hundred miles before you reached them. One set of signs I remember had a little black jackrabbit silhouette painted on them; each sign counted down the number of miles to go. When we finally got there, we found a black rabbit the size of a two-story house that had souvenirs for sale inside.

Our journey was not entirely smooth sailing. The car's engine had an oil leak that drip, drip, dripped tiny specks of greasy black liquid on the highway across eight states. We stopped several times in the desert and crawled underneath, trying to figure out a way to staunch the flow, but it was no good. We just made ourselves filthy. Eventually we started going to gas stations and saying, "Fill her up with oil and check the gas." It was getting expensive until one garage owner suggested we use some of the drip-back oil he'd drained from other cars. It was an awful idea, but we had no choice. We drove out of there with several gallon-sized glass jugs full of dirty oil.

At one point, a shimmy developed in one of the front wheels, and when we got out to check it, the hub was steaming. It sizzled when Rich spit on it. We had worn out a wheel bearing. A farmhouse down the road had a bunch of old cars rusting in a nearby field. Rich was a good mechanic and had brought a nice set of tools. He figured he could find a decent set of wheel bearings from one of the old cars — the only problem was that no one was home at the farm and worse, a big German shepherd came running out into the front yard and bit Rich hard on the back of his leg as we retreated to the car. His jeans were torn and he was bleeding profusely from the wound. He sat there steaming for ten minutes, then said: "Dammit, I'm going to get the wheel bearings."

And he did. When he got back, we cleaned out the hub of the wheel as well as we could and smeared a bunch of grease into it that he'd scooped from the old farm truck when he took the bearings. We got it all back together, and it worked fine for the rest of the trip.

But those weren't the only problems we had with the car. The muffler was falling apart, making the car sound like a top-fuel dragster as we rumbled through each tiny burg. In one small town in New Mexico, a sheriff came running out of a café with a napkin still tucked in his shirt and stood in front of our car to stop us.

"Why ain't you kids in school?" he snarled, ketchup dripping down his chin.

"It's Saturday," we said.

"Yeah, but you didn't leave home this morning!"

True . . . but somehow we finessed our way out of it — or, I should say, Rich did. He was smooth. The sheriff finally wished us luck on our trip, turned, and strode back into the café. Rich slowly pulled out a comb and dragged his Brylcreamed dishwater blond hair back, carefully making it stand up in front, Long Beach hood style. Slipping on his shades, he lit up a Camel, smirked at me, then fired up the engine — *VRROOOOM; VRROOOM* — and we were off, with nothing left to stop us.

We continued on. Sleeping in the car. Living on cans of beans that we put on top of the engine as we drove to heat them up. I never told my mom we didn't have enough money for food and lodging. Rich taught me the trick of sitting at a lunch counter in a truck stop café and ordering a cup of tea. Instead of dropping the teabag into the hot water container, he would pour half a bottle of ketchup into it, salt and pepper it liberally and voilà — instant tomato soup, with plenty of crackers at the table for bulk. After finishing the meal, he would wipe the cup out with his napkin and ask for a refill of hot water, which he would then use to make a real cup of tea. Only problem was, the tea tasted like Heinz ketchup.

We finally got to Centerville after four days on the road, and at first we couldn't find anyone. We drove up and down the main street of the tiny Midwestern town then expanded our search into the countryside. Eventually we spotted a light green Ford Falcon sedan with Colorado plates cruising slowly along the edge of a field. We first spotted the immature goshawk perched bareheaded on the backseat and then the North American Falconers' Association decal displayed prominently on the rear window. The two falconers in the car invited us to go hawking with them, and together we walked across a nearby field in search of rabbits. We tromped around for a while without success, and the goshawk finally flew up to a tree and perched contentedly as the sun dipped below the trees and dusk began to descend on the vast fields of corn stubble. The blond kid who owned the goshawk called his bird down and took it back to the car. His name was Bill Heinrich, and he was the same age as me. When the Peregrine Fund was formed a few years later and began breeding peregrines in captivity and releasing them to the wild, Bill joined the staff, and he is now the species restoration manager, working with California condors and other critically endangered raptors. We met again many years later working on a peregrine falcon banding program on Padre Island, Texas, and became friends.

By this time it was getting dark, and we had no place to stay, but some other falconers we ran into in town told us about an old, vacant schoolhouse nearby. We decided to spend the night there. Although it was dusty and unheated, it was out of the wind and had a couple of long tables we figured we could sleep on. We quickly wiped off the dust and unrolled our sleeping bags. My bag was thin and way too short. I'd had it since I first joined the Boy Scouts, and I couldn't afford to get another one. I think I slept for about an hour before it got so cold I started shivering violently. I rolled up into a fetal ball with my head stuffed inside the bag and that helped. It was almost tolerable, and I thought I might be able to fall asleep again — until I heard footsteps. It sounded like the tread of a human walking slowly along the old hardwood floor, creaking with each step. Then when the sound got right beside me, it stopped. And everything was silent for the longest time — it could have been five minutes; it could have been five hours. I lay there trembling with terror, afraid to move or call out. It was impossible to sleep after that. I was still young enough to think that I might have had an encounter with something scary like a ghost. I lay awake till the daylight streamed through the dirty cracked windows, illuminating the gloomy classroom. Turns out, Rich was awake the whole time, too, and like me had been too scared to yell.

"Must have been a raccoon," he said.

"Yeah. Must have been," I said. But there was no way either of us would spend another night in there.

The falconry meet was great. The town of Centerville seemed genuinely pleased to host the group. A massive cake with a stooping falcon and "Welcome Falconers!" emblazoned across it in decorative icing sat in the window of the town bakery. All of the greats of the sport were there, including the famous British falconer and author Jack Mavrogordato — who was like a Victorian gentleman and had lived for years in the Sudan, flying falcons with a toweringly tall black manservant named Hakim at his side.

I was completely in awe of Jack. He was one of those remarkable figures sometimes encountered in falconry. Trained as a barrister, he became a Queen's Councilor. In the Sudan, he was a prominent colonial judge and later drafted the country's constitution as it gained its independence. You might say Jack Mavrogordato was larger than life, except that he was incredibly short — probably less than five feet tall.

He had been quite an active falconer in the 1930s when he was young. He and his friend Bobbie Spens would go on long hawking excursions to Ireland and other far-flung parts of the British Isles, flying casts of falcons (a cast is two raptors, usually of the same sex, flown together) at magpies and other challenging quarry. I've seen several pictures of the two of them taken in the 1930s. Bobbie looked great, like a character from Evelyn Waugh's *Brideshead Revisited*, clad in baggy tan pants and a sport coat, sometimes accented with a fedora and pipe — and always with a falcon on his fist (except for one boyhood picture in which he wears a fencing mask and is holding a pet cormorant he had trained to catch fish).

Unfortunately, like all too many of the promising young British falconers of his generation, Bobbie did not come home from the war. His ship was sunk as he was being taken to Italy as a prisoner of war. He left behind a wife and child as well as a good friend who had lost his closest hawking companion.

Jack was well known among falconers worldwide because of his excellent book, *A Hawk for the Bush*, which he had written a few years earlier. It was mostly about flying sparrowhawks, a small Eurasian accipiter somewhat similar to a North American sharp-shinned hawk, but the information was directly applicable to Cooper's hawks, goshawks, and even buteos such as red-tailed hawks. It didn't address falcons, but shortly before the meet he published a sequel named *A Falcon in the Field* to address that deficiency. He had a single copy with him and was taking orders from falconers at the meet. Of course, I wanted one badly, but there was no way I could afford the nine-dollar price tag. I gave Jack my name and address so he could put me on his mailing list. I thought maybe he would send me a note or an advertisement for the book and I could keep it as a souvenir.

As it turned out, I misunderstood what the mailing list was for. A few weeks later, Jack sent me a copy of the book, with his signature and the date written in red ink inside. I was both thrilled and horrified. How could I possibly pay for it? In a strange bit of irony, somewhat like O. Henry's "The Gift of the Magi," I ended up having to sell the book to pay for it. I let my friend Mac have it for the price on the invoice and sent a money order to Jack. Years later, in an act of amazing generosity, Mac gave the book back to me as a gift. (By then it was a rare collector's item, easily worth more than $1,500.) Mac knew how much the book meant to me, and I'm proud and grateful to have it on my bookshelf, right beside *A Hawk for the Bush*.

Jack was also a great admirer of Frederick II, although he detested the 1942 English-language edition of the book and sometimes poked fun at the poor quality of the translation. Late in his life, he worked closely with a Latin scholar on a new translation, but as far as I have been able to find out, it was never completed. I hope the manuscript turns up someday.

At the meet, Rich and I met a student from Purdue University named Greg Thomas. He came to the meet with an eyas red-tail that hadn't caught any game yet. We watched his hawk take its first rabbit, followed by several more during the course of the meet. Jack Mavrogordato saw Greg's red-tail fly a few times and was quite impressed by the bird. This only made me more depressed about not bringing my hawk. Of course, I got to talk with Jack about all the cottontails and jackrabbits I'd taken with a red-tail during the past season, but there's nothing like actually flying a hawk for someone and catching game. I ran into Greg again this past fall at the 2006 falconry meet in Kearney, Nebraska. We had both gone gray in the forty years since we'd last met. He is still an avid red-tail hawker.

We met a lot of interesting characters at the Centerville meet, including the legendary Cornelius McFadden, a tall, stocky, white-haired man with a booming voice, who wisecracked endlessly with everyone. Corny, as he was called, had taken part in an amazing 1950 gyrfalcon trapping expedition to Greenland that people still talk about to this day. Then there was Hal Webster from Colorado, who, with coauthor Frank Beebe, wrote *North American Falconry and Hunting Hawks*, a seminal work on falconry in the United States and Canada published a couple of years earlier. When that book came out, American falconers could, for the first time, read a book specifically about the raptor species and game we have on this continent, instead of having to adapt the information from British and European falconry books to fit our special needs.

One somewhat sad memory I have of the meet is Hal Webster calling out one day, "Anyone lose a camera?"

"I did," I said. I had brought an old 35 mm rangefinder camera with me — the only camera I owned. I had been carrying it around, stuffed in the pocket of my coat, and apparently it had fallen out one day when I got into Rich's car. Hal came over and put his arm around my shoulder.

"Well, son," he said, puffing on a huge cigar, "I think you better get a new camera." He handed me a brown paper bag containing the crushed remains of my treasured camera, which had been run over by a car. This was a tragedy for me. I couldn't afford to get another decent camera for the rest of my teenage years.

We also got to know Frank Beebe, Webster's coauthor on the book. He was a gifted artist who worked at a museum on Vancouver Island, and he created all the paintings and line drawings in *North American Falconry and Hunting Hawks*. The first edition came with a set of high-quality reproductions of the paintings, suitable for framing. Beebe was one of the great inventors and gadgeteers in falconry, coming up with remarkable innovations never before seen in the sport — such as the spring-closing hood. The falconer could hold on to the hood's ingenious closing mechanism with his thumb and forefinger, holding the hood open as he slipped it over his falcon's head. As soon as it was in place, he could let go and the hood would close automatically. This was much easier than having to cinch it up with the leather ties called braces. He also invented the large latex lure with flapping wings that mimics the flight of a duck when swung around on the end of a line. And don't forget the pole lure. Beebe would take a large fishing rod blank — the kind avid fishermen buy so they can build their own rods from scratch — and attach a lure to it using a length of elastic surgical tubing in between as a shock absorber. This keeps the lure away from the falconer, minimizing the risk of a collision between the falcon and its trainer, and improving lure control. (My only complaint about the pole lure is that it's not portable enough. I like all my equipment to fit into my falconry bag. I make an allowance for my telemetry receiver and its folding antenna, but there's no way to make a pole lure truly portable. However, a number of people still use them effectively.)

Beebe and his wife and daughter drove out to the field one day with Rich and me. For some reason, Rich had installed drag-racing-style seatbelts on the front seats of his car, with harnesses that went over both shoulders and a wide, flat leather belt that went over the lap and locked with a big metal clasp. (This was at a time when few people used seatbelts of any kind.) Beebe was mightily impressed by those seatbelts; no doubt his inventor's mind was trying to figure out a new gadget he could make based on this design.

Years later, I visited Beebe at his home near Victoria, British Columbia, and watched him catch a mallard with his five-year-old eyas gyrfalcon. I also went to the museum where he had worked, though he was already retired by then.

Like most falconers, Beebe could be quite opinionated, and when debating he would sometimes become borderline cantankerous, his voice rising to a shrill pitch guaranteed to grate on everyone's nerves. (Maybe that was a debating ploy.) But I always found him fascinating, and he is still going strong in his early nineties. Hal Webster, who recently turned eighty-seven, now lives in Montana and is still active in falconry. I received a letter from him just the other day, congratulating me on my first issue as editor of the *Journal of the North American Falconers' Association*.

Another thing that made the 1966 meet so interesting was that it took place just one year after the famed peregrine falcon conference of 1965, convened by ornithologist Joe Hickey at the University of Wisconsin–Madison. Falcon researchers from around the world had converged on Madison to compare notes and examine the peregrine falcon's plight. They learned that the situation was much more dire than anyone had thought and that the bird had already been extirpated as a breeding species in the entire eastern United States. A number of key figures who had been at that conference — Fran Hammerstrom, Jim Enderson, Heinz Meng, and others — were in attendance at the falconry meet, continuing the discussion they'd begun a year earlier, and it was fascinating to hear them speak, and shocking; I'd had no idea we were in such imminent danger of losing the peregrine falcon.

A new group named the Raptor Research Foundation (RRF) had formed virtually right after the Madison conference, spearheaded by Don Hunter — a gentleman farmer and falconer who lived in Centerville — and several other falconers. I'm still a member of the foundation, but it was in its infancy at that time and held its second meeting at the falconry meet. I have a copy of the RRF's first publication, a simple, unadorned newsletter printed in black ink on white typing paper — barely a step above a mimeograph. Now four times a year the group publishes *The Journal of Raptor Research*, a respected scientific journal with an attractive color cover.

Hunter had a beautiful white gyrfalcon, which he treasured. This was before the advent of radio-telemetry devices for tracking falcons, and on the rare occasions when he lost his falcon, he was a wreck. He also had a nice goshawk, and one day he went out pheasant hunting on horseback with the bird — the first time I'd seen someone use a horse in falconry. I ran into Don Hunter again decades later at a California Hawking Club meet, just a couple of years before he passed away, and we had a nice talk about the 1966 meet.

Each night the falconers got together in a hall in Centerville and had long discussions about falconry. When Rich and I walked out of the meeting on the second night, we realized we didn't have a place to sleep. Even though the hotel rooms in town were only four or five bucks a night, we didn't have enough. In fact, we already had barely enough cash to pay for gas to get home. And after our experience the night before with the ghost or whatever, we definitely didn't want to stay in the old school again. We ended up sleeping beside a river with Jim Weaver and another falconer from Illinois. A few years later, Jim would head the Peregrine Fund's falcon breeding facility at Cornell University.

Famed Cornell ornithologist Tom Cade launched the Peregrine Fund in 1970, to try to figure out how to reverse the catastrophic decline of the peregrine falcon in North America. You could say the organization launched itself. Various falconers started sending checks to Cade to help with his research efforts, so he set up a bank account he called the Peregrine Fund, and the organization fairly quickly morphed into a powerhouse in raptor conservation. Falconers were the key contributors to the organization from the start, giving of their time, their money, and even donating falcons to be used in the captive-breeding program Cade envisioned. At that time, the concept of breeding raptors was largely theoretical.

A great deal of the success of the peregrine falcon reintroduction in North America was thanks to Jim Weaver's efforts. At the 1966 meet he was fairly recently back from Alaska and had two nice peregrines — an adult female and a first-year male — perched next to his sleeping bag. His friend had a sleek gray gyrfalcon. He had trapped the bird a short time before the meet, and she was already remarkably tame. They were cooking pheasant on their campfire, which they shared with us, our first meal of the day.

Jim looked like a real mountain man, with a bushy handlebar mustache and wild, dark red hair. He was definitely in his element in that cold. Of course, Rich and I had come from a balmy climate and had thin sleeping bags. And that night there was a cold snap. My own shivering kept me awake, so I lost another night's sleep. By the time we got up, the river beside us had frozen enough to skate on.

Rich and I shambled around town the next morning like shell-shocked refugees, dark rings beneath our eyes. We paused beside the bakery, gazing longingly at the falconry cake inside. The next thing we knew, the woman who worked there, Mrs. Steadman, had waved us inside and was giving us some free Danish rolls. She got excited when she found out we were from California; her daughter lived there. She asked where we were staying, and we mumbled about the trees beside the river outside of town. Then she invited us to stay at their place with her husband, a retired farmer. We were in heaven. Mr. Steadman was a hunter, and she was a fabulous cook. We ate pheasant, venison, and homemade apple pie every night. And it was so warm in their home. It wasn't long before three or four other falconers heard about our good fortune and tried to horn in. The Steadmans graciously took them all in. I sent them Christmas cards for years.

The hawking was great at the Centerville meet. South Dakota is famous for its pheasant hunting, and these birds were the primary quarry of the falconers flying longwings at the meet. (The term "longwings" refers to gyrfalcons, peregrines, prairie falcons, and other true falcons, which have long pointed wings in proportion to their bodies. "Shortwings" are the accipiters such as goshawks, Cooper's hawks, and sharp-shinned hawks, which have short, rounded wings and long tails. It is perhaps worth mentioning that a falcon is a type of hawk, so all falcons are hawks, but not all hawks are falcons. But hawking and falconry generally refer to training any kind of raptor.) The pheasants seemed remarkably strong, blasting from the corn stubble as if they were shot from cannons. We went hunting with Jim Weaver several times. His intermewed female peregrine was a solid performer. ("Intermewed" refers to a bird that has molted in captivity and is thus in adult plumage; a hawk that has molted into adult plumage in the wild is called a haggard.) Although she was not a high flyer, she caught at least a couple of pheasants during the meet. But his young tiercel was the real star, for me at least. He always flew high and fast, making terrific vertical stoops, swooping back up almost to his original pitch and then stooping again. I knew immediately that this is what I wanted in a falcon — the finesse, the sheer exuberance of flight — and his bird's example may well be the reason I almost always fly male peregrines.

We flew several times with Roy and Eddie Bigelow, a father and son from British Columbia who brought with them some superb intermewed Peale's falcons — the large, dark race of peregrine found along the coast and islands of the Pacific Northwest. And Mike Arnold, a falconer from Southern California whom I met in Centerville, was flying a juvenile female Peale's he had taken that spring from a nest cliff on the Queen Charlotte Islands, off British Columbia. We watched him catch his first head of game with the bird — a hen pheasant. And we were also with him, sadly, a day or two later when he lost her. We had a dog on point and were walking in a line across a corn stubble field with his bird ringing up above us. As she circled, our view of her became blocked by the trees in a shelterbelt at the edge of the field. We all expected her to reappear in a few seconds as she completed the arc of her circle, but she never did. I finally turned to walk over to the trees to see if I could see her. Pheasants were suddenly bursting out all around in front of me. They knew the danger had passed. Pheasants are extremely difficult to flush with a falcon right above them.

We started searching immediately, checking a nearby farm to see if she'd gone after some barn pigeons, but it was starting to get dark. We couldn't see her or hear her bells anywhere, and at nightfall we went back to the meet headquarters empty-handed. Although everyone searched for the rest of the meet, the falcon had vanished without a trace. Such was life in the days before telemetry.

On the last evening of the meet, we had a banquet in nearby Yankton. Jack Mavrogordato presented a wonderful talk. I remember the simple rule he told us about how to have a happy marriage —"one hawk, one wife; two hawks, no wife"— of course, this was coming from a man who generally owned several hawks at a time and had never been married. He also showed us a movie he had taken of hawking in Arabia. Some of the men were riding in a Cadillac convertible with the top down, holding their falcons. There was one hilarious scene in which the Cadillac had become stuck in the sand, and the men in their Arab kaffiyeh headdresses were out of the car pushing on it as the tires spun uselessly, kicking up dust everywhere. At the end of the evening, we all exchanged addresses, promising to keep in touch, and I did correspond with some of the falconers for several years.

As we were leaving to drive back to California, Mrs. Steadman handed us two grocery bags full of Danish rolls from the bakery to take with us, and that's all we ate for five days. I've never since liked Danish rolls.

7

THE LONG SPIRAL
DOWNWARD

LESS THAN A month after the Centerville falconry meet, I trapped my
first large falcon — a first-year prairie falcon I named Josie. I had gone
to the desert with my friend Ed, who worked as an alligator wrangler at
the California Alligator Farm, a now-defunct tourist attraction in Buena
Park. He used to let me into the farm after-hours to shoot house sparrows with my BB gun when I was raising young hawks. It was always a
race to pick up the fallen sparrows before the big alligators got them.

Ed drove me to the desert a couple of times that fall to go hawk
trapping, and on our final trip, in the late afternoon, we caught Josie.
She seemed like the most beautiful bird I'd ever seen, with her huge
dark eyes, her cream-colored breast with dark markings, and her buff-
brown back. She was perfect — except for one thing: she had a big thorn
jammed into one of her toes, which was red and infected. I pulled it out
first thing and let the wound drain. I also soaked the foot each night in
warm water with Epsom salts, and it quickly healed.

You could say this was like Androcles, who pulled the thorn from
the biblical lion's paw, because Josie had none of the legendary ferocity I
had been expecting. Most wild-trapped prairie falcons are famously bad
tempered, often screaming in a rage and biting their trainers. (Some of

them will deliberately reach beyond the end of the falconer's gauntlet to bite the unprotected flesh of his forearm.) I don't know why that is. Maybe it has something to do with the prairie falcon evolving in such a harsh environment, having to scratch out an existence in the parched, unforgiving landscape of the desert.

Josie seemed as good-natured as the most easygoing peregrine. Of course, this might have had something to do with the fact that she practically lived on my fist during her first two weeks of captivity. This was during Christmas vacation in eleventh grade, and I was also between jobs, so I had unlimited time to spend with her. I would put a hood on her and walk over to visit Mac and my other Buena Park friends, then I'd sit and talk with them for hours, taking off her hood and letting her sit on my fist, looking around with great curiosity. One day I hitchhiked to Seal Beach with her to visit my friend Steve. I got stranded and had to walk all the way home — about fifteen miles — in the middle of the night.

I had Josie flying free quickly. My only problem was that because I didn't have a car, it was difficult to get to a good field every day. I ended up often flying her in some nearby big fields that were broken up with factories and warehouses — far from optimal habitat for flying a large falcon. There were some pheasants scattered here and there, plus feral pigeons along the edges of the fields and around the railroad tracks, but it wasn't great. I ended up mostly doing speculative hunting, having Josie wait on above me as I used my speed and stamina as a runner to race across the fields, kicking brush here and there, hoping to get a lucky flush. I did get some nice flights but few kills.

In one memorable early flight with Josie, I think I was probably actually losing her. She rang up higher and higher into a brilliant-blue sky until — even through binoculars — she was just a tiny speck passing in and out of the puffy cumulus clouds high above me. And she completely ignored the lure. I finally put it away in my game bag and took off sprinting — through the field, across the drainage ditch, along the railroad tracks, through another field. I didn't even know if she was still above me. I finally flushed a small flock of pigeons, maybe five or six, and watched them fly away, not knowing if anything would happen.

The pigeons scattered away from each other just before I saw Josie, plummeting downward, looking more like a falling rock than a living creature. She struck one of the pigeons with her feet, knocking out a small puff of feathers, but the bird rolled, avoiding the full impact of Josie's colossal stoop. The pigeon took off toward a distant factory yard with the falcon in fast pursuit.

I ran as quickly as I could to get there. A huge chainlink fence — perhaps eight feet high with barbed wire on top — surrounded the factory and its yard. It was closed for the weekend. I walked around the fence, looking and listening, and finally heard the sound of a bell coming from inside the factory yard. I draped my coat on the barbed wire and climbed over the fence. I found Josie plucking the dead pigeon behind some stacks of pallets.

Getting out of the factory yard proved to be much harder than getting inside. I had to climb over the fence with one hand, while holding Josie on my other fist. By the time I got over, my arms were bleeding from barbed-wire gouges, and my pants were torn. I spent that evening sewing them up. I had only two pairs to wear to school.

I FLEW JOSIE for the rest of the season and then drove to the desert with Mac, Robert, Philo, and Hollis (a new friend), and we set her free. We planned to camp there for the weekend, below a rocky butte. I fed Josie early in the morning and cut off her jesses. I was hoping to see her circle up until she disappeared into the desert sky, but she was too full of meat to feel like flying. She made a couple of circles and landed atop the butte. There she sat for a couple of hours while we ate breakfast and got ready to go looking for nesting prairie falcons.

Although we searched most of the day, exploring all the rocky buttes and cliffs in the area, we found nothing — except for a couple of raven nests and a mountain lion we flushed as we looked over a deep, rocky gully. When we returned to our campsite, Josie was gone. I climbed up to the ledge where she had perched, and I sat there for a while as a stiff breeze blew across the desert, bringing tears to my eyes. Two years later, Hollis and I found a prairie falcon nest within a mile of this spot. I've always liked to think that it was Josie's nest, but I'll never know.

I RELEASED JOSIE in the spring of 1967, when I was in eleventh grade. This was right before the famed "Summer of Love," when many people in my generation broke away from their parents and went off to live the hippie life in San Francisco and other places across the country. Drugs had already begun to descend on us like a great gray fog, threatening to swallow us up. No one my age — at least, no one I knew — was immune. I used to think I was. I held out a couple of months longer than Mac and Robert, but before long we were all smoking pot together and going to love-ins, pop festivals, and other hippie gatherings in the hills of Southern California.

I had met Hollis earlier that spring. He lived in Long Beach and had known my friend Steve — the blond kid from Seal Beach — for several months. They were both avid surfers and ran into each other a few times at the beach before finding out they were both interested in falconry. Hollis came to our apartment one day, driving a white '59 Ford station wagon and eager to head out to the hills to search for hawks and adventure. He had just finished rebuilding his car's engine — taking it completely apart; replacing all of the rod, crankshaft, and camshaft bearings; replacing the gaskets and seals and valves; and putting it all back together again.

Mac and I were best friends by then. We were always eager to search for hawks, especially in late winter and early spring when they paired up and began nesting. We welcomed the chance to go exploring with someone new — especially a person who had his own car.

In some ways, it was a shock the first time I saw Hollis. Mac and I were definitely hippie wannabes — we went without haircuts for so long we started getting hauled into the vice principal's office regularly and threatened with suspension if our hair got any longer. But Hollis had already reached the pinnacle of hippiedom. He looked like someone from a psychedelic rock band like Big Brother and the Holding Company. Dressed in a baggy white T-shirt and blue jeans, Hollis had straight, dark-brown hair well past his shoulders and broad dark sideburns growing all the way to his jawline. He had a mellow, amiable disposition, and we all instantly took to each other.

It was early on Saturday, a bright spring morning in late March. We grabbed our binoculars and a few snacks and were on our way, headed for a remote canyon on the far side of Orange County. Mac and I and a few other friends had gone there many times before to search for raptors. We had rappelled several times to an eagle's nest on a rocky cliff and had also found the nests of red-tailed hawks, great horned owls, and long-eared owls. Although we had seen a pair of Cooper's hawks doing some early-season courtship flights there, we had not found a nest. That's what we were really after. Mac and I hoped to take young Cooper's hawks again that spring.

Unfortunately, we didn't get far in Hollis's station wagon. We'd gone only five or six miles on the Santa Ana Freeway when we heard a loud bang followed by the clatter of broken mechanical parts. Hollis stepped on the clutch and steered the car onto the shoulder of the road. He opened the hood and propped it up. Inside, a broken connecting rod protruded through a ragged hole in the side of the crankcase. (I don't know why it happened; maybe Hollis didn't tighten a bolt sufficiently when he rebuilt the engine.) I'll never forget seeing Hollis stick his hand into the gaping hole, staring as the engine's hot, oily lifeblood spilled over his fingers onto the asphalt below.

We had no intention of letting that stop us. We immediately hitch-hiked to Mac's house to see if his older brother Willy would let us borrow his car. It was an old, faded-blue Opel sedan, which we used often on our hawk-searching expeditions. Amazingly, Willy said it was fine. He flipped the keys to Mac, and we were on our way. As we retraced our journey up the Santa Ana Freeway, we noticed Hollis's car was already gone; it had probably been towed to the county yard. The only trace left was a pool of motor oil. We never saw the car again. Hollis took the loss in stride, but at least a couple of years went by before he had a car of his own again.

We had no idea what adventures we might still face that day. We parked in a secluded spot, where the car was hidden from view behind some live oaks, and took off overland, climbing up a high ridge through pungent, shoulder-high sagebrush. By this time, it was nearly noon. The sun hung high overhead, searing us and filling our eyes with burning salty sweat. The loud calls of California quail echoed around us — *chi-CA-go* . . . *chi-CA-go*. Thrashers scolded incessantly. Occasionally a huge mule deer would burst from cover and bound off quickly, making a mockery of our pathetic efforts to pass through its domain.

While clambering up the steep hillside, we had a couple of close encounters with rattlesnakes. Once Mac, who was in the lead, jumped back on me to avoid a red diamondback coiled at his feet. The snake rattled endlessly, probably more in fear than anger. We gave it a wide berth and continued upward to the crest of the ridge. From there, the tree-filled canyon spread out below us, a mix of live oaks and sycamores and other native California trees and clumps of prickly pear and cholla cactus. A tiny creek glinted through the foliage.

We scrambled down the hillside to a dirt road running along our side of the canyon. A few beef cattle grazed nearby, which gave us pause. It's not that we were afraid of cows but of the cowboys who might be watching over them. We had rarely seen cattle in the canyon before. We knew it was serious trespassing to go there. People had been thrown in jail or given big fines for getting caught on some of these huge ranch properties. But in many ways that was a good thing. It kept out the kind of people who might harm the hawks, owls, and other wildlife. It was a de facto sanctuary. No one could hunt there. For us, it was a dream. And we figured we were sneaky enough to avoid getting caught. Since we weren't doing anything noisy like shooting guns or riding dirt bikes, we could step quietly through this peaceful, near-pristine place and experience California as it had been in centuries past.

But we should have stepped quickly into the cover of the trees and brush. Instead, we foolishly strode down the dirt road, talking and laughing. We were eager to get to the eagle nest to see how far along the birds were in their nesting cycle. Eagles nest much earlier than most other raptors, because it takes so long for them to raise their young. We were excited and just didn't think.

The pickup truck appeared around a bend in the road about a hundred yards ahead of us. The cowboy inside locked his eyes on us and sped up, raising a great cloud of dust as he raced to get to us. Without a word, we took off running, Hollis going to the right, Mac and I to the left, trying to reach cover and hide as quickly as possible. The two of us ducked through the trees, ran full out for a few minutes, then dove into some knee-high grasses and lay still. It suddenly felt like it was a hundred degrees outside. I was breathing hard and could barely catch my breath. My heart pounded in my temples and a bitter taste flooded my mouth — probably adrenaline. Were we safe? Or would he find us?

A twig snapped maybe sixty yards away. I peeked through the grass and could see the cowboy treading slowly and carefully toward us, following our trail like Tonto in a cowboy hat. Occasionally he seemed to peer straight at Mac and me but didn't see us, motionless and watching. He wore a sweat-stained gray Stetson and looked to be in his midthirties — clean-cut and no-nonsense. More worrisome, he packed a six-gun in a leather holster at his side. I whispered to Mac: "On the count of three, let's run." He glanced at me and nodded.

"One ... two ..." Before I finished the countdown, Mac grabbed my shoulder and threw himself up and over me, running like hell for the dense brush on the other side of the canyon. I was up and running an instant later, but Mac was already thirty feet away, sprinting like an Olympic champion.

"Stop or I'll shoot! ... I'll shoot!" screamed the cowboy.

Maybe I was braver back then, or maybe just crazy, but I crouched down and went zigzagging through the woods like a scared rabbit.

BAM! ... BAM-BAM! Bullets whizzed through the woods around me. BAM-BAM-BAM! A bullet slammed into an oak tree in front of my face, splattering bark fragments in my eyes, blinding me momentarily.

This just scared me more and made me all the more determined to escape. As the cowboy stopped to reload, I crashed through some heavy cover and into the shallow creek, where I went bounding like a deer from rock to rock upstream, moving almost as fast as if I were running on flat ground, determined not to leave a trail that he could follow. I finally jumped over the brush beside the creek — careful not to crush any plants he might spot. From there, I ran all out for another ten minutes before I collapsed and lay with my back against a large oak, my chest heaving as I struggled to catch my breath.

I wiped my forehead with my right hand and set it down beside me — right on a snake, which hissed loudly and coiled. I don't know to this day whether it was a rattlesnake or just a harmless gopher snake or king snake. I didn't wait to find out. I was already in panic mode and that was all I needed to push me over the top. I sprang like I was hurled from a catapult and continued sprinting. I finally fell to my knees and crawled, burrowing deep into some shrubs, where I lay gasping for air, repeating over and over, "I'm never going to Vietnam" (pant, pant, gasp); "I'm never going to Vietnam" (pant, pant).

I have no idea how long I lay there. Eventually my breathing slowed, and I began to feel sluggish, almost languid. I may even have fallen asleep for an hour or so. It seemed much later when I carefully emerged from cover, peeking out and listening intently before showing myself. The sun had dimmed, and everything was quiet except for the din of buzzing bees and the calls of the ubiquitous quail on the hillsides. I decided to take the long way back to the car, climbing up to the ridge through an area with more cover than where we had gone through earlier. It would take much longer, I knew. It might even be dark before I got to the car, but more than anything else, I didn't want to run into that crazy cowboy again. I have no idea if he was really trying to shoot me, but if he just wanted to scare me to get me to stop, his bullets were coming much too close — especially the one that splattered oak bark in my face. I could easily have dashed one way instead of the other and been hit.

As I slipped through a stand of oak trees, I noticed a shadow move above me and turned to see a Cooper's hawk flying stealthily away. I examined the trees carefully with my binoculars and finally spotted a tightly constructed stick nest, not much bigger than a crow's nest. Bingo. I'd found it by accident: a Cooper's hawk nest.

I considered just continuing on my way but then thought — *I came here to find a Cooper's hawk nest and now that I've done it, I'll be damned if I don't climb up and check it out.*

I jumped as high as I could to reach the lowest limb and then hauled myself up onto it. The next step was a little hairy. I would have to stand balancing on top of the limb, bend my knees, and jump as high as I could to reach the next-higher limb. I didn't want to think about what might happen if I fell and sprained my ankle or broke my leg. I was determined. I sprang up, caught the limb, and started scrambling to pull myself up. At first my feet slipped, and I was hanging from the limb. Then I did a chin-up and eventually pulled myself on top of the limb and finally stood on top of it. For the next twenty feet I was able to find branches when I needed them, but I had to shinny the final ten or twelve feet. It was a proud moment when I peered over the edge of the nest and looked inside. There was only one egg, and it was freshly laid. I knew the female hawk would come back each day and lay another until she had a clutch of four or five eggs.

But I'd seen enough. I was ready to get back to the car. Just as I was about to hit the hillside and make my big climb, Mac popped out of some bushes where he'd been hiding. Apparently he'd had the same idea as I did about where to go over the hill. By this time, it was close to sundown. We wondered what had happened to Hollis and how we could find him. We were so tired and spaced out we couldn't even remember his name. We'd only met him that morning, and Mac kept calling him Hans.

We slithered up the steep hill, trying to keep as low a profile as possible, while at the same time watching out for snakes in the sagebrush and pickup trucks full of cowboys with shotguns. Mac and I became so energized as we neared the summit we ran the last twenty feet almost straight up and burst over the crest. The downhill part was a snap. We couldn't help wondering, though, if that cowboy might be sitting down there, leaning against the car with his arms folded — maybe smoking a cigarette and drinking a cool beer, waiting for us to drop into his little trap. But at that point, there was nothing else we could do. If he had the Opel, we were done for.

We finally saw the car and approached it as quietly and carefully as possible, scanning constantly to see if there were any other vehicles around. We couldn't see anything. Maybe it was OK. Maybe we'd get out of there without any more problems.

It was the best feeling when we reached the car. We got inside, closed the doors, and started laughing hysterically. Then Mac suddenly tensed up. "Hey, we're not out of this yet," he said. "I won't feel good till we're at least on the freeway again." He put the key in the ignition and then a shadow fell across his face. "Shit," he said. "What are we going to do about Hans?"

"I don't know," I said. "Maybe we can get Philo and some other people to come back and look for him tonight. But I don't think he's called Hans."

Mac nodded. "I know it started with an H," he said, then started the car and drove slowly back toward the paved road.

A second later, I caught sight of something big moving in the oak tree up ahead. My heart sank. It was a man. Then suddenly I saw it was Hollis, dropping to the ground in front of us like some crazed Sasquatch. I opened my door and bent the back of my seat forward so he could climb inside.

As soon as the door closed, Mac howled and threw the car into first gear, peeling out on the dirt road. "Let's get the hell out of here," he said. "Just a few more miles . . . just a few more miles . . ." It was starting to get dark as we reached the paved road. Mac turned left and sped away.

Hollis had a wild tale to tell. It turned out that when we split up and he ran to the right, there was nowhere to go. He tried to hide in a little gully, but the cowboy was on him instantly. "Freeze or I'll blow your fucking head off," he yelled, pointing his gun at Hollis's face, just three feet away. Hollis opted to come out quietly. The man seemed incensed by Hollis's appearance. He grabbed him by the hair and held the barrel of his gun hard against the back of Hollis's skull as he marched him to the pickup truck. He told him to get inside the truck and that if he wasn't there when he got back, he'd hunt him down like a mad dog and shoot him dead.

Then the cowboy went off after us, bending down frequently to examine footprints or places where we had bent the foliage as we ran. Hollis had sat in the truck obediently for a while, but when he heard all the shooting, he was afraid the man might have killed us, so he panicked and fled. He had been sitting in the tree near the car for hours.

Hollis's story bothered Mac. "I hope that asshole isn't sitting in his pickup somewhere," said Mac. "He knows this is the way we'd have to come to get out of here."

"Don't worry about it," said Hollis. He reached into his pocket and pulled out a huge ring with maybe twenty keys on it, including the ignition key of the cowboy's truck. "The guy left in such a hurry to chase you, he left the keys in the truck."

Mac and I both blanched and looked at each other. Hollis rolled the window down and threw the keys as far as he could into the sagebrush along the side of the road.

The saddest part of the story is that we loved that canyon, but we knew we could never return again, at least not in our youth. I did make the mistake of going back about thirty years later and, like most places in Southern California, it had been ruined. It is now a warren of planned communities, shopping malls, and high-priced faux mansions.

VISITING HOLLIS'S HOUSE for the first time was, well, a surprise. He lived with his father and his extended family in a large single-level ranch-style house in Park Estates, one of the wealthier areas in Long Beach. But his family was different from any other family in the neighborhood. They could all have been characters in *The Beverley Hillbillies*. Hollis's father, Bill; his uncle, Hughes; and his grandmother, Mabel (whom everyone called Nanny) were originally from east Texas, where they had been dirt-poor farmers, and they all spoke with a broad country drawl. They also sometimes still acted as if they were living in a homestead surrounded by hundreds of acres of open land, miles from the nearest neighbor.

I remember one time they cooked up a scheme to set up a chicken farm in their backyard to produce eggs to sell. They bought fifty or sixty huge white leghorns and put them in a long cage they'd built along the edge of the fence, a few feet from the swimming pool. Not long later, the chickens somehow all escaped and scattered throughout the neighborhood. Hollis and I spent days chasing the huge squawking white birds up and down the street and through people's backyards and gardens. They were still getting calls about them weeks later.

Another time, one of Hollis's other uncles, Freeman, brought over several bushels of fresh-picked black-eyed peas. There were way too many to eat, so Nanny decided to can them all. We sat around for days snapping the peapods so Nanny could put them into Mason jars. She finally had thirty or more jars stacked in neat rows in the pantry, but she must have made a crucial error in the canning process. A month or so later, she opened one of the jars, put the contents in a saucepan, and started heating it. I was in the living room with Hollis and Bill, when suddenly a putrid odor wafted through the house, as though the combined stench of all the sewers in the county had been dropped like a megaton stink bomb in the kitchen.

It was the black-eyed peas, and Nanny didn't even notice it. As she brought a bowl of the stuff to Bill we took it from her and buried it in the backyard, then opened all the windows in the house. Each of those jars was probably filled with pure essence of botulism, enough to wipe out half the county. They meant to throw all the jars away, but somehow didn't get around it to it for a while . . . until they started exploding. I was there when one of them went off like a shotgun blast in the pantry, spreading putrid stinking pea slime all over the walls and ceiling. It was not a fun cleanup.

$\backsim$

BILL WAS A disabled World War II veteran who had spent years in a wheelchair. He had joined the navy as a teenager after Pearl Harbor and gone off to fight in the Pacific. His ship was sunk by the Japanese, with a huge loss of life, in the naval battle for Guadalcanal. He was hospitalized with a severely injured back. This might not in itself have been a crippling injury, but he was also coming down with rheumatoid arthritis. The trauma of being injured in battle, of floating for an extended period in a life jacket, and then having to stay in bed for weeks to convalesce was the worst combination for his emerging arthritic condition. His joints began freezing up, and he was never able to walk again. Bill married the nurse who had cared for him during his long hospital stay. They eventually had a son together and named him Hollis, after Bill's eldest brother, who had become a wealthy farmer in the San Joaquin Valley. But the marriage didn't last. Bill's wife took Hollis and moved to the San Francisco Bay area, more than four hundred miles away.

Nanny moved in with Bill to take care of him. But she also had a full-time job. She would set Bill up in an easy chair each morning, and he would sit there alone all day, smoking cigarettes and staring out the window. A few years later, Hollis's mother got married again, and her new husband wanted to start a new family that didn't include her first-born child. She put Hollis on a plane bound for Long Beach, leaving him in the care of some stewardesses. He was six years old, quiet and shy. He spent the rest of his youth with Bill and Nanny and eventually his uncle Hughes and his two kids, Mark and Frances, when they moved into Bill's house.

Bill always welcomed people into his home, and there were always one or two friends, relatives, or various misfits who would show up and sometimes stay for weeks at a time.

Bill was in his forties and had striking blue eyes and black hair, slicked down with Brylcreem and combed straight back. He sported a pencil-thin, carefully trimmed mustache right above his lip, Clark Gable style. Hughes was at least four or five years older than Bill and had graying hair and a similar mustache. They were the most hospitable people I've ever met — sometimes to a fault, because it was hard to leave once they'd latched on to me. "What's your hurry? Set a spell. Get yourself a cup a coffee," they'd say as I tried to dash away. They were both big Western movie fans, and they thought I looked like Clint Eastwood. Whenever his friends visited while I was there, Hughes would get me to strike a gunslinger pose, squint, and pretend to draw a pistol from an imaginary gun belt. He'd laugh and say: "See? . . . See? What'd I tell you? Just like Clint Eastwood."

I never heard Hollis call his father Dad. He just called him Bill like everyone else did. And Bill usually called Hollis "Brother." He'd say: "Fetch me a cup of coffee, would you please, Brother?" Sometimes the two of them would argue, especially when Hollis was in his teens, but they were devoted to each other. Hollis would've done anything to protect Bill. (The last time I ever saw Hollis was years later in the early 1980s at Bill's funeral; then he seemed to vanish off the face of the earth.)

MY LAST YEAR of high school was a strange one. I became completely disengaged from school. It wasn't just drugs. I'd begun working swing shift in a factory to help my family and also to save up to take trips to faraway places to look for falcons. I had lied about my age — I was seventeen — and about my status as a high school student, and the company where I worked didn't check. My grades suffered. I remember one day being so tired in class that I had to put my head down on my desk. In what seemed like an instant later, I heard peals of laughter and sat up quickly. Almost forty-five minutes had passed, and the students in my class were standing in the doorway looking back at me as they left the room. My face was creased from the desk.

It didn't get any better as the year progressed. I arranged my schedule so that I had only four classes in my last semester. I was out of school by lunchtime, at work by 3:30, and home in bed by 1:30, if I was lucky. Any dreams I'd had of going to college were fading, at least for now. I hoped maybe someday I might be able to get an education, but for the time being, as far as my eyes could see, my life would be one long factory shift, interspersed with falconry.

I did graduate. And I even attended the graduation ceremony at John F. Kennedy High School, wearing a dark green cap and gown — but I was stoned on LSD and barely lucid enough to maintain the proper distance between the student in front of me and the student behind as I walked up to get my diploma.

8

DESOLATION ROW

I'D BEEN OUT of high school for a few months and was working the graveyard shift at a factory in Fullerton. It was basic grunt work. I would stand in a line of people, stuffing coupons into sample boxes of detergent as they moved past on a conveyer belt. A lot of the workers were old and down and out — deeply entrenched members of the working poor. Most had broken or missing teeth. One middle-aged woman had lost an eye at some point in her life but had never gotten a glass eye to replace it. She had a piece of cardboard taped over one of her eyeglass lenses to hide her disfigurement. But standing beside her on the assembly line, I sometimes caught a chilling glimpse of her vacant eye socket, her eyelids curved back into her skull revealing a gaping red hole.

The factory workers were mostly nice people, though the supervisors were always tense and stressed out, pushed to the breaking point by higher-ups in the company, and they would constantly drive us to work faster.

Hollis and I started work at midnight and usually got off at 8:30 in the morning. Sometimes we'd work two shifts back-to-back if we needed extra money. It worked out well with our falconry. We both liked flying in the morning. As soon as we got off work we would pick up our birds and head for a good field, either in Long Beach or Seal Beach, or sometimes we would drive all the way to the fields around Orange County

Airport, which always had lots of rabbits. We had both gone back to flying red-tailed hawks that season. The simplicity of hunting rabbits with a red-tail was appealing, and it was easy to fit it in with our work schedule. Birds such as Cooper's hawks, merlins, and large falcons need to be flown almost every day to keep them in top hunting condition. But red-tails thrive on much less flying time and can cope with an irregular schedule. Flying them every other day is fine, and it provides you an opportunity to give them a good feed each time they fly and then let them have a day off to digest the food.

I had a nice male red-tail called Moby, named after the rock band, Moby Grape. He was a great bird — fast, aggressive, and deadly for catching cottontails right from the start. I knew the minute he attacked our trap, folding up and diving straight down from the top of a lofty high-voltage power pole in the desert, that he was a keeper. Hollis had a big female red-tail he had trapped near Seal Beach. We usually hunted them at rabbits together, and they got along well.

Later we made a mistake and flew them when they were too fat because we wanted our friend Chuck to take 8 mm movies of the birds hunting. They had done well the day before, but we had fed them too much and we should have given them the day off to digest their food. We'd gotten so used to their dependability, we thought we could get away with it. It was a disaster. The birds would make short flights at rabbits, barely trying to catch them, and then fly to a telephone pole and sit there sunning with their wings spread, ignoring us completely. To get them to come down, we had to throw a rabbit carcass up in the air again and again. We should have just gone home the first time that happened, but instead we pushed on, beating the brush for more rabbits and hoping the birds' attitude would improve as the morning wore on.

Before long, as the day warmed up, our birds went off soaring, circling higher and higher above us — a risky thing to have happen with wild-trapped red-tails; it's so easy for them to revert back to the wild, which is just what Hollis's bird did. I managed to get Moby to come down one last time to the dead rabbit as I threw it as high as I could while blowing my whistle frantically. He finally folded up and came swooping down. Hollis was not so lucky. His hawk soared into the clear blue sky until she was a tiny speck, finally vanishing as she drifted southward into the vast fields of the Naval Weapons Station, never to be seen again. For her, this was not such a bad thing. The weapons station was a wildlife sanctuary, where shooting was forbidden and people other than the guards entered at their own risk.

e~

SOMETIMES ON PAYDAY I would spend $10 on an ounce of marijuana: something to share with my friends on the weekend. It usually lasted me a long time. I was more or less a social pot smoker and didn't use much. I didn't like the way my mind seemed dull the morning after smoking it, and I was afraid it might affect my skills as a falconer.

One night, Andy, a friend I'd known in high school, dropped by with a flashy blonde named Vivian, who drove a blue Austin Healey sports car and seemed to have money to burn. She and Andy were planning a camping trip in the desert and wanted to get some pot before they left. He had taken her to Holder Street (a local doper hangout) and a couple of other places looking for drugs, but they struck out. He wanted to know if I could spare any pot for their trip. I had just bought some the night before. They started begging me to let them have it, offering to give me more money than I had paid for it. I said they didn't have to do that. I finally agreed to let them have it for $10, just what I'd paid for it, but they let me roll a couple of joints from it. I knew I could get more in a day or two, so I didn't mind doing them a favor.

It was crazy. I should have known better, but I was just eighteen and lacked street smarts. It turned out right after they left, Vivian made an excuse about having to go home to get her camping equipment and ditched Andy. I had assumed he had known her for some time, but this was actually the first time they'd met. She had bought the pot and disappeared.

I knew it was over. Weeks before the police came for me early one morning, I knew that I'd be going to jail. I just didn't know when and for how long. The fact that I had recently turned eighteen meant that I would be tried as an adult, and it would be classified as a felony. (Had I still been a minor, I would've gotten a slap on the wrist and juvenile probation.)

A couple of days after I sold the pot to Vivian, a man came to my door asking to buy marijuana. He was obviously a policeman, and I said, "I don't know what you're talking about." When I thought about it, everything pointed to this being a sting. Vivian was a Mod Squad wannabe. One morning, returning from a trip to the desert to look for nesting prairie falcons, Hollis and I spotted her driving her blue sports car out of the police station parking lot. If I'd still had any lingering doubts that clinched it: she was a cop.

What should I do? Should I leave town, maybe move back to Canada? But what about my mom and my sisters? What would happen to them?

In the end, I did nothing. I just sat waiting for the guillotine blade to drop. One night, Hollis and Steve came by about midnight and asked if I wanted to go to the desert with them and check out some prairie falcon nests. This was something I enjoyed more than anything, and I never said no. I loved the desert in early spring when the wildflowers were in bloom and everything was coming alive. Nesting birds, foxes, snakes — the overwhelming abundance of life emerging from the depths of winter, long before the blazing summer sun baked the ground into a shimmering inferno again. Somehow I think I knew it was all over. It was time for me to enter the next phase. I told them I didn't feel like going with them to the desert.

A few hours later, just after my mother left for work, the police swooped in, four of them, all in plain clothes, led by Detective Smock, a burley red-haired detective in his thirties with a goatee. When one man asked if they should search the entire apartment, Smock took a glance around and said no. They should just search my bedroom. It was obvious that this was a family apartment and not some drug den. They read me my Miranda rights, then cuffed my hands behind me and left me sitting on the couch in the living room as they ransacked my bedroom. I had 8 × 10 black-and-white prints of hawks taped all over the walls. Smock came out a short time later and asked me about the pictures. I said I was a falconer and had a hawk I was using to hunt rabbits. I asked if it would be all right to feed him before we left, because I had no idea how long I would be gone.

"Where's your hawk?" he asked.

"Out in the backyard," I said. He was surprised to see Moby sitting on a bow perch under a shelter outside. Our yard was tiny.

"OK, you can do that," he said and unsnapped my handcuffs. I took a couple of cottontail hind legs from the refrigerator and opened the sliding glass picture window that led to the yard. Rex came bounding in, and one of the policemen knelt down and petted him. Smock went outside with me and watched as Moby jumped to my glove and began stripping the meat from the rabbit legs. He seemed genuinely interested and wanted to know all about how I hunted with hawks. After I set Moby back on his perch, I threw away the rabbit bones and washed my hands. They put the handcuffs back on and led me to one of the squad cars outside. We talked about falconry as we drove along, Smock riding shotgun in the front seat, me behind him in the back seat.

When we got to the police station, Andy was already there, just finishing being fingerprinted by a clerk. "I'm really sorry, Tim," he said as we passed. The clerk took my right hand and rolled each finger individually in black ink, then rolled the fingers one by one on a piece of white card, leaving a distinct impression of each fingerprint. He also took an impression of my palm and then repeated the procedure with my left hand. I was then led back to a holding cell, where I sat alone.

A deputy finally opened the cell door and took me to a room where Detective Smock stood leaning against a table with his arms folded. "Come in," he said. "Can I get you a cup of coffee or a Coke or anything?"

"No, thanks," I said. "I'm not that thirsty."

He motioned toward a chair at the side of the table and I sat down.

"You really screwed up, Tim," he said. "We've been trying to shut down Holder Street for months, and you're the first person we busted." He grimaced. "They'll probably throw the book at you."

I stared at him and said nothing.

"You know, it doesn't have to be like that, though," he said. "If you help us, I'm sure we can help you. Who knows? You might not even have to do any time."

"What would I have to do?" I asked.

"Just be our eyes and ears on Holder Street. Let us know who's doing what and when — that kind of thing. We'll do the rest. No one would have to know you're involved in any way."

"I couldn't do that," I said.

"Sure you could," said Smock. "Don't you think every single one of those guys would do the same thing in your shoes? Believe me, they would. I've been in this business a long time." He sat down at the table and leaned closer to me. "You don't want to go to jail," he said. "You have no idea how bad it is. You seem like a good kid ... not like a lot of the people we get in here. You don't belong in jail. You should be out flying your hawk. You go to jail ... it'll change you. Your life'll never be the same again."

I nodded. "I really couldn't do that. I'm sorry."

"Can you tell us anything? Give me something to work with so I can help you. Tell me who you were selling the pot for or at least where you got it?"

"I want to remain silent."

He shook his head angrily and walked out. "Lock him up," he told the deputy outside and then strode away down the hall.

"Can I make a phone call?" I asked the deputy. "I never had a chance to talk to anyone yet."

Calling my mother was one of the hardest things I've ever done. She had worked so hard to keep the family together, faced so many hardships. It wasn't fair that I should ruin everything. I called her at the hospital, where she worked as a medical transcriber. I told her not to worry. I was in jail on a drug charge, but it was all a mistake. It was just because of the people I hung around with. It would all soon be straightened out. She wouldn't need to get a lawyer or put up bail. I'd get a public defender. Everything would work out fine.

A short time later a deputy took me to a room with several other prisoners. We were all handcuffed to a single, long chain and led single file outside to a sheriff's bus with windows covered by an iron grid-work and then driven to the municipal court to be arraigned.

The arraignment is the first reading of the charges and the moment a defendant enters a plea. Almost everyone who goes through an arraignment enters a not guilty plea to begin with. It's far too early to make a decision yet, and there may be an opportunity to cut a deal of some kind later — plead guilty to a lesser charge or agree to a shorter sentence and probation, and the county is then spared the trouble and great expense of a jury trial.

I was still in shock as they led me into the courtroom chained to the other prisoners. It seemed like hours before it was my turn to be arraigned. Some of the prisoners waiting there were from the big jail in Santa Ana, dressed in sweatshirts and jeans with "Orange County Main Jail" stenciled in gleaming yellow paint on their clothing. The color of their sweatshirts indicated whether they had been sentenced already or were still awaiting trial and couldn't afford to pay bail. The men in gray sweatshirts — the majority of those in court — had not been tried and sentenced yet. Sometimes they would serve months like this before they could begin working off their sentence. Their pretrial incarceration was usually dead time — it didn't count as time served when they received their sentence.

A public defender spoke with me for three or four minutes, asking about my background and how I got in trouble. He was young — in his midtwenties at most, with unruly brown hair parted on the side, and a cheap suit. Like all of the other prisoners around me, I claimed to be completely innocent. He nodded, jotting a few notes on a yellow legal pad, then asked where I lived and if I'd ever been in trouble before.

As I stood before the court a short time later, the district attorney read my charges to the court. He was a middle-aged, humorless man, with graying brown hair and a perpetual scowl. He told the judge how serious my charge was, selling drugs to an undercover police officer, and recommended that bail be set at $6,000. Then it was the public defender's turn. He looked sheepish, almost painfully shy. He said I lived at home with my mother and sisters and was not a flight risk. I had recently graduated from high school, and this was my first offense of any kind. The judge was in his sixties, with thinning gray hair and thick glasses. He looked bored. He said I was to be released on my own recognizance. The district attorney let out an audible sigh of disgust, which seemed to annoy the judge. He banged the gavel and turned to the next case.

I looked around the court and saw that my mother and my sister were sitting in the courtroom. My mother's eyes were red and she looked more depressed and worried than I had ever seen her. I didn't tell her the truth behind the case for several weeks. I wanted to spare her some of the pain and anguish for as long as I could.

This was a dark time for me — a period of endless waiting. I was caught up in a process over which I had no control and was heading into the unknown. I knew I'd soon be serving time, but how much? And what would it be like? And what would I be like by the time it was all over? Would I even survive? People kept telling me how hard-nosed Orange County judges were. Orange County was the heart of conservatism, the birthplace of Richard Nixon. The legal system there was anything but soft on crime. Would my sentence be in months? Years? I had no way of knowing. One person I heard about had recently gotten five years to life for selling one five-dollar tablet of LSD. It was not a good time to be facing a drug-selling charge in Orange County. Meanwhile, in nearby Los Angeles County, first-timers were getting two or three years of probation with no jail time for a crime like mine. It didn't make sense.

Other things started falling apart. Our apartment owners came up with a new rule that no dogs were allowed. What could I do with Rex? Where could I keep him? I couldn't get a place of my own. I knew I was about to enter jail. And my mother couldn't afford to move. But then I talked with Hollis's dad, Bill, and he said I could keep Rex at their house. Hollis would feed him and take care of him. That was a dream situation — or so I thought. Rex seemed to enjoy it when I took him there. The yard had a swimming pool with a wheelchair ramp for Bill. To get a drink from the pool, Rex would walk down the ramp until his mouth was below the level of the water, and then drink enough to quench his thirst. And sometimes he'd go swimming.

But there was a problem. Rex wanted to be with me, and I was twenty miles away, staying at my mother's apartment while my case was progressing through the court. Rex started escaping from Hollis's house. He would jump up on the wooden gate, putting his front paws over the top and holding on as he scrambled up and over, then walk more than half a mile to the intersection where Seventh Street, Pacific Coast Highway, and Anaheim Street came together, and cross over the busy highway to get to the drive-in restaurant. It was one of those places where the waitresses come up to the car, take orders, and bring people's food on a tray they hang on the car window. This was a gold mine for Rex. He'd hang around for hours, scrounging food from the customers. Kids loved him and were always eager to share their hamburgers with him.

The restaurant would eventually call the dog pound to pick him up. He was a big hit with the animal control staff because he was so friendly. They called him "Old Red," and he became like a mascot, riding around up front all day as they picked up stray dogs and cats. When they saw him, they'd just open the truck's door and he'd jump inside. They would deliver him to the pound at the end of the day, and I'd have to bail him out.

To try to deal with this, I spent one weekend building a high fence behind Hollis's garage so Rex couldn't possibly escape. But he would sit there and howl for hours until someone let him out. Then he'd haul himself over the gate and escape. I tried tying him to the back of the house with a long rope, but that had the same result: he howled until someone unsnapped the rope.

In the meantime, I had gotten a better-paying job at a plastics factory a few miles from home and had trouble getting to Long Beach to spend time with Rex. He got worse and worse about escaping, and sometimes I couldn't get to the dog pound for days at a time to bail him out. I started calling the animal control office every day to tell them to be sure not to euthanize Rex: I'd be there in a day or two to bail him out.

It was such an awful time. I loved that dog. I'd owned him since I was twelve years old, when he was a tiny pup, back when King had gotten sick and died. He'd been there when I started in falconry and had shared the backyard with all of my hawks. Couldn't he understand? Couldn't he just wait a few months? When I got out of jail, everything would be fine. I'd work hard. I'd rent a house. We would be together again. What was I going to do with him? And what about Moby? Why was all of this happening now? Why did the damn landlord have to kick our dog out now? Why did Andy have to bring that cop to my house that night? Why did everything have to go to hell at the same time?

The cost of getting Rex out of the dog pound started to add up. One day when I went to pick him up they told me I'd have to pay fifty dollars to get him back, an unbelievable sum for a person making less than three dollars an hour. A dogcatcher who had picked up Rex a few times was there in the office and had a talk with me.

"You know you really ought to think about giving him to someone else," he said. "We had a nice couple come in here just the other day. They loved him and wanted to take him right home. We had to tell them he already has an owner, but I told them we would ask you if you might give him up."

I nodded. "Well, who are they? Where do they live?"

"They're middle-aged," he said. "I think they live somewhere in Orange County. They seem to really like Old Red." He said I just had to sign a paper releasing him to the dog pound.

"How do I know they'll come back," I said. "I don't want him to end up getting put to sleep."

"Don't worry about that," he said. "He's a great dog. If they don't want him, someone else will. I'm sure of it."

They let me in to see Rex before I left. I petted him, gave him a hug, and then walked away. A couple of weeks later, I got a call from a dog shelter in Orange County. They had picked him up and had tracked me down through his license tag. I was just about to go there and pick him up, when I got another call, this time from his new owners. He had escaped from them, and they were going to get him at the pound. They told me what a great dog he was.

"I know," I said. "He's really great." That's the last I ever heard of him.

A SHORT TIME later, I borrowed my sister's car and drove Moby to the back of the Naval Weapons Station. I climbed over a fence, carrying my hawk on my fist, then went down into a drainage ditch and walked through the water to the other side. I sat on the far bank for a while, slowly feeding him a rich meal of raw steak. Before he had finished eating, I opened my pocketknife and carefully cut through both his jesses.

After he took his last bite of meat, he wiped his bill against my glove. As I stared at him, he fluffed up his feathers, and then shook them vigorously in what falconers call a rouse: a sure sign of contentment. Stroking his breast feathers with my hand, I felt his bulging crop — enough meat to last two or three days. I smiled at him and tried to memorize what he looked like. He'd been one of my favorite hawks, and I had been planning to keep him through the molt. I finally stood up and walked to the chainlink fence surrounding the weapons station. I raised my arm above the level of the three strands of barbed wire at the top and rested my arm on top of it. He just sat there, so I had to cast him off as hard as I could. He was heavy with his full crop and went lumbering along, eventually landing atop one of the big grass-covered bunkers. I knew he'd be all right there. I put my glove into my falconry bag and walked back to the car. At least I'd never have to worry about Moby again.

MY MOTHER DIDN'T like the idea of using a public defender to represent me. Maybe she thought public defenders wouldn't do a good enough job with my defense. Or maybe she thought they were something reserved only for poor people and beneath our dignity. (Of course, we had already been living below the poverty level for more than two years, but that was our little family secret.)

She ended up hiring Marvin Warren — the man who had arranged my parents' divorce — to represent me. He let us pay when we were able, a little at a time. My father had been the one who had originally hired him but, as the divorce progressed, he became more sympathetic to our side in the case, because Dad had been so stingy. He refused to pay a penny of alimony. My mother said that was fine; she didn't want anything from him anyway. But he also didn't want to pay child support. Of course, child support was legally mandated, so it had to be included in the divorce settlement, but we didn't receive a single payment from him. My mother wouldn't go after him, and she had too much pride to apply for welfare, so my father got a free ride, and we barely scraped by for a couple of years.

Mr. Warren was well meaning, but I think he was over his head with my case. He was a civil lawyer and had little experience in criminal law. I remember visiting him at his office soon after I was released on my own recognizance. He was young, perhaps in his midthirties, and seemed good-natured and kind. He smoked a pipe as we spoke about my case.

I had already decided before I went to his office that I would be completely open with him. He seemed surprised when I told him I was more or less guilty as charged, that I had indeed sold an ounce of marijuana to an undercover policewoman. The only things he'd heard about my case previously had been what my mother had told him.

Andy's lawyer was in some ways the opposite of mine. Although Theo Lacy, Jr., didn't seem much older than Warren, he knew criminal law inside and out. He and his family had a long history in the county's legal system. This may not have been an auspicious sign for us, but Theo Lacy Branch Jail had been named after his father, the former county sheriff. The first time Andy and I had a meeting together with both of our lawyers, Lacy laid out clearly the grim prospects we faced. Something in the neighborhood of six months in the county jail with three years of formal probation was about the best we could hope for, even if we went through a long, expensive superior court jury trial, and he thought he could arrange a deal with the district attorney and get us a similar sentence without a trial. It was clear he knew what he was talking about. Warren blanched when he heard this. I think he felt great sympathy for my family and me and had hoped that I could avoid serving time in prison. But I think I actually felt better when I heard what Lacy had to say. My future didn't seem so nebulous anymore. A punishment for my crime was taking shape — something concrete, with a beginning and an end — and I was ready to move on and start working my way through my punishment.

$\backsim$

MY APPEARANCES AT the Orange County Superior Court were some of the worst times for me in this process. Something about standing up before the court and having my case name read aloud was chilling: "The People of the State of California vs. Timothy William Gallagher." I felt all the weight of this colossal institution and the millions of people it represented united against me, and it was dizzying. I had a constant dread as I stood there that I might pass out and come crashing down dramatically in front of the court and the spectators.

The attorneys finally worked out a deal that would allow Andy and me to plead guilty to a lesser charge. It was a classic good news–bad news scenario. The charges would be dropped from sales of marijuana to simple possession — good. It would still be a felony — bad. The state prison sentence would be suspended and we would get three years of probation — good. Under the terms of the probation we would serve five months in the county jail — bad. Also bad was the fact that on probation people can be sent up to serve their original suspended sentences for a less-serious crime without much in the way of due process. Three years can be a long time to stay out of trouble. And the authorities can keep extending the probation more or less indefinitely if a person commits even minor infractions. But if I could make it through without having my probation violated my conviction would be set aside and the record would be sealed. That's the part that was most attractive to me — that someday, if all went well, it would be almost as if I had never committed a crime. That meant a lot to me. And besides, I didn't see any alternative. I couldn't afford a superior court trial. Even the pretrial attorney costs I'd incurred were backbreaking. I jumped at the chance to end this court ordeal and start working off my time.

But Andy balked. He couldn't imagine spending even a single night in prison. This was not what he had in mind at all, and he quickly backed away from the deal. It didn't affect me. Our cases were split from one another. Andy opted to hire a high-priced lawyer (the same one who had successfully defended Timothy Leary in a high-profile marijuana case). This moved Andy back to square one and started the entire bargaining process with the district attorney again.

When I entered my guilty plea, my lawyer arranged a two-week stay in the imposition of my sentence so I'd have time to get things in order and prepare myself mentally and emotionally for prison. But the judge made a special point of telling me that if I was late turning myself in at five-thirty P.M. two Fridays from then, I would be considered an escapee and would automatically face an additional year and a day of imprisonment (which meant I would go right to state prison; one year is the maximum county jail sentence in California).

꙳

MAYBE I SHOULD have taken a look at the municipal complex in Santa Ana a few days before I was scheduled to begin my sentence. I just didn't think it was necessary. I had seen the huge, square, three-story gray concrete edifice of the Orange County Main Jail before. And it was scary-looking. The only windows in the building were long, narrow slots — large enough to let in a little light, but too small for anyone to squeeze through if he smashed out the glass. Because I knew where the building was, how could I possibly get lost? I just didn't take into account that we would hit heavy rush-hour traffic on the way to downtown Santa Ana, and I would arrive within minutes of my deadline in a rush, not knowing how to get inside the building. My sister Maureen was driving her black-and-white '56 Ford sedan, which my friends and I always called her cop car. I sat in the front passenger seat and my mother and Janet rode in the back. There were no parking spaces anywhere, so I said goodbye and dashed out of the car in heavy traffic.

The wilting-hot summer sun blazed down as I ran up and down along the side of the gray concrete building, searching for an entrance. I couldn't see one anywhere. What if I'm late? What if I get sent to state prison for a year just because I can't find the damn door to the jail? I ran along a sidewalk leading into an open area between the buildings in the municipal complex. By this time, I was breathing hard and sweating, in a complete panic. And I was already five minutes late. I finally spotted a sheriff's deputy. Almost in tears, I practically threw myself at his feet.

"Excuse me, could you help me?" I asked. "I was supposed to start serving a sentence at five-thirty. I got here on time, but I don't know where to go . . . I can't figure out how to get inside." He looked at me in amazement, then he explained how to get to the door where prisoners turned themselves in.

It's funny. In some ways I expected the cops to be waiting at the door for me with handcuffs ready. It wasn't like that at all. Inside the iron door was a small room where perhaps a dozen men sat in chairs along the wall. Most of them were weekenders. They'd been sentenced to serve ten weekends in jail so they could work at their regular jobs during the week. They would turn themselves in each Friday night and spend Saturday and Sunday engaged in various menial projects like picking up trash along the freeway or hoeing weeds in public places. At that time, the courts never gave weekend sentences or work furloughs to people who'd been convicted of drug charges; they were afraid the men might try to smuggle drugs into prison.

I was surprised there weren't any deputies around. We all sat there waiting for someone to open the iron door at the end of the room and take us inside. But nothing happened. I sat there for almost two hours. Some of the other men asked me what I was charged with and how long my sentence was. When I told them I'd be in for five months, they all said I should get out of there right now and head for Mexico or someplace. None of them could imagine serving five months in prison — even though most of them would be spending each weekend there for a couple of months or more. But I think they rightly saw that you cross an invisible line when you become a regular inmate. Weekenders all go in together and never really become part of the inmate population.

I didn't know what to expect. I had stopped to say goodbye to Mac and Robert earlier in the day. They seemed genuinely upset that I was going to jail. It was as if they hadn't really thought about it until that moment. Jail is a fearful place to people who have never been there — a great unknown conjuring up frightening images of unspeakable humiliations and tortures: muggings, rapes, razor slashings, murder, and who knows what else?

Many of my friends had ideas and suggestions about what to do to get by in jail. "I'd start screaming like a maniac so everyone would think I was crazy and leave me alone." "I'd crap in my pants if someone tried to rape me, and then they'd be too disgusted to go through with it." Or the best one I heard: "The first chance you get, attack the biggest, meanest guy in the jail, so everyone'll know you're too tough to mess with." That friend was right about one thing: no one would ever mess with you again — because you'd be dead.

9

O TANK

I WAITED IN the room at the main jail for a couple of hours before a guard finally called my name and let me inside, but that was just the beginning. I was put into a cell with some Mexican farm workers who had obviously been picked up on immigration charges. They were still dressed in their field clothes and one wore an old straw cowboy hat with a small leather tassel in the back. They didn't speak English. From that holding cell I was finally led to another holding cell to wait my turn to be processed, fingerprinted, and issued jail clothes. I struck up a conversation with another prisoner. He seemed friendly enough, and before I was led away, he said: "Be sure to tell them you want to go to O Tank."

I had to turn in all my belongings, including my clothes. The guards took me to a shower room where I washed up, and then they sprayed a whitish liquid — some DDT-laced lice-killing concoction — onto my hair, armpits, and pubic area. It burned, but they wouldn't let me wash it off. I had to leave it on and get dressed in the white boxer shorts, jeans, and dark blue sweatshirt I was issued. They also gave me white athletic socks and flip-flops.

A guard took me to a room to pick up a thin, rolled-up mattress, a blanket and sheet, and a pillow to take to my cell. As I was walking there, I asked him, "Would it be OK if I stayed in O Tank?"

He frowned. "Oh, you're just going to sit on your duff, huh?" he said.

I shrugged. I didn't know what he was getting at. By this time it was almost midnight. I'd been at the jail for more than six hours. I was spaced out and exhausted, and I just wanted to sleep. A few minutes later, we entered the cellblock containing O Tank and P Tank. A call went up immediately: "Man walking. Man walking!" I found out this was how prisoners spread the word that a guard was coming, so if prisoners were doing anything illegal, they would have time to stop. When the guard left, they'd shout: "Man got a hat. Man got a hat!" And everyone knew the coast was clear.

The cellblock looked like a set from a classic prison movie: two tiers of cells — P Tank above and O Tank below — with a bulletproof-glass-enclosed catwalk where the guards would walk past, right across from P Tank. The only thing missing was the machine-gun turret. But at the Orange County Main Jail, none of the guards carried firearms. They were too afraid an inmate might get hold of a gun if any were around.

I followed the guard down the iron stairs and stood in front of Cell 2 in O Tank. Inside, three prisoners sat around a long metal table that was permanently attached to the bare concrete floor. Behind it was a sink, a toilet without a seat (or any kind of enclosure), and an open-fronted shower stall. To the right, in a different section of the cell, I saw eight flat metal bunks, at least two of which had people sleeping on them.

The men at the table were rough looking. Although most of them were probably not more than four or five years older than me, they had the pallid, dull-eyed look of longtime inmates. They glared menacingly at the guard but seemed oblivious to me. I wondered why they weren't in bed sleeping; it was well past midnight. It turned out that in O Tank it didn't matter what time of day it was — no one worked; no one left the tank except for the twice-a-day walk to the mess hall and back for breakfast and dinner. O Tank inmates didn't get lunch. And the lights were always on; they were just dimmed a little at night.

I later found out I'd been the butt of a little prison joke. O Tank was a punishment area where inmates were sent if they refused to work, wouldn't obey the guards, or were serious troublemakers. None of the cells in O Tank had televisions, and the prisoners could not have playing cards or even books, with the exception of the *Holy Bible*, which most inmates just used to make tattoos. They would tear out a few pages at a time, burn them in a tin ashtray, and mix the dark ashes in water to get the printer's ink from the paper. They would then take the fuzz off the end of a pipe-cleaner, sharpen it to a point on a matchbook cover, dip it in the ink, and poke it repeatedly deep into someone's flesh to get the ink under their skin — an incredibly painful process. But I'd learn all about that later.

As I stood in front of the cell, a guard up on the catwalk operated the controls and the cell door slid open automatically and then shut behind me with a great clang as I walked inside.

It's an odd moment entering a jail cell full of strangers, with all the fear and awkwardness of being the new kid in school multiplied a thousandfold. For someone who had never done time, that moment was horrifying.

I carried my bedding inside and laid it on the only open bunk. One of the prisoners who had been sitting at the table suddenly appeared behind me, and I jumped for an instant, but he was just going past to get something from his bunk. He pulled a deck of cards from under his pillow. This was contraband in O Tank, but sometimes the prisoners would make deals with the trustees (prisoners who worked in the jail) to slip them some playing cards along with the commissary items people ordered each week if they had money in their prison account. They usually paid for contraband (or lost wagers) with packs of cigarettes, the unofficial coin of the realm in most jails.

"Wanna play cards?" he asked.

I shrugged. "What kind?"

"Hearts."

"I've never played it," I said. "I don't know how."

"It's easy," he said. "Come on."

I was too tired and scared to say no, so I followed him out to the table and sat down next to a tall thin Mexican named Cruz. The man with the cards, Eldon, sat across the table from me, and another man named Wayne sat beside him. Eldon carefully explained the rules of hearts to me — about how the object of the game is to avoid getting points and that each card in the hearts suit is worth one point and the queen of spades (nicknamed "the bitch") is worth 13 points. If I got her, he said, I'd be done for — unless I could "shoot the moon" successfully. If one person manages to get every point card, everyone else automatically receives 26 points each, he told me.

I stared blankly at him, and he repeated the whole thing again . . . and again. I was still in a daze about being in jail and was physically exhausted; I couldn't focus my mind. Eldon shook his head finally and said we should just start playing. Wayne smirked. I'm sure he sensed some easy pickings. We were betting packs of cigarettes — which was odd for me, because I didn't smoke. And it was all done on credit. If I lost, I'd have to order cigarettes from the commissary using the ten or twelve dollars in my account — all the money I had in my wallet when I was booked into the jail.

I played a few hands and got behind, which only encouraged everyone to up the ante. There was so much riding on the final hand, I was afraid I wouldn't have enough money to pay for all of the cigarettes. I felt sick. I didn't know what these guys would do to someone who tried to welsh on a bet. And I kept getting more and more hearts. Then I got the queen of spades. And then it suddenly dawned on everyone — lastly on me — that I had taken all the points. I'd shot the moon successfully without even knowing it.

Everyone was stunned. Eldon stared at me and suddenly started laughing. "Shit, we'll probably find out his dad's a riverboat gambler in New Orleans," he said.

Cruz slapped me on the shoulder. "Way to go, Slick," he said, laughing. (The nickname "Slick" stuck with me after that for the rest of the time I spent in jail.) I glanced at Wayne, but he wasn't laughing. He stared sullenly at me with a blank face that chilled me. I looked away and laughed along with Cruz and Eldon.

Cruz was the oldest prisoner in the cell — probably at least twenty-six, with black slicked-back hair, a mustache, and dark, melancholy eyes. He wore the sleeves of his dark blue prison sweatshirt pulled up, revealing several crude jail tattoos. The inside of his left forearm had a side-view sketch of a long skinny lion with the words "Krazy Kool Kat" written underneath. He had a sad personal story — as do most prison inmates if you scratch beneath the surface. He was born to an illegal immigrant mother in a small Texas border town but had been living in Santa Ana for a few years. He met a woman from Mexico, and they married and had a daughter together. Then she became pregnant again. At the time, he was working nights at a factory at this time but then got laid off. Desperate for cash, he was told by a friend he could make decent money transporting stolen goods. He set Cruz up with a band of thieves operating from Los Angeles. Cruz would pick up the items — furniture, televisions, and appliances mostly — from the back of stores and warehouses in Los Angeles and drop them off at a warehouse in Santa Ana. In most cases, the storeowners or employees were in on the theft, and they were looking to collect insurance. Someone else set everything up, and Cruz knew nothing about the business.

One night, a police squad car pulled Cruz over en route to Santa Ana, and he couldn't explain why he had stolen property in his van. He ended up in the main jail and spent months as an unsentenced inmate before he was convicted. He couldn't afford bail, and the judge wouldn't let him out on his own recognizance because Cruz had originally come from out of state and was considered a flight risk.

Cruz called a friend to send a message to his wife. She was still an illegal immigrant; they had never gone through the process of trying to get her a green card. She never visited him, because she feared being arrested by Immigration and Naturalization Service (INS) agents and deported to Mexico. And she only sent one letter, but that was months after he had been sentenced to one year in the county jail, and it had no return address. She said she was moving to another city where she had a chance to work as a housekeeper for a wealthy family, but she couldn't tell him where. She enclosed a snapshot of his tiny daughter and his infant son, whom Cruz had never seen. He kept the picture on the wall beside his bunk.

The thing I remember most about Cruz was his singing voice. Late at night, he'd lie in his bunk singing beautiful, mournful ballads in Spanish. His voice was so mellow and pure, no one ever told him to stop singing. Sometimes when I lay awake in my bunk at night listening to him sing, I'd find myself weeping.

Eldon had a mustache and dark shoulder-length hair and always wore a blue bandanna tied in the back to form a headband. He seemed to be the one in charge in the cell, perhaps because he'd done more time than anyone else — for burglary, car theft, drugs: I heard he'd even been charged with manslaughter once but had pleaded guilty to a lesser charge. I later found out that his older brother and his brother's fiancée were the ones whose deaths he had caused. Apparently he insisted on driving them someplace when he was so stoned on liquor and Seconal he could barely walk. He was in a terrible accident that killed both of them, but he was hardly injured. He would carry the guilt for the rest of his life. He had a small laminated card with a picture of his brother on one side and the fiancée on the other.

Then there was Wayne — the scariest person in all of O Tank. He was short and stocky with medium-length light-brown hair that he combed back behind his ears. He had done a couple of tours in Vietnam and enjoyed the violence and destruction there, but he had gotten in some kind of trouble and been busted out of the army. He was serving a nine-month sentence for selling drugs. Wayne had been at Theo Lacy — a branch jail in Orange County — for several months but was sent back to the main jail because he was considered too dangerous. He was the prime instigator in a planned prisoner uprising. One of the inmates at Lacy who worked at the police pistol range had been stealing ammunition for several months to get gunpowder so Wayne could make a bomb. Another inmate who worked at the dog pound adjacent to Lacy had somehow gotten a handgun he kept stashed inside a barrel of dry dog food at the pound.

Lacy jail at that time was laid out with four glass-fronted barracks arrayed in a semicircle facing a central control booth, which was also glass-fronted so that the guards could see into every barracks night and day. But usually only one guard sat there at night, and sometimes he would read a book or even doze off, so guard coverage was light. Wayne was going to sneak out in the middle of the night and place a gunpowder bomb against the control booth. There was a guard Wayne particularly hated. He planned to wait outside with the pistol and shoot the guard dead as he fled the control booth after the explosion.

I was surprised by Wayne's glee as he told me the story. The odd thing is that this plan had nothing to do with escaping from jail or anything that even remotely made any kind of sense. Anyone could escape from Lacy. It was then a minimum-security prison. All an inmate had to do was jump over the chainlink fence out back and run along the bed of the Santa Ana River. Of course, escapees usually got caught, which meant they would automatically get a year and a day added to their sentence and go straight to a state prison. And they would be considered "rabbits" by the prison system and forever after would only be housed in maximum-security facilities. That's what kept most people from running. But none of that mattered to Wayne; his plan was all about mayhem and revenge and had no other purpose.

The scheme collapsed when a guard found the pistol at the dog pound. A massive follow-up search at Lacy unearthed a bag of gunpowder hidden in Barracks C, and Wayne was the prime suspect. He was the "house mouse" in that barracks — an inmate whose sole duty is to keep a barracks clean and well maintained; it's considered a plum job. The guards all knew Wayne was involved in whatever destructive act had been planned, but they couldn't prove it. No matter how they tried to break him, he stayed mum. But they knew how dangerous he was, so they quickly whisked him away to O Tank to serve out the rest of his sentence.

A couple of weeks into my jail time, I got into a brief scuffle with Wayne. I can't even remember what started it — probably a joke that went bad. He suddenly made a lightning-fast commando move on me, sweeping my legs out from under me with his foot and throwing me hard onto the concrete floor. And he was on me instantly in a death hold, his legs holding my torso from behind and squeezing my lungs, his hands gripping my throat firmly. He seemed as strong as a wild animal — like a grizzly bear or a lion. I couldn't move. I couldn't make a sound. I couldn't inhale or exhale. It was a strange sensation, like being paralyzed from the neck down. It didn't hurt. I lay there completely detached from my body, watching myself die. Just before I blacked out, I heard Eldon say, "Let him go. NOW!"

It's always weird coming to after being unconscious. I didn't know where I was for a couple of minutes as I lay on the floor staring up at the neon lights. I heard Wayne laughing.

"We was just kidding around," he said. "I was showing him how to off people without making a sound, like in 'Nam."

Eldon stood over me. "You OK, Slick?" he asked.

"Yeah," I said, clearing my throat. "I'm OK." He reached for my hand and pulled me to my feet.

I was amazed Wayne had backed off. I guess even he realized that with someone like Eldon, who didn't care if he lived or died, there was no telling what he might do if he went off.

Two other people also lived in Cell 2 for part of the time I was there. I had so little contact with them I can't remember their names. One was serving thirty days and as far as I know slept the entire time he was there. The other was a short guy with a beard who had once tried to commit suicide when he was on LSD. He had so many deep, ghastly razor scars up and down his arm it made me cringe to look at him. I can't imagine how he had survived. The guards gave him Thorazine, an antipsychotic drug, every day, and he rarely spoke.

Looking back, my days spent in O Tank all seem to run together, because there was no break between them — no real difference between night and day. Sometimes we'd go two or three days at a time without sleeping, playing cards when we had them or trying to play chess in our minds without a board or chess pieces when we didn't. Other times we might sleep for a couple of days, just getting up to walk to the mess hall. This was a way to break up the routine, a way to make time pass. That was the worst part: time moved so slowly.

It was unbearable for me at first. I'd been such an outdoors person my whole life. Now I had to spend every minute of every day in a bleak, depressing place with no sunshine or fresh air — just the constant glare of neon tube-lights, bright during the day, dim at night, but never dark. The only windows to the outside in the entire prison were thin slots and they were only on the upper level of our cellblock, behind the guards' catwalk. In O Tank we saw only solid concrete walls.

Each day at five in the morning they herded us into a vestibule at the top of the stairs before taking us to the mess hall. I always paused to gaze out the window toward the street far below, where a bail bonds sign gleamed perpetually through the mist. I remember enviously watching a wino stagger down the street just before dawn one morning and thinking that he had far more freedom than I did.

When we were all gathered in the vestibule, the thick iron door would buzz loudly, then open to let us into the long hallway. "Single file! Hands in your pockets!" a guard would bark, and we'd all line up along the institution-green wall and wait to be escorted to the mess hall.

Privacy is the first casualty in a prison. I never had a moment alone the entire time I was at the main jail. Everything is wide open. The toilet stands just three or four feet from the table where everyone sits, and there is no partition. The single-stall shower has no curtain. Any modesty a person might feel has to die quickly. A guard walking along the catwalk can see everything going on in a cell, but a guard's presence doesn't really give a prisoner much if any protection. A lot can happen outside the scrutiny of the guards. But the lack of privacy does add to the humiliation and dehumanization of being a prisoner.

I started pacing back and forth in the cell within a couple of days of being there, which really bugged the others, especially Wayne. And I had a small calendar I was using to check off my time served. One day Eldon saw me looking at my calendar, and he shook his head.

"You gotta stop that, man," he said. "It'll drive you crazy. You're pulling hard time. It don't make time go by any faster. It makes it worse. You should just relax, do your time, don't think about it. You'll be out of here before you know it." I finally took his advice and threw away my calendar.

A few weeks after starting my time a curious thing happened. The guards gathered all the inmates in O Tank and marched us upstairs, where we crammed into the cells in P Tank along with the prisoners already there. Together we watched Apollo astronauts Neil Armstrong and Buzz Aldrin land the first spacecraft on the moon. I've never heard of anything like that happening before or since at a jail. I suppose someone made a decision that this was too historic an occasion not to share it with us, and for that I'm grateful. Many years later I was at an Explorers Club dinner in New York City, receiving a conservation award, when I met Buzz Aldrin. We had a nice conversation, but I never told him I'd been watching the moonwalk from a jail cell on that historic day.

The guards were not always that understanding — far from it. Some seemed to delight in humiliating us. The worst was a guy we called Cutter. He was always doing shakedowns in O Tank, pulling people's bunks apart and dumping all their belongings on the floor. He'd frequently come into our cells with three or four other guards and put us through a strip search. We'd have to take off all our clothes and stand in a line in front of the cell as they searched through our hair, our armpits, and every other potential hiding place. As a final humiliation, each of us would have to bend over and spread our butt cheeks apart as a guard shined a flashlight up our anuses. I don't know what they expected to find there.

Cutter was a burly man in his thirties with a close-cropped flattop. He would strut around the cell like a Marine Corps drill instructor, often going too close to each prisoner in the line, invading the prisoner's personal space, daring him to strike out. He also had an annoying habit of suddenly turning on the cell lights to full strength at 4:00 A.M. and opening and closing the cell doors again and again and again — *clang, clang, clang* — until every man in every cell was up and dressed. It was the rudest of awakenings.

One morning when Cutter was opening and closing the cell doors, Wayne said someone ought to stick his arm in the door so Cutter would get in trouble. I glanced at Eldon and saw him staring blankly at the door as it slid back and forth — *wham . . . wham . . . wham!* I grabbed his wrist.

"Don't do it, man," I said. "Please . . . don't do it."

He looked up, surprised, then smiled. "Don't worry about it," he said.

∼

I SPENT MY nineteenth birthday at the main jail that summer. I didn't tell anyone about it. I just bought a huge cigar from the commissary and lay on my bunk smoking it to celebrate.

"I didn't know you smoked, Slick," said Cruz.

"I don't," I said, laughing as I blew out a cloud of acrid gray smoke.

O TANK WAS the strangest place I've ever seen. It had its own code, its own rituals — even its own language. The prisoners would always say "radio" instead of "shut up." "Hey, radio that shit!" they'd yell if someone was being too loud or saying something they didn't like.

Every so often, the police would raid several of the local bridges frequented by homeless winos, called "grapes" by the inmates. They would end up in P Tank, drying out before being sent on to Theo Lacy or to the honor farm, another branch jail in Orange County. Some of them suffered from serious delirium tremens as they went without alcohol and would cry out and moan or talk to imaginary people in the middle of the night. This infuriated the other prisoners, who would shout: "Radio, grape!"

EVERY SATURDAY INMATES could have short visits with their friends or family. The guards would herd us down to the visiting room if someone came to see us, and we would each sit in a little stall with a glass partition separating the prisoner from the visitor. I remember the first time my mom and my sisters came to visit me they just started talking, and I couldn't hear a word. I finally tapped on the glass and pointed to the telephone receiver we each had to use. I didn't get many visitors outside of my family. For the most part, I was forgotten. Three or four people I knew came for a single visit shortly after I began my sentence, but they were not close friends and I think had come more out of curiosity than anything else. I wrote back and forth a few times with a girl I knew, but her letters soon petered out. It's hard, especially for a young person, to keep interested in someone who is locked away in prison. But Hollis visited me a couple of times, later, when I was at Theo Lacy. And Jeff Sipple sent me some postcards he'd made with pictures of trained hawks on the front, and I stuck them on the wall beside my bunk.

I BARELY MISSED being sent to the hole one night. I don't remember exactly what triggered it — probably just boredom and frustration — but suddenly everyone was throwing stuff out of their cells up and down O Tank. Torn mattresses with the stuffing hanging out, blankets, pillows, clothes, toilet paper, garbage — everything the other inmates could get their hands on. Wayne started to tear his mattress apart with his bare hands, but Eldon stopped him.

"Hey, I don't want to go to the hole," said Eldon. "I've been there enough times already, and I don't like it." That was enough to stop us. As the other O Tank prisoners continued their destructive rampage, we reversed the process in our cell, cleaning up the floor, making our bunks, putting everything neatly back in its place. Soon, the whole cell row was a shambles — except our cell and the space in front of it. The first guard who came by on the catwalk was aghast. He called for backup, and when they arrived, one of the guards got on the loudspeaker: "Roll it up," he said. "You're all going to the hole . . . except Cell 2."

The prisoners rolled up the remnants of their bedding and headed up the stairs where even more guards had arrived to take them to the hole. And we didn't see any of them for the next five days — the standard minimum time spent in the hole. It's a miserable place — a series of small one-man cells with only a toilet inside: no seat, no bunk, no bedding. And it can get cold in there, lying on the bare concrete floor. The prisoners don't even get to go to the mess hall to eat. These guys from O Tank had it worse than most, though, because the jail didn't have enough cells in the hole to accommodate them all. The guards had to put five or six of them in each one-man cell.

⁓

ONE DAY WAYNE expounded to me on his long-term vision and philosophy. He was a survivalist long before that lifestyle had a name. He dreamed of gathering together a tribe of misfits and going off to live in some remote mountains, apart from society, existing on whatever they could scrape together, kill, or steal in the wilderness. Of course, this involved having a full complement of various guns and other high-tech weaponry in case the government ever came after them. He happened to ask me if I was a hunter, and I said yes. But I usually hunt with hawks, not guns, I told him. His eyes lit up. He wanted to know everything about the birds. How I caught them. How I trained them. What kinds of game they could take. After a few days of this, he started trying to talk me into joining his group in the mountains — although at this time he was the sole member. He opened up about everything he'd been thinking about for years, speaking with all the zeal of a prophet. He had a vision he was sure would catch fire and eventually spread across the world. And I could be a major part of it — along with my falcons.

I had mixed feelings about suddenly becoming Wayne's new best friend. On the one hand, there might be less chance he would flip out and kill me while I was in prison. But on the other hand, who'd want to be hooked up with this nut case? I tried to stay noncommittal, but he was always there, talking in detail about the great things we'd be able to accomplish. Eldon and Cruz overheard some of this a few times. They'd look at me from behind Wayne's back and smirk.

Some bad things eventually started happening in our cell. Cutter had taken a strong dislike to Eldon, and he did everything he could to get to him. One day when he was going through a cigar box where Eldon kept a few of his belongings, Cutter squirted a tube of shaving cream all over the inside. We didn't see him do it, because we were all lined up naked facing the other way for a skin search, but he was the only one who went back in the cell where the box was kept. Another time, Cutter was searching our bunks and saw the picture of Eldon's brother stuck on the wall. He pulled it off and looked at it.

"What the hell is this?" he said. "A goddamn pinup?"

I could sense Eldon tensing without even seeing him.

"It's mine," I lied. "It's my brother. His wife's on the back."

I was a nonentity to Cutter. He barely knew I existed, so he let it go. He just turned the picture over to look at the other side then tossed it on the bunk. I'm sure he never realized how close he came to having his head slammed into the concrete wall by Eldon.

But that wasn't the end of the troubles between Cutter and Eldon. One day when we were lined up for another skin search, Eldon made a crack about Cutter under his breath, and we all laughed for a second.

Cutter rose up in Eldon's face. "What's the joke, huh? You got something to say to me?" They glared at each other eye-to-eye, just inches apart. Eldon kept silent. "I didn't think so," said Cutter. "Well, turn around and spread 'em."

Eldon bent over and spread his buttocks, and just as Cutter knelt down behind him with his flashlight, he broke wind right in his face.

Cutter shot up in a fury, beet red and shaking with anger. "Roll it up, you bastard! You're going to the hole!" he shouted.

"What for?" said Eldon.

"Contraband," said Cutter as he pulled a deck of cards from his own shirt pocket and slammed it on the floor.

Eldon calmly got dressed and gathered his bedding together. "Could you take care of my stuff for me?" he asked.

"Sure," I said and watched as he walked up the stairs in front of Cutter. A moment later, he went through the heavy iron door, and it slammed shut behind him. I picked up the cigar box he left on my bed and looked inside. It held a razor, an old toothbrush, a couple of packs of cigarettes, and a laminated plastic picture of his brother and his brother's fiancée.

A RUMOR SWEPT through the jail a few days later that Eldon had jumped a guard and then been beaten severely by some other guards. He would be in the hole for at least two more weeks. I immediately thought of Cutter, but no, it turned out that Twiggy was the guard Eldon attacked. (The prisoners nicknamed him Twiggy after the English fashion model, because he was so thin.) That surprised me. Twiggy was one of the more amiable guards at the main jail. I couldn't imagine what set Eldon off.

A couple of weeks later I heard Eldon was out of the hole but wouldn't be coming back to O Tank. He'd had his hair cut short and was now a trustee living in a ward on another floor. I was stunned. Later that day during dinner at the mess hall, an O Tank prisoner sitting across from me started talking about Eldon, saying he was a snitch. I shot up instantly, knocking my tray off the edge of the table with a clatter.

"That's fucking bullshit!" I said. Everyone at the surrounding tables stopped eating and stared as I stood there. "He'd never snitch!"

The man backed off. "Well, I don't know," he said. "Maybe I'm wrong. I just think it's strange he punches out a guard one day and now he's a trustee."

To have a "snitch jacket" — the stigma of having given information to police or guards — is a virtual death sentence for a prisoner. It's a brand that follows a person to any prison across the country where he may serve time someday, and there's no way to erase it. That's why I had to stop that rumor before it started. But I still wanted to find out what happened. I wanted to see Eldon somehow and talk with him about the rumor.

The next morning, I wrote a note to the guard on duty saying I wanted to transfer out of O Tank and become a trustee. The funny thing is I had written several notes like that before, beginning with my first day in O Tank, when I said I'd made a mistake. I didn't know what O Tank was. I wanted to work. I wanted to go to Lacy or the honor farm. All of my letters had been ignored. But this time was different. Within an hour, the guard called me out of my cell to talk about my transfer.

"So, you're ready to work?" he asked.

"Sure," I said. "The sooner the better." A short time later I was back in Cell 2 rolling up my bedding. Wayne came up to me.

"What is this?" he asked. "What's going on?"

"I'm getting out of here," I said. "I'm going to be a trustee. I'm hoping maybe I can get transferred to Lacy after that."

He was astounded. "Why the hell would you want to do that?" he said. "They're all a bunch of faggots at Lacy."

"I don't know," I said. "I just can't stand never getting to go outside. I really hate this place. I want some fresh air and sunshine. I want to be able to see birds again, you know?"

"Yeah, I know that's important to you," he said, frowning. "But you're making a big mistake."

I ignored him as I pulled my hawk pictures down from the wall and gathered together my toothbrush and razor and Eldon's cigar box.

"Well, don't forget, Slick," said Wayne. "We got to get together again on the streets, when we're both out of here. I got big plans."

"I'll definitely keep in touch," I said. "See you around." I turned and saw Cruz sitting at the table where I'd first seen him. "I hope everything works out OK for you, Cruz," I said. "And I hope I see you again sometime." He stood up and embraced me. "I hope so, too," he said.

And with that I was out of it. After more than two months I walked up the stairs and out of O Tank and never saw that place (or Wayne) again.

ELDON DID A double take when he saw me walk into the mess hall for the first time in my new trustee sweatshirt. We were both gold shirts now, which meant we were trustees who worked only on the first floor. His group was just getting up to leave as I was lining up for food. I barely recognized him at first without his long hair and bandanna. They'd given him a buzz cut before letting him be a trustee. Only prisoners in O Tank or in the cells for unsentenced inmates could have long hair at the county jail. The barber did the same to me, although my hair had been nowhere near as long as Eldon's. The guard took me downstairs to the barbershop — a cell with a barber's chair inside — and asked the inmate who worked there to cut my hair.

"He's from O Tank," the guard said. The haircutter winked at him and pulled out the electric clippers. He switched the power on and buzzed it across my head like he was mowing a lawn — the shortest haircut I've ever had.

After that the guard took me to get my bedding and my trustee sweatshirt and showed me where I'd be staying, in an open ward instead of a cell. It was still a sterile place with a door the guards locked at night, but we had a little more freedom. When we got off work, we could hang around a large common area and watch television, play cards, read, or talk to other prisoners.

I finally got to see Eldon that evening after work. (I was a custodian mopping the holding cells and hallways on the first floor and doing other menial work.) His face looked like it had been roughed up. Although it was mostly healed, he still had a few faded bruises and scabs. He also had a huge bandage on his right thumb. He'd already had a badly infected thumb for a few weeks in O Tank, but it looked worse now. We sat at a table together in the common area.

"So you beat up Twiggy?" I said.

He smiled. "I feel bad about that," he said. "Too bad you weren't there to stop me." We both laughed. He told me how tense he was after two or three days in the hole, and then his infected thumb flared up again. He showed it to the guards, and they arranged to take him downstairs later so the medic could examine it. Twiggy was one of the guards who took him out of his cell, and he gave Eldon a little shove as he walked behind him.

"I snapped," said Eldon. "I just turned around and tackled him, and we both went to the ground." The other two guards were on him instantly, but Eldon was in such a rage, they couldn't budge him off Twiggy — until one of them grabbed hold of his infected thumb and squeezed with all his might. Eldon nearly fainted from the pain. As soon as they got him off Twiggy, they beat him senseless and threw him back into the hole.

"You know, Twiggy came back later and apologized, said he was out of line," said Eldon. "Can you believe that? If it'd been Cutter . . . I don't know."

Eldon told me he had to see his probation officer a couple of days after that, and the man laid it out straight for him. He had never before had to violate the probation of someone currently serving time, but he was about to do it with Eldon — which would mean he would immediately start serving the state-prison sentence that had been suspended as part of the terms of his probation. But he offered him one final chance. If Eldon would stop being such an incorrigible rebel — if he would cut his hair, become a trustee, and try to become a more productive, positive member of the inmate population — his probation would not be violated. And Eldon agreed, which, for him, was an amazing act of contrition. I'm sure it had a lot to do with the fact that Twiggy apologized to him. He was impressed by that and felt bad that he had attacked him.

The next day brought a surprise: Cruz showed up in the trustee common area. He had transferred from O Tank.

"Wayne was driving me crazy," he said. "He wanted me to join his damn army and go live in the hills someplace." We all laughed. It was great having the three of us back together again. And after spending a couple of months in O Tank, this place seemed like a holiday resort. I'll never forget how great it was being able to take a container of trash outside to a dumpster for the first time. I couldn't see much. It was in a small asphalt-covered area with a twenty-foot wall blocking my view. But for just a minute I was out in the fresh air and sunshine, and for the first time in weeks I felt alive. And the guards let us go up to a fenced-in exercise area on top of the jail a couple of days a week. There we could play shuffleboard and other games or just lie in the sun relaxing. At the time, it seemed as good as being on a cruise ship.

After three weeks of being a trustee, I found out I was being transferred to Theo Lacy in a couple of days. Suddenly I had mixed feelings. This was something I'd been wanting for the entire time I'd been in jail. But now, when I finally had a chance to go there, I felt conflicted. I had friends now. I felt reasonably comfortable with my environment. But now, once again I'd be going off into the unknown.

I told Eldon and Cruz that evening. "That's great," said Eldon. "That's what you wanted all along," he said.

"Yeah, I know," I said, wistfully.

"Hey, you'll do fine," he said.

"That's right, Slick," said Cruz. "You don't want to be in this damn place anymore."

But it was sad. We'd become like a family. I knew that if someone attacked me, Eldon and Cruz — and Wayne, too, for that matter — would throw themselves into the fray to help me, against the most hopeless odds. And I felt the same way. We all knew that instinctively. You don't see that kind of devotion in day-to-day life. I suppose it's the kind of camaraderie soldiers experience in combat. I would have died for those guys in a heartbeat back then. Hell, I'd do it now. Only I'm sure Eldon is long dead. And Wayne's probably a whacked-out survivalist in the mountains of Idaho with his own squad of trained killers. Cruz might have made it. I like to think he's sitting on a porch someplace singing to his grandkids.

The night before I left, the three of us got together. Eldon had somehow gotten a bottle of raisin jack some guys working in the kitchen had made. It was awful. We mixed it with water but it still scorched my throat and left me with a killer headache the next day. We laughed like giddy children that night until tears streamed down our cheeks, and it was good. It was the best. And then it was lights out. And then it was time for breakfast. And then I was climbing aboard another sheriff's bus with wire-mesh-covered windows and being driven away from the main jail. And once again in my life I was leaving friends I knew I'd never see again.

THEO LACY WAS the home stretch. It was the last month and a half or so of my sentence, and I saw the warm days of summer and early fall end and a chill set in as November began. On our work crews we started wearing denim jackets with "Orange County Branch Jail" stenciled in gaudy yellow paint on the back. It wouldn't be long until it was all over. I was amazed how open Lacy was. During free time after work, the prisoners could walk around most of the compound, which included a huge grassy field where people played baseball or other sports. The first day there, I strolled to the chainlink fence at the edge of the field and looked at the dog pound, which stood a hundred feet or so away. I could see the dogs in the last row of cages, and I looked closely at them on the off chance that Rex might be there. I started doing that every day as new dogs came in. I only once saw a dog that looked like Rex, but it wasn't him. Probably just as well. I don't know what I would have done if he had shown up.

I was lonely. I entered Lacy not knowing anyone. I was assigned to work on a flood-control crew, which each day went to various manmade ditches and canals in the county to hoe weeds or shovel mud or swing a pickax or move rocks — basic unskilled grunt work. It was OK. I worked hard and came back exhausted at the end of the day. But I screwed up badly one day.

We would be driven to our work site each morning in a big covered truck that carried about twenty men, who sat on wooden benches along the sides. It was open in the back, and we always towed an outhouse on wheels behind us. The area at the far back of the truck was the most desirable place to sit, because the prisoners got to look into passing cars and stare down at the drivers — which included quite a few pretty women.

One day at the end of work, I was the first one into the truck, and I took one of the best seats in the back. A few minutes later everyone else started climbing aboard. The last man was a stocky, muscular Mexican whom everyone called Zorro, because he always wore big wraparound sunglasses like a mask. He swung up onto the back step bumper of the truck and towered above me as I sat.

"What the fuck you doing in my seat?" he snarled.

"Oh, sorry," I said and got up quickly. I made my way to an empty part of the bench toward the front. Everyone burst out laughing. The prisoner sitting beside me leaned toward me.

"You shouldn't have done that, man," he said. I looked at him but didn't say anything.

The seat at the back didn't mean anything to me. I just sat there because it was the first place to sit that I came to, so I didn't think anything about giving it up to Zorro. But something else had happened. I'd shown weakness, and that's never a good thing in jail. Zorro started bothering me after that, calling me names like Sweetie and Bitch and making comments about me to other prisoners and laughing.

Zorro was a maniac about working out. Although he didn't have weights to lift, every time we stopped for lunch or had a chance to sit around for a while, he'd find whatever heavy object was available — a big block of broken concrete or a huge rock — and he'd lie on his back, lifting it up and down above him as his arm muscles bulged. Most people were terrified of him and laid low so he wouldn't notice them.

We had only one person watching us when we went out on our flood-control crew, and he was not an official guard. He was old — a retired army master sergeant with a thick Alabama accent, whom everyone called Grits. He couldn't have done anything to stop the prisoners on our crew from escaping, but I suppose none of us were thought to be a flight risk. He usually would just sit around all day smoking cigars while we worked.

The situation between Zorro and me began escalating. One day in the mess hall he bumped into me hard, making me drop my tray of food on the floor. He walked away laughing as I stood there, mortified. A few days later we were all working in a flood-control channel, wearing rubber boots in the shallow water as we dug out aquatic weeds with our shovels. Zorro came up behind me and pinched me on the butt.

"Don't you EVER do that again!" I said.

He laughed. "Aw, what's the matter, Sweetie? You got a sore bottom?"

I stood there trembling with anger as he walked away. I stared after him for a moment then went back to weeding. A while later I felt him pinch me again. I spun around in a blind rage and punched him in the face with all of my might, his sunglasses flying off behind him into the murky water as he fell back. I'll never forget that. The loud *thwack* of my leather work glove as I struck his face; the way the energy of the punch shot all the way through my body from my fist to my foot, connecting perfectly; and the way Zorro went down, tumbling like a great tree uprooted and landing on his back in the water. And I was on him instantly, flailing away with punch after punch. His face was an inch under the water, and he kept trying to raise his head to take a breath, and I kept punching him down, with ditch water and blood from his mouth and nose splashing up all around me.

It took four or five inmates to pull me off him. Zorro raised himself on all fours coughing and choking as he struggled to clear his lungs and get a breath. He looked like he was trying to puke. He finally got up on his feet and stood shakily a couple of feet in front of me shouting in my face as the others held me.

"I'll get you in the shower with a razorblade!" he screamed.

I lurched forward and smashed my face right into his face, which caused as much damage to me as to him, and that got him. I saw the same look of terror I'd seen on my father's face when I was about to throw a brick at his head. I knew he was beaten.

After they let go of my arms, several prisoners congratulated me and tried to shake my hand, but I didn't want any part of it. I stood there for a few minutes as the blood streaming from the cut on my forehead clotted up and began to dry. Then I splashed some ditch water on my face and went back to weeding.

When we finally walked back to the truck, I saw old Grits sitting where he had been when we left him three hours earlier, smoking a cigar and enjoying the sunshine. His eyes opened wide when he saw us.

"What happened to you men?" he asked.

"We fell down in the channel and hit our heads on the rocks along the side," I said. He looked at me and then at Zorro and shook his head.

"Let's get these tools put away," he said. We loaded everything up and drove back to Lacy, arriving just before sunset.

I've thought about that incident many times over the years. How ridiculous it was, really. I could never have beaten someone like Zorro. It was the murderous rage I felt at that instant — uncontrollable, beyond any kind of thought process, supercharged by adrenaline. And the lucky punch. And the fact that he was standing off balance and hadn't expected it. And that he was stuck in the mud with water covering his face, unable to take a breath. But it was mostly because in that horrible moment, I fully intended to kill him, and that gave me a strength, a sheer physical power I never knew I possessed. I'm just glad the other prisoners stopped me.

IT WAS MID-NOVEMBER when the guards released me from Theo Lacy. They got me up early, long before sunrise. (Inmates are always released before breakfast.) They fingerprinted me again (to make sure I was the same person they admitted months earlier) and gave me back the clothes and other personal items I'd brought with me to the main jail. After I signed some papers, they opened the front door and let me walk out into the darkness.

I came out of jail the same way I went in — alone. But there was a long dark passage in between, and I was a different person when it was over. My mother and my sisters were parked outside. As I climbed into the car, my mother handed me my leather fringe hippie jacket and hugged me. The sky was just beginning to lighten in the east as we drove home. I never looked back.

PART II

MY FREDERICK II YEAR

10

IN FREDERICK II'S
FOOTSTEPS

IF THIS BOOK were an old movie from the 1940s, this part would be a montage indicating the passage of time — an image of a calendar blown by a powerful wind, with pages flipping wildly to show the months and years flying past. Here I make the mighty jump from the age of nineteen to fifty-five, from early adulthood to middle age. Many interesting things happened in the intervening years, when I turned my life around and became a successful, productive member of society. But this narrative is not about that. It's about my time as a falconry bum — both before I went to college and began my career as an author and editor and later in 2006, when I went back to my life as an itinerant falconer, spending much of the year either hawking at home with Macduff or in Wyoming, Scotland, England, Kansas, Idaho, and Italy, watching other people's hawks being flown. It was the kind of year I dreamt of as a teenager — especially visiting the places where Frederick lived and hawked more than seven centuries ago.

Before delving deep into my Frederick II year, I take a side trip in this chapter, departing from the narrative about my own life and exploring the world of Frederick to provide an overview of his life so readers will understand the references to him during my later travels through Italy. I also want to show why this figure from the distant past has had such a hold on me for so long and why he means so much to me.

I ALWAYS LOVED the story of Frederick II — especially the first part, long before everything in his life went to hell. Perhaps it was his audacity, his supreme confidence in himself and his ideas that so attracted me. Here was a person who even as a boy knew what he wanted and went after it.

Frederick was a polarizing figure in his lifetime. People either loved him or hated him. To his admirers he was the Stupor Mundi — "the Wonder of the World." Piero della Vigna went so far as to call him "the God-sent Savior, the Prince of Peace, the Messiah-Emperor." Pope Gregory IX, who led the Church for almost half of Frederick's thirty-year reign, held a vastly different view: Frederick II is "the beast that surges up from the sea laden with blasphemous names, and raging with a bear's paws and a lion's maw, his other members in the likeness of a leopard, his gaping mouth offending the Holy Name, unceasingly even hurling his lance at the tabernacle of God and His Saints in heaven."

Frederick would have been a wonder in any age, but in the thirteenth century he stood without equal. Easily the most intelligent and charismatic monarch who ever ruled in Europe, he spoke six languages fluently, including Arabic and Greek. He thrived on learning, and his court became the greatest cultural center of its day, attracting scholars, scientists, mathematicians, physicians, artists, and poets from all of the Germanic and Mediterranean cultures. Through Frederick II, algebra and Arabic numerals (as well as the concept of zero) were introduced to Christian Europe. He eliminated internal tariffs throughout the Empire, creating the world's first free-trade zone. He established the first secular university, challenging the Church's monopoly on formal learning. He was the only monarch in Christendom who had read and studied the Koran and knew all of the precepts of Islam. And he corresponded frequently with Arab scientists and scholars. Throughout his life, Frederick associated without restriction with Muslims, Jews, and other sects the Church considered unacceptable. For these and other heresies he was excommunicated — twice.

Frederick II also led the first and only bloodless Crusade to the Holy Land, negotiating with the Arabs instead of fighting them. In the Constitutions of Melfi, which Frederick established after his return from the Crusade, he abolished trial by combat and restricted the Church's land holdings. He also determined that all secular government officials would be appointed by the Emperor, not by the Church, which further undermined the authority of the Church in state matters.

Frederick had an unusual childhood. He was the son and grandson of emperors. His paternal grandfather was the great Frederick Barbarossa, the popular and charismatic Emperor who had ruled Germany and northern Italy before dying during the Crusades.

Frederick's father, Henry VI, also became Holy Roman Emperor, but he did Barbarossa one better by marrying Constance of Sicily and acquiring her kingdom. At that time, Sicily included not only the island of that name but also most of southern Italy. This was the nightmare scenario for the Catholic Church, to have the Papal States bounded on the north, east, and south by the Empire. The Church would be powerless to resist if the Emperor decided to annex Church lands or exert imperial authority in other ways. But a showdown between Henry VI and the Pope was averted by the Emperor's untimely death at the age of thirty-six.

Frederick was only three years old when his father died; a few months later, he was crowned King of Sicily in Palermo. This was the only crown his mother, Constance, wanted for him. She was against the idea of Frederick becoming Emperor and embracing the entirety of his kingdom in Germany and northern Italy. But in November 1198, within a year of Henry's death, Constance herself had passed away, leaving instructions in her will that Frederick was to become the ward of Pope Innocent III, who would be regent over Sicily until Frederick came of age at fifteen. But Frederick was a ward of the Pope largely in name only. Innocent III kept aloof from the boy, never once making the journey from Rome to Sicily to visit him.

Frederick showed the strength and fieriness of his personality at an early age. In a blatant power play, the German nobleman Markward of Anweiler seized six-year-old Frederick at his castle in Palermo. (Markward sought the power to be able to rule in Frederick's name.) Frederick was betrayed by a guard, who let Markward enter the castle and showed him where the young King of Sicily was hiding. Frederick sprang at Markward and his followers, attacking them in a furious rage. When that failed, Frederick tore his own clothing to ribbons and ripped his flesh with his fingernails. Rainald, the Archbishop of Capua, described the event to the Pope in detail and added: "a worthy omen for the future ruler who cannot be false to his own nobility, who with royal instinct feels himself, like Mount Sinai, outraged by the touch of a beast of prey."

Markward died a year later. Various papal legates and noblemen continued to be ostensibly responsible for Frederick, but by and large he was poorly cared for and often went without the most basic necessities. Much of his property had been squandered. At the age of eight and nine, he lived the life of a waif, wandering the streets and gardens of Palermo without oversight.

Pope Innocent III did not act in Frederick's best interest. To avoid the dreaded scenario of being surrounded by imperial lands again, he offered the crown of Holy Roman Emperor to Otto, with the understanding that Otto would never attempt to add the Kingdom of Sicily to his empire. Crowned in 1209, Otto IV had barely left Rome before he began conspiring with others from Pisa and Apulia to invade Frederick's kingdom. Innocent III prided himself on having eyes and ears everywhere, and he quickly learned of Otto's plans. He immediately went to work behind the scenes, instructing all of the bishops of the realm to try to foster opposition to Otto. By the time Otto marched on Sicily in late 1210, the Pope was ready. He excommunicated Otto and released the Emperor's subjects from their oath of allegiance to him, but it wasn't clear these maneuvers would be enough to stop him.

Town after town on the mainland of southern Italy yielded to Otto as he marched southward. Then Calabria and Basilicata — the two provinces closest to the island of Sicily, where Frederick was holed up — declared themselves in favor of Otto. No entreaties from the Pope or Frederick could dissuade Otto from his goal. The most they could offer him were territories or properties he already held or was about to seize. Otto's army stood waiting only the arrival of the Pisan fleet to ferry them across to the island of Sicily so they could attack Frederick and claim all of southern Italy.

Frederick — only sixteen years old and with few supporters — didn't have the resources to fight a force this size. He kept a galley at anchor near his fort in Palermo ready to flee to Africa if the need arose, but it was a slim chance. His doom seemed near. But just as Frederick's situation appeared hopeless, the Pope's machinations began to bear fruit. At the urging of Innocent III and his bishops, the German princes decided to throw their support to Frederick as Emperor. No doubt all of them, including the Pope, thought it far preferable to have a weak-willed, easily controlled boy at the helm instead of a strongman like Otto. They obviously didn't know Frederick.

A messenger from Germany came to Otto's camp just as he was about to complete his conquest. The messenger warned Otto that many German princes were defecting to Frederick. Otto decided to return at once and consolidate his power base in Germany — a remarkable tactical blunder. If Otto had spent a few more days there and captured or killed Frederick, the Empire would have been his to keep, without dispute.

What was Frederick to do? To claim his northern realm, he would have to journey to Germany, traveling unprotected through hostile areas of Lombardy and across the high passes of the Alps. How could he be sure the fickle German princes wouldn't change their minds again and throw their support once more to Otto? And what of Pope Innocent III? Would he continue to back Frederick as Emperor? All of Frederick's advisers and the nobles of Sicily warned him against going to Germany. They urged him to remain in Sicily and retain his kingdom — to give up his imperial dream, a fool's quest that he could never hope to attain.

Frederick didn't hesitate. It was but one of the moments in his life when he seized the initiative, proceeding boldly, against all odds, risking everything to achieve his destiny. "As torn and ragged as a beggar boy," as one chronicler put it, with "fair and gracious countenance: merry the brow and merrier yet the sparkle of his eyes." Frederick set off from Palermo with only a handful of men and no money to conquer the Empire.

The journey took months. All the main roads were unsafe and the Pisan fleet, still loyal to Otto IV, kept watch at sea. After finally reaching Genoa, Frederick had to wait weeks before attempting to pass through the vast swath of hostile territory that lay before him en route to the city of Cremona. His enemies in Milan and Piacenza knew he had to cross the river Lambro to get there, so they patrolled the river constantly, stopping every boat to search for the boy.

Frederick and his men rode all night, reaching the Lambro at dawn. As they took a brief rest on the riverbank, a force from Milan arrived to seize Frederick. Jumping onto a bareback horse, he plunged into the river, swimming across in a hail of arrows. He was met with wild rejoicing in Cremona, where the townspeople believed a miracle had taken place. From there, Frederick seemed an unstoppable force. He rushed to Mantua, then on to Verona and up the Adige Valley to Trent. The dukes of Meran and Bavaria, who still supported Otto IV, blocked the Brenner Pass, so Frederick turned west, searching for another way to get through the Alps. He and his tiny band finally crossed into German territory, reaching Chur in September. The Bishop of Chur received him warmly and escorted him to St. Gall, where three hundred horsemen joined his force.

Frederick and his men raced toward the city of Constance, only two hours' ride from where Otto and his army lay encamped at Überlingen. Otto had already succeeded in re-establishing much of his power in Germany and was just about to visit Constance. His servants and cooks were already there, preparing a great banquet to celebrate Otto IV's entrance into the great city. Suddenly Frederick appeared at the gates of Constance, demanding to be admitted. The Bishop of Constance refused to allow him inside, but Archbishop Berard of Bari, who accompanied Frederick, read out Pope Innocent III's declaration of excommunication against Otto IV and his support for Frederick. The Bishop finally yielded, allowing Frederick and his retinue inside. They set to work immediately, fortifying the bridge across the Rhine and manning the city gates with a fighting force.

By the time Otto arrived three hours later, the city of Constance was barred against him. If Otto had entered the city first, Frederick could never have hoped to succeed in Germany. As it was, tales of this great coup spread quickly through the land. It was taken as another miracle — a sign from God of His approval of Frederick. The size of Frederick's following grew by the hour. Just days later, all of the princes and noblemen of the Upper Rhine joined him. People thronged the streets wherever Frederick went, weeping with joy and cheering as he entered their towns and villages. In a few short weeks he had conquered all of southern Germany without a fight.

The people called Frederick the "Child from Apulia" (a province in southern Italy) or sometimes just "Our Boy." He stood in stark contrast to Otto IV in every way. Where Otto was tall, stern, dour, and tightfisted, Frederick was of medium height, with golden blond hair and a radiant smile, warm and generous, and dripping with natural charisma. One Italian said, "It is a joy merely to gaze on the handsome Hohenstaufen boy." And there was something magical about the way events in his life unfolded — like a fairy tale: the beggar prince arising to claim his throne or young David's miraculous victory over Goliath.

It would be several years later, in 1220, before Frederick made the journey to Rome for his official coronation by Pope Innocent III's successor, Pope Honorius III. With full imperial pomp, Frederick rode along the Via Triumphalis, the ancient coronation road to Saint Peter's Basilica and was crowned by the Pope. But even in this most hopeful time, the seeds of Frederick's next crisis were already planted. For Pope Honorius III, the most important challenge facing Christendom was to recapture Jerusalem — which had been taken by the great sultan Saladin in 1187 — and he wanted Frederick to lead a Crusade.

Frederick was not in a position to depart quickly for the Holy Land. Some areas of the Empire — particularly the major cities in Lombardy, such as Milan — still swirled with plots and intrigues aimed at overthrowing his rule. He could not afford to be gone for a lengthy period at such a crucial time. He was also shrewd enough to use the Pope's desire to launch a Crusade as a bargaining chip with the Church in working out the terms of his rule. He finally agreed, under threat of excommunication, to mount a Crusade in the late summer of 1227.

Shortly before Frederick was due to leave for the Holy Land, Honorius III passed away, and Gregory IX became Pope. The new Pope was quick to sense the potential danger of an independent-minded man like Frederick II controlling the Empire, and he soon made it his main mission in life to bring the Emperor into line or destroy him. His obsession with Frederick eventually turned into bitter hatred.

As Frederick made preparations for the Crusade, an endless stream of pilgrims from Germany and other parts of the realm poured into Brindisi on the coast of southern Italy to join him. As they waited to embark in August 1227, a plague broke out — perhaps cholera or dysentery, which was always a danger at that time of year in the hot southern climes, particularly for people from northern Europe. Scores of crusaders and pilgrims died, and to escape the contagious disease, thousands more fled the area and scattered throughout Italy.

Many noblemen from Germany died of the illness, and Frederick himself became sick. He decided to postpone the Crusade until the following spring, when he would be fully recovered and able to reorganize an army. Frederick sent two emissaries to the Pope to explain what had happened. Gregory IX refused to receive them. Two weeks later, he excommunicated Frederick. He also spread bizarre rumors that Frederick had deliberately infected his men with this illness to avoid going on the Crusade.

Frederick said he would undergo any penance the Church required, and he promised to launch the Crusade the following May. The Pope refused his entreaties. The only condition Gregory IX would accept for Frederick's absolution was for him to cede control of the Kingdom of Sicily to the Church. This was something Frederick would never agree to, but what could he possibly do? If he didn't lead a Crusade that spring, it would prove the Pope's point that he had forsaken his pledge to the Church and should relinquish his Empire. But how could an excommunicated man lead a Crusade — a person who had been condemned to eternal damnation by the world leader of the Church? He knew the minute he left, the schemers would emerge and attempt to carve up his Empire. And the odds were stacked mightily against his achieving victory over the Sultan of Egypt, al Kamil, a nephew of Saladin. To be defeated in the Crusades, to be forced to turn back and return empty-handed would be the worst outcome of all. His defeat would be viewed as a judgment from God for daring — as an excommunicated man bearing the curse of the Church — to enter the Holy Land. But what if he won? What if by some miracle he did retake Jerusalem? This would be a crushing defeat for Pope Gregory IX.

Once again, Frederick risked everything — his wealth, his Empire, his very life — with the slimmest chance of success. In June 1228, he sailed from Brindisi with a fleet of forty galleys. He was thirty-four years old.

Pope Gregory IX was furious and sent emissaries to Syria where Frederick's forces were massed, commanding that no one should follow the banned Emperor. The pilgrims split into two hostile groups, one supporting Frederick, the other the Pope. In this weakened position, Frederick prepared to face the mighty al Kamil.

What he lacked in military might, Frederick made up for in charm and personality. He was a master conversationalist, widely read, quick, and witty. His knowledge of science, philosophy, medicine, mathematics, logic, and other branches of learning was astounding. He had read all of the Arab poets, and, of course, was a master in the art of falconry — the most popular field sport in the East.

Al Kamil was almost a mirror image of Frederick in terms of his interests and passions. He loved nothing better than discussing deep philosophical or scientific questions with learned men. In his castle, "fifty scholars reclined on divans round his throne to provide his evening conversation." He promoted learning throughout his realm and founded a school in Cairo.

Frederick set about winning Jerusalem through friendship and negotiation with the Sultan's representative, Emir Fakr ad-Din. For weeks they met secretly. Finally on February 18, 1229, Frederick emerged with a treaty. In addition to his other titles, Frederick would thenceforth be called King of Jerusalem. (He had earlier wed Isabella, Queen of Jerusalem, giving him the right to the title through marriage.) All of the city would be his except for the sacred enclosure of Haramu'sh Sharif, with the Temple of Solomon and the Mosque of 'Umar — but Christian pilgrims would be able to visit the area to pray, and Muslims would have the same rights in Bethlehem, which was also ceded to the Emperor. Also, a ten-year truce went into effect immediately.

And so, Frederick had accomplished what no Crusader had been able to do since Jerusalem fell to Saladin — he had opened up the Holy City to the Christian world, without a drop of blood being spilled.

Rejoicing broke out immediately when he announced the treaty to his knights and pilgrims.

Frederick decided to lead the pilgrims into Jerusalem himself and visit the Church of the Holy Sepulcher. Shortly before he entered the city, al Kamil received a note from one of the Pope's henchmen, letting him know about Frederick's plans and where he would be if the Sultan wished to kill him or take him prisoner. Disgusted by this treachery, the Sultan had the letter delivered to Frederick.

One of the most unusual coronations ever recorded took place on the day the Emperor walked through Jerusalem. With his friends and followers, Frederick strode into the Church of the Holy Sepulcher — the most sacred site in all of Christendom. Without a bishop or any intermediary of the Church present and without a coronation mass to bless the event, Frederick walked up to the altar, picked up the crown, and placed it on his head himself.

Pope Gregory IX had been busy while Frederick was in the Holy Land. Immediately after hearing of the Emperor's departure, the Pope had released all of Frederick's subjects from their oath of allegiance and issued orders for them to take up arms against him. Gregory IX sent an invading army made up of his own soldiers and rebels from Lombardy into Frederick's Kingdom of Sicily — an unprecedented move. "This war is necessary for the Christian faith that such a mighty Persecutor of the Church be driven from his throne," wrote the Pope. Gregory IX was on dangerous footing here: sending a papal army into battle against a Christian monarch while he was off fighting for the true religion in the Holy Land. So both men engaged in a daring, all-or-nothing gamble for control of Christendom. Gregory IX also sent messengers throughout the land, announcing to everyone that Frederick II was dead.

Frederick's triumph in Jerusalem was a disaster for Gregory IX, but he refused to admit defeat. His general, John of Brienne, had orders to watch the ports of Apulia and take the Emperor prisoner as soon as he landed. But Frederick's ship outdistanced those of his fellow crusaders and landed at Brindisi in early June. The townspeople were stunned when the imperial banner was unfurled and they saw Frederick stride into view with his retinue of knights and pilgrims returning victorious from Jerusalem. So once again, Frederick had triumphed, seemingly through a miracle. People thronged the streets, overjoyed by the return of their beloved ruler. He sent out a stirring proclamation, announcing his return to his subjects, and his followers poured in from everywhere. By chance, a large group of Teutonic knights had been forced by a storm to land at Brindisi, and they pledged themselves to Frederick. An amazing army was forming — German crusaders, Sicilians, as well as Saracens — to fight against the Pope and his Lombard allies.

But the battle never took place. The papal army fled in terror before the Emperor, streaming from the cities and towns they held, retreating all the way to Rome in a complete rout. An increasing number of cardinals strongly opposed Gregory IX's policy toward Frederick and pushed him to seek reconciliation with the Emperor. The Pope finally relented, lifting his excommunication, and in the summer of 1230, greeted Frederick as the "beloved son of the Church." Frederick had again achieved a spectacular and bloodless victory.

Of course, it would not last. Throughout the remainder of his reign, Frederick II had to fight to hold his imperial realm against the power of the Church. There were victories and defeats — but ultimately, he lost. And because Frederick lost, his enemies wrote the final footnote to his story: He was a heretic who tried to destroy the Church, and the world is better off without him. His greatness was interred with his bones. What might have happened if he had succeeded — how much different the world might be — we can only speculate. The Middle East would certainly be a different place today.

11

WINTER IN WYOMING

MY FALCONRY SEASON with Macduff ended as they all do in upstate New York — with all of the duck ponds frozen solid as concrete and no game for him to chase. Still, he put on some great flights and ended the year with no mishaps, so I had no complaints. But I did feel a little guilty. I would soon be sneaking off to Wyoming with my wife to watch other peoples' falcons hunt. And I was not only ditching my falcon — worse, we would be leaving our children behind.

It was an almost unheard of occasion for the two of us to be traveling together. My wife, Rachel Dickinson, is an author who writes articles for various national and international magazines. We both travel frequently, but someone always stays home to take care of our children — as well as the falcon, the dog, and the other assorted livestock and pets that make up our household.

Over the years, we've worked out a fair arrangement to make sure we both spend roughly the same amount of time at home. But this year would be more complicated than most. Rachel already had tentative plans in the near future to travel to China, Tibet, and Colombia as well as several areas in the United States. And I was in the middle of a book tour and lecture circuit to discuss the rediscovery of the ivory-billed woodpecker and my book on this elusive species, *The Grail Bird*. In the months ahead I would be endlessly crossing and recrossing the country, going as far away as Alaska, to talk to eager audiences about the history of the ivorybill's decline and the search I launched with my friend Bobby Harrison to determine whether the bird still exists, which ultimately led to our sighting of a lone ivorybill in February 2004. I also had trips planned to Britain and Italy later in the year.

Childcare is no small task at our house. We have four children — a twenty-one-year-old daughter, Railey; a thirteen-year-old daughter, Clara; a twelve-year-old son, Jack; and a seven-year-old daughter, Gwendolyn. We basically have every developmental stage covered, so life is pretty interesting for us. Railey is a senior at Smith College in Massachusetts, so she's usually too far away to help take care of her siblings, but this time she agreed to come home so we could go to Wyoming.

This would be an important trip for both of us. For me, it would be the start of my Frederick II year — twelve months devoted to falconry. And for Rachel it would be another chance to spend time with well-known falconer Steve Chindgren, about whom she is writing a book. We would be spending a week with him at his hunting lodge in Wyoming.

In an endeavor such as falconry, which seems to attract the most intense, obsessive, over-the-top devotees, Steve is exceptional — one of the most hard core of the hard-core practitioners of the sport. Steve has lived and breathed for falconry since childhood. His exploits are legendary, and not because he's a braggart who plays up everything he does — on the contrary, he's low-key and matter-of-fact about his accomplishments.

Steve is a master of hawking sage grouse — one of the most challenging quarries a falcon can catch. The grouse are enormous, some of the males topping seven pounds, whereas Steve's favorite falcon, Jomo — a male gyrfalcon/peregrine falcon hybrid — weighs less than two pounds. Many times sage grouse fly off completely unfazed after being struck hard by a stooping falcon. Or they will tumble to the ground only to rocket away the instant the falcon drops down on them. And they are powerful flyers. It's not unusual to see flocks of sage grouse flying hundreds of feet overhead, moving from one feeding area to another. To people accustomed to hunting lesser game birds such as pheasants, partridge, and quail, sage grouse seem like freaks of nature — tireless, unstoppable, invincible.

Sage grouse hawking is actually a relatively new branch of falconry, made possible by advances in technology. Before lightweight radio-telemetry devices were developed in the late 1960s and early 1970s, enabling falconers to track down their hawks quickly and efficiently, the risk of losing a falcon in a sage grouse flight was too great to be worthwhile. The problem is that if a falcon doesn't disable the grouse in the initial stoop, the flight will often continue in a long tail-chase and may take the falcon several miles away across the endless sagebrush before it catches the grouse or breaks off from the flight. Contrary to what many people think about falconry, trained falcons do not retrieve their kills. If a falcon catches something, it will sit there and feed on it until the falconer finds the kill. And if he doesn't reach the kill in time, the falcon might gorge completely and then just fly away with no interest whatsoever in returning. (The term "fed up" comes from falconry and describes the disinterested attitude of a hawk after it has stuffed itself with meat.) Before telemetry, all we had — for centuries — were tiny brass bells to help us find our falcons in cover. But now, using a receiver and a directional antenna, we can often walk right up to our birds on a kill, even if they have flown miles away and are sitting on the ground in the middle of wall-to-wall sagebrush. So in the 1970s, the wonderful world of sage grouse hawking opened up.

Each fall and winter for more than twenty years, Steve has come to Wyoming to pit his falcons against this king of North American game birds. He's never been the kind of falconer who takes a two-week vacation once a year to go hawking. He builds his entire life around sage grouse hawking, spending up to five days a week at it, from late September to March each year.

Although Steve is a devoted husband and the father of two teenage daughters he adores, they see little of him when he's flying his hawks. On weekends during hunting season, he presents bird shows in Salt Lake City at the zoo and other venues, using raptors, parrots, and other birds to entertain and educate the public. But as soon as his last show is finished on Sunday night, he blasts eastward, headed to his hawking hideaway, a three hours' drive away near Eden, Wyoming, where he stays until Friday night.

For many years, Steve camped out next to a river in a tiny Scamp trailer with his falcons and a couple of pointers. And he would stay in it through the most bone-chilling nights of winter, when temperatures sometimes dipped to minus-thirty degrees Fahrenheit or lower. Then a few years ago, he pitched in with Dave Kennedy, a Georgia falconer, and bought a lodge and the surrounding 40-acre parcel of land. (The property backs up to Bureau of Land Management [BLM] land — millions of acres of undeveloped sage.) Sage grouse fly in every evening to drink from a pond on his land, but he never hunts them there. He enjoys seeing them and doesn't want to discourage them from returning.

AS RACHEL AND I walked out of the airport terminal in Salt Lake City, Steve was waiting at the edge of the sidewalk in his Toyota truck. After handshakes and hugs, we loaded our bags into the back of the truck, where the falcons usually sit, and climbed aboard to drive to his home in the suburbs. When he first moved into his house, more than twenty-five years earlier, the area was much more rural, but the city has steadily encroached on him, and now he is surrounded by houses — and neighbors, some of whom occasionally complain about his birds. He has quite a menagerie, including various parrots and cockatoos and eagles he uses in his shows. His falcons sit on block perches on the back lawn, enjoying the afternoon sun.

Inside the house, it quickly became clear that we were in the home of a falconer. Exquisite sketches and paintings of raptors adorned the walls; books and journals on falconry sat on every bookshelf, with handmade leather falcon hoods scattered here and there as accents.

After visiting briefly with Steve's wife and one of their daughters, we started loading up the truck and getting ready to leave for Wyoming. As in most things he does, Steve seemed driven, racing to finish everything he could think of so we could get out of town. He picked up his falcons, hooded them, and carried them one by one to the perch inside the enclosed shell at the back of the truck. Steve asked me if I'd mind getting Jomo for him, and of course I said, "Not at all." I considered it an honor to be entrusted with a bird as legendary as Jomo — the best falcon Steve has flown in a lifetime of falconry.

Seeing Jomo sitting on a block perch in Steve's backyard, you'd never know what a powerful flyer he is. At eighteen years old — ancient for a falcon — this remarkable bird is starting to look his age. When I picked him up, he seemed stiff, perhaps a little frail, and I could see he was missing a couple of talons — battle scars from the many sage grouse he's tackled in the course of more than a decade and a half of rough-and-tumble game hawking. But take him out into the vast sagebrush country of western Wyoming, hold him into the wind with a good dog on a solid point nearby, and the years seem to strip away as Jomo explodes from the fist and rings up into the sky, with the boundless energy of a bird in its prime. He may well be the best sage grouse hawk ever flown, which is remarkable considering his size — only 729 grams (1.58 pounds). (Sage grouse range from four to more than seven pounds.) Most of the other falcons Steve has flown at sage grouse weigh at least three or four ounces more than Jomo. But Jomo is all heart, with boundless endurance and fierce enthusiasm for the chase.

Rachel and I had seen Jomo fly many times, but now — at his age, facing battle-hardened winter grouse — we had no idea how he'd do. As difficult as sage grouse are for falcons to catch at any time, in winter the balance shifts significantly in the grouses' favor. Winter grouse are survivors — the strongest, wiliest members of their species. They have toughed out brutal blizzards and subfreezing weather and thrived in it. Falcons catch very few sage grouse at this time of year. But that's just the way Steve likes it. He has an area on one wall in his grouse lodge reserved only for pictures of falconers and their birds that have caught winter grouse.

After picking Jomo up, I stroked his chest briefly with the hood then slipped it over his head. I carefully cinched tight the leather drawstrings at the back (called braces) using my teeth and the thumb and forefinger of my right hand, and tied his leash securely to the long perch in the truck. And then we were off. As soon as we got out of Salt Lake City, we were blasting into the hills with nothing but wide-open western highway ahead. And it's stunningly beautiful country with snow-swept vistas of open sage. We stopped only once en route at a grocery store in western Wyoming to get food supplies and some bottles of wine. As we talked enthusiastically all the way, the miles slipped past quickly, and we soon turned onto the dirt road, now covered with crunching snow, leading the last couple of miles to the lodge. I'd never seen it so stark here. A bitter wind blowing across the snow sent the wind-chill figures well below zero. We hurried to unload the truck and get inside.

The lodge is great — a falconer's dream, with raptor paintings on every wall, taxidermied game birds, an enormous trout on the wall, plush leather couches, and enough room for several guests and their falcons. Entering the side door and walking down the hallway toward the kitchen and living room, visitors pass a "walk of fame," the walls lined with pictures of the falconers who have come here to hawk sage grouse over the years. On one table stands an enormous cock sage grouse, killed years earlier by Jomo.

Steve immediately fired up the pellet-burning heater inset into the fireplace. It's the kind of thing I can stare at for hours, watching the tiny fuel pellets being sucked into the burner and flaming up, giving off enormous heat. But for now, we needed to finish putting the supplies away and prepare a meal. Steve is a dynamo who usually cooks every meal, but this time Rachel insisted on doing it. As she prepared chicken and biscuits, Steve poured a couple of glasses of single-malt Scotch and we sat beside the fire, talking about the history of falconry.

Like me, Steve is a Frederick II freak. The 1942 translation of Frederick's treatise was the first book on falconry he encountered as a second grader. He actually became interested in hawks by way of dinosaurs, which his class was studying. Steve was completely enthralled with them — the tyrannosaurus rex and all the other wicked-looking creatures that once roamed the primeval world — and he checked out every dinosaur book he could find in the library. Then one day he saw a Cooper's hawk catch a pigeon at close range, right behind the house, and he locked eyes with it as it sat on the ground, struggling with the pigeon.

"He looked at me with his bright red eye — this magnificent bird," he told me. At the time, Steve had no idea what the bird was, so he looked it up in an encyclopedia and found out it was a hawk. The encyclopedia also mentioned that hawks were sometimes trained and used in falconry. That was it for Steve. He switched his admiration from dinosaurs — which had vanished from the earth millions of years earlier — to birds of prey, which were here and now, something tangible he actually might be able to work with himself.

This was in the late 1950s and Steve was seven years old. He was absolutely determined to become a falconer. The first step was to visit every library in the area, searching for books on the sport, but he completely struck out — none of them had anything. Then he found a copy of Frederick II's treatise in a huge bookstore in Salt Lake City. The only problem was its price: twenty dollars — a lot of money for a kid his age. So he started picking apricots from his grandmother's tree and selling them door-to-door in his neighborhood, pulling them behind him in a red wagon.

"They asked me what I wanted the money for, and I told them for a book — not a bike or a baseball glove," he said. "It made it pretty easy to sell the apricots."

Steve was finally able to buy the book, and he studied it thoroughly, gleaning rich nuggets of wisdom to help him train hawks effectively. But at first he wasn't able to get real birds of prey, so he had to use substitutes. He would put jesses on various chickens and pigeons his family owned, and carry them around on his fist like a real falcon. Eventually, he trained a male red-tailed hawk he named Shoulders, because it would ride around on his shoulder like some huge predatory parrot. Years later, he started flying gyrfalcons, the favorite species of Frederick II. Now Steve prefers gyrfalcon/peregrine hybrids, which often have the best qualities of both species. These hybrids of course did not exist in Frederick II's time, but Steve is convinced that if the great emperor were still around, this is the kind of bird he would fly.

Steve still keeps his copy of *De Arte Venandi cum Avibus* nearby, on a night table beside his bed, and I can't think of anyone who has embraced the falconer's way of life professed by Frederick II more fully than he. Years ago, Steve began a tradition in the Utah Falconers Association of having a fall get-together called the King Frederick Meet. He set up an elaborate competition — an obstacle course of sorts — based on the qualities of the ideal falconer, which Frederick II had enumerated in his great treatise centuries earlier. The competitors had to take time to untie a leash from a perch and go through the motions of releasing a falcon into the air. From there it was a madcap scramble of running through rough cover, jumping over fences, swimming across a river, climbing up a rope high into a tree and rappelling down, and dashing back to the finish line. Steve won it every time for years.

As we sat beside the fire at the grouse lodge, I told Steve all about the amazing adventures Frederick had when he was growing up — the many close calls in his lifelong struggle, first to become emperor and then to hold onto his empire. Steve's eyes lit up and he sat enthralled as I described each story in detail.

"Where did you learn all that?" he asked.

"I just read a lot of books about him," I said, laughing.

A SHORT TIME later, Tony Huston pulled up in front of the lodge, driving a Ford pickup with a camper shell on the back. He had called to say he was in the area, and Steve invited him to stay for a few days. He had three falcons and his dog with him.

Tony is a tall, thin man in his midfifties with graying dark hair, brown eyes, and a scraggly beard. He was born into a famous family. His father was legendary film director and actor John Huston, his grandfather actor Walter Huston, and his sister is Anjelica Huston. All three won Academy Awards for their work: Walter and Anjelica for acting and John for directing. (One of Tony's earliest childhood memories as a boy in Ireland was seeing a wild-eyed, bearded Gregory Peck roped to the top of a simulated whale as buckets of water were thrown on him during the filming of *Moby Dick*.) Tony has a distinctive, booming voice, remarkably similar to that of his father.

Tony had an Oscar nomination himself for writing a screenplay adaptation of James Joyce's short story "The Dead," in which his sister played a starring role. It was his father's last film and was released posthumously. As a child, Tony also once acted in a film called *The List of Adrian Messenger*, a 1963 whodunit starring George C. Scott. But Tony has mixed feelings about the world of moviemaking.

"I've always had a kind of schizophrenic relationship with Hollywood," he told me. "I really don't like the way Hollywood operates; the kind of pecking orders there don't agree with me."

So instead, he prefers to go hawking. Tony is a self-described falconry bum who spends each hawking season on a circuit, working his way from his home in Taos, New Mexico, through Nebraska, Wyoming, Colorado, and other places, searching for prairie chickens, sharp-tailed grouse, and sage grouse. His only companions on the yearly trip are his pointer, Frankie, and his falcons: Clara, a female peregrine falcon; Manassa, a wild-trapped female prairie falcon; and Johnny, a striking, nearly pure-white gyrfalcon/peregrine hybrid. En route, he sleeps in his truck, camps out, or visits other falconers.

Falconry is the kind of all-consuming obsession that seems to draw this kind of devotion. (I've certainly felt the pull of the road many times in my life.) At any given time in autumn, far from the comfort of towns and cities in places like Wyoming, you can find falconers — if you know where to look. They'll be parked just over a rise, out of sight of the highway, perhaps close to a stream where they can get water for drinking and cooking. And they'll be in tiny trailers, like the one Steve used to use, or in big cabin tents with built-in cook stoves, or in tiny dome tents, or maybe just sleeping with their dogs in the back of a truck. Many of them don't have much money, just an overpowering passion for falconry that eclipses anything else. They sacrifice everything for their sport.

I can't think of any other place in the world where falconry takes place in quite this way. In most countries, it is very much an affluent person's sport; falconers must lease vast areas of hunting land. The falconry-bum syndrome is strictly an American phenomenon, made possible by cheap gas, liberal game laws, and miles and miles of wide-open BLM land, where anyone can go to camp and hunt.

I've always been fascinated by the varying ways in which lifelong falconers came to take up the sport. Tony's story is interesting. He grew up in Galway in western Ireland, within an hour-and-a-half's drive of the home of Ronald Stevens — one of the most influential falconers of the twentieth century and the author of several falconry-related books such as *Observations on Modern Falconry* and *Laggard*. (He is the same man Henry Swain told Mac and me all about years earlier during our hitchhiking adventure to Riverside.) One day his mother's friend Ralph Blum, a well-known author, asked Tony if he'd like to go with him to visit Stevens. Blum had heard of the famous falconer during a trip to Iceland, where Stevens had earlier gone to take a young gyrfalcon (which he had written about in his book, *The Taming of Genghis*). Tony was just seven years old.

"It's the first day I remember in its entirety," he says. "Ronald had a peregrine on a block perch on the lawn." They went hunting together that day, and Tony saw the falcon stoop at a pigeon, finally catching it in an old abandoned cottage, a relic from the great potato famine. Then they went back to Stevens's manor house for tea, and he gave Tony a falcon's hood for a souvenir of the day.

As soon as he got home, Tony dug out his father's copy of Frederick II's falconry book and found a pattern for a falcon hood printed inside. He got a piece of leather, made a rudimentary hood, and sent it to Stevens.

That was the extent of Tony's interest for several years. But then at the age of twelve, he went browsing through a secondhand bookshop and found a copy of *Country Pastimes for Boys*, which has a section on falconry. So the fire was instantly relit. Tony began corresponding with Ronald Stevens, and about a year later, Stevens gave Tony a young merlin, his first falcon. He's rarely been without a falcon since.

ON THAT COLD, crisp morning in January, we got up early, well before the sun rose over the hills, illuminating the endless expanse of snow-covered sagebrush. We loaded two pickup trucks with falcons, dogs, and gear, and headed east — Rachel in Steve's truck; me following behind in Tony's. In the darkness, I felt like I might as well be traveling through outer space; I was completely clueless about where we were going. But Steve has been traveling the same roads for decades and could probably drive to the grouse areas blindfolded.

Tony and I went blasting along after Steve and Rachel, driving fast to keep up with them — which was fine on the paved highway, but as soon as we turned onto the snow-covered dirt road running through the BLM land, Tony's pickup truck started slipping. We stopped and got out. His truck has the kind of front hubs with the inset dials that have to be turned to the locked position so the four-wheel drive will work — otherwise the front wheels spin freely. By the time we got back inside, Steve had almost vanished in the distance up ahead, the running lights of his truck quickly fading in the darkness.

Tony pushed down on the gas pedal, driving hard to catch up with Steve. I reached unconsciously for the seatbelt, stretching it over me and pushing it into the buckle — it wouldn't snap. I smiled to myself and looked off toward Steve and Rachel, now a distant twinkle on the horizon. At least we had tracks to follow in the snow, though in some places there were deep drifts. We smashed through them, sometimes careening wildly for a few seconds before the tire treads dug in again and the truck blasted ahead.

The sky eventually began lightening in the east, casting a pinkish purplish hue on the snow and illuminating the rugged form of the Wind River Range, but it was well before sunup. Steve likes to fly his falcons as early as possible, before the golden eagles start cruising high overhead, searching for a morning meal.

Steve finally stopped his truck and went around back to the tailgate. As we pulled up, he was opening one of his built-in wooden dog compartments, inset just in front of where the falcons are perched. Tucker, the wonder dog, burst out and leapt to the snow-covered ground to take a grateful pee against a sagebrush plant. Steve attached a radio-telemetry collar to Tucker's neck. A wide-ranging pointer like Tucker can vanish in this vast country in seconds, so the collar is vital. In addition to enabling Steve to determine his location, the dog-telemetry unit shows whether or not he is moving. Most times when Tucker is still, he's on point, locked on a grouse scent.

Before letting him go, Steve took a day-glow-orange vest from the back of his truck and tied it around Tucker's neck like a scarf so he'd be a little easier to spot in the snow, and then Tucker was gone, running and leaping through the sage, frantically searching for a grouse scent. The distance Tucker covered was incredible, especially in this snow. Although it was not deep — probably only six or eight inches in most areas, it had drifted much deeper in some places and was piled all over the sage, giving an odd, lumpy appearance to the landscape.

We kept losing sight of Tucker and then spotting him again. Several times, we thought he might be on point, but then he started moving again. When Tucker finally locked onto a solid point, Steve jumped into action. He had Jomo out, unjessed, unhooded, and ready to release in a matter of seconds. Out there in such open country, it is vital to get a bird up as soon as possible to pin down the grouse, or they will fly away before the falcon can get into position for a stoop. Jomo shook his feathers, defecated, and was gone, climbing powerfully into the quickly lightening sky. He was soon a tiny speck, and we were moving forward, walking quickly at first and finally running full out across the sage as he came into position above us. Five sage grouse blew from the cover just ahead of Tucker. I lost sight of Jomo for an instant as he turned over, but spotted him again as he pumped his wings and finally folded up into a blistering vertical stoop. He hit a female sage grouse hard, causing her cover feathers to explode in a thick cloud. I saw the grouse go down in the sage. Any other game bird would be stone dead after an impact like that, but with a sage grouse, you can never be sure. Jomo remounted, and Steve invited Rachel to reflush the grouse. It took off again flying strongly, with Jomo making punishing stoops from above. The grouse hid in the sage, and still Jomo climbed up again high into the sky. But on the next flush, the grouse made good its escape, flying hard down a gully and vanishing from view. Jomo came back overhead, and Steve called him to the lure.

One of the most amazing things about Jomo is the way he remounts like this — again and again and again. He doesn't like to crash down on a sage grouse unless he's sure it's disabled. This is his key to success and probably one of the main reasons he's been able to avoid an eagle attack for so long. After bashing the hell out of a sage grouse, most falcons will drop immediately on the bird, hoping to dispatch it quickly. But the grouse usually have other plans, and this is when they often make their escape, blasting across miles of open sage. A determined falcon can still catch a grouse in this situation, but the kill might take place five miles from the falconer, leaving the falcon vulnerable to any high-soaring golden eagle that might have witnessed the flight. This is when a falconer will drive full out in his truck, telemetry antennae held out the window, racing to get to the bird in time to prevent disaster.

Steve's been there, more than once. In his forty-plus years of falconry, Steve has lost three birds to golden eagles and another to a great horned owl. Probably one of his closest calls with Jomo came several years ago when the bird chased a sage grouse over a rise and perhaps several miles away. As Steve was reaching for his telemetry, he looked down with horror at the two transmitters still clipped to his vest. He had forgotten to attach them to Jomo's legs. So there he was with his falcon out there somewhere in an endless expanse of sage, probably gorging on a grouse, with no way to track him down. Steve spent the entire day in the kind of private hell all falconers have experienced at one time or another. Guilt. Worry. Horror.

At the end of the day, long after the sun had dropped below the hills and darkness spread across the sage, Steve sat in his truck alone, in sheer desolation. Suddenly he heard a loud thump on the top of his camper shell. Jomo had returned.

WE CONTINUED SEARCHING for sage grouse. The area we traveled through is right along the old Mormon Trail, where settlers rode in oxen-drawn Conestoga wagons or walked more than a century earlier, on their way to Salt Lake City. It seemed somehow appropriate to be here with Steve, whose family members are Mormon; his ancestors trudged through this very spot in the 1800s, pushing handcarts. At one point a few years earlier, Steve took Rachel and me to a pioneer grave, marked only by a couple of large stones with no inscription. We could tell he was deeply moved.

WE DROVE FOR a half an hour or so down the long, straight dirt road that bisects this broad valley, then Rachel spotted a grouse sitting on top of the sagebrush, its dark coloration standing out in stark contrast to the snow-covered plant. The bird immediately jumped into cover and vanished, but it was a good sign. Sage grouse are rarely alone. This time it was Tony's turn. We stopped the truck and walked back to the end of the tailgate. As soon as Tony opened up the back, his dog Frankie jumped out. Like Tucker, she's an English pointer with ginger patches on a white coat but she is smaller and daintier.

"Get on, Frankie," said Tony. "Get on." He motioned with his arm in the direction of where Rachel saw the grouse, and Frankie began quartering back and forth as she worked her way out into the expanse of snow-covered sage, with head held high to detect the scent of the grouse. Tony turned back to the truck and untied Johnny from his perch (and yes, Tony did name his dog and his falcon after the old ballad, "Frankie and Johnny"). He carefully attached two small radio-telemetry transmitters to Johnny's legs, then removed his leash, swivel, and jesses, leaving only the leather anklets the jesses slip into.

Johnny is a stunning bird, gleaming white as snow in the morning light. Although he is a gyrfalcon/peregrine hybrid, he looks just like some of the wild white gyrfalcons I saw during a couple of expeditions to northern Greenland I took part in a few years earlier with Peregrine Fund researchers.

Far up ahead, near where the lone grouse had disappeared, Frankie started slowing down, pausing to lift her head and suck in air. Moving ahead again, she treaded more and more carefully and finally froze. This was it. Tony loosened the braces on Johnny's hood and lifted it off. He then held him up into the wind. Johnny looked around intently, bobbing his head as he scanned the horizon. He soon spotted Frankie on point and knew what that meant. He shook his feathers then defecated — the typical falcon routine. Pumping his wings for a few seconds, he abruptly exploded from the fist, flying hard away upwind. The stiff morning breeze pushed him higher and higher. By the time he turned back, he was already two or three hundred feet up and continuing to climb. Tony gave him plenty of time to mount, circling ever higher to gain a lofty pitch above us.

Tony, Steve, and I started jogging slowly toward where Frankie was on point, more than a football-field length away. Rachel opted to stay near the trucks with her camera, hoping to take pictures of the action. As Johnny drew into perfect position overhead, the three of us ran faster and faster until we were sprinting all-out and leaping like hurdlers over the sagebrush.

Johnny is so white that from below he was difficult to spot against the stark winter sky, especially with our eyes filled with tears from the wind. We stopped for a moment to scan the skies. I looked straight up with my 10x binoculars and suddenly: "There he is, right overhead. Flush 'em."

We charged past Frankie, clapping our hands loudly. In a cloud of snow, the grouse burst out all around us, five or six or more, and started flying in the direction of the trucks. I looked up and locked my binoculars on Johnny as he folded his wings and came hurtling down on them at a steep angle. He came right in on one of the grouse but didn't connect. What went wrong? Did he see that it was a huge cock grouse and think better of colliding with the bird? It's hard to say.

Rachel had the ringside seat for the flight. Johnny came within ten feet of her when he made his pass at the grouse. We all ran to her like giddy children. "Did you get the picture? Did you get the picture?"

"No," she said.

"Why not?" I asked her. "It was right in front of you."

"This from the man who didn't get the shot of the ivorybill flying past the front of his canoe," she shot back. We all laughed.

Johnny came back and started remounting above us, but we couldn't find any more grouse, so Tony pulled out a leather lure with a bird wing attached and swung it around to call him down. As Johnny approached, Tony tossed the lure onto the snow. The falcon put on his airbrakes and slowed down, finally landing gently on the lure. Tony picked him up and fed him on his gloved fist. It was time to move on. We had more birds yet to fly.

❧

BY THE TIME we finished eating dinner each night, we were dog-tired. We had all been going full-speed-ahead since 3:30 in the morning, and by the third or fourth day, it was taking its toll. It didn't take much — maybe a glass or two of Scotch — for us to start spilling our guts about our wretched lives. Steve's wicked half brother, who spent years tormenting and torturing his younger sibling — he actually threw a dart at Steve when he was five years old, blinding him for life in one eye. Rachel's dairy farmer dad, who one day when she was a teenager loaded all of the cows into a truck and drove out of their lives forever. Or my drunken father, who made my life — as well as my mother's and my sisters' — a living hell until we escaped. It strikes me you don't need to dig very deep beneath the surface with an avid falconer — the kind who has sacrificed everything for the sport — to find a screwed-up childhood. It's certainly true with Steve and me and many other falconers I know.

It's amazing how early we conked out each night. Often by 7:00 we were all laid out and snoring on the plush leather couches and chairs or on the carpet beside the fireplace. Sometime around midnight or so we would get up and drag ourselves to our various rooms. Then a couple of hours later, the alarm clock would chime, and the whole cycle would begin again.

❧

LATER IN THE week, Jomo flew extremely high, with Tucker below on a solid point. We moved in quickly and flushed maybe twenty sage grouse. *Whoosh!* A long vertical stoop. *Whack!* A grouse tumbled. Jomo remounted, and we flushed again. *Whomp!* It went down even harder. Jomo started to remount again, but then changed his mind and slammed into the grouse in cover — finally a sage grouse in the bag. Steve's other bird, Tava, also caught one the following morning, and that was it: all we had to show for a week of hard flying on the frigid sagebrush plains of western Wyoming — except, of course, for the wonderful flights, which we will remember for the rest of our lives.

On the final evening, we feasted on sage grouse, staying up long into the night, talking about old times and hawks and good friends. Inevitably, we talked about Jomo. His name, Steve told me, is a Swahili word for "hunter." In Jomo's case, the name is well earned. But Steve must sometimes wonder how things will end with him. Jomo is approaching his nineteenth season. How much longer can he keep it up? Will he soon become stiff and arthritic and end his days quietly in retirement? Will his luck with eagles finally run out? And when it's all over, how will Steve celebrate the life of such a distinguished falcon? He laughed when I asked him and said maybe he would give him a true Viking sendoff and burn up the old Scamp trailer with Jomo's body inside. I hope I'll be there to drink to his memory.

12

HIGHLAND FLING

IN AUGUST, I finally did something I'd dreamed of since the 1960s: I visited the Highlands of Scotland to hawk red grouse. I'm just surprised it took me so long. Ever since the days when I first started reading British falconry books at Jimmie White's house, I had wanted to experience grouse hawking in all its glory for myself.

I left for Britain just as Heathrow Airport had a big clampdown after a terrorist scare and barred all carry-on luggage. I had to put my computer, all of my camera equipment, clothes, and rubber wellies into uninsured check-in luggage, where they ended up being lost for three days. I arrived without having slept for more than thirty-five hours and had to step immediately into a stick-shift, right-hand-drive car and blast for three hours along a Scottish roadway, driving on the opposite side of the road from what I was used to and having to negotiate endless confusing roundabouts.

I was supposed to meet Roger and Mark Upton at two o'clock in the afternoon at their cottage near Dunbeath, in the heart of Caithness. It was just past noon when I picked up my rental car, and Dunbeath was a three-hour drive away. I knew I'd be late, and I had no way of getting in touch with them, so I just hit the A-9 highway and went speeding northward — across bridges and causeways, sometimes driving on two-way roads so narrow they would have been single lanes in America.

I finally got to Dunbeath, following Mark Upton's explicit directions — the best directions anyone has ever given me in Britain. I turned left off the highway and skirted the village, driving up a single-track road, where if someone is coming the other way, one of you has to back up all the way to a wide spot to let the other person's car get through. After going across an old stone cart bridge, up a hill, and through a gate, I found myself driving on a narrow gravel track cutting right through the bushes and shrubs, so close together they scratched and scraped the sides of my car as I burrowed through. But I found the place. And Roger and Mark were standing in front, miraculously just loading up their dark blue Land Rover. They had kindly waited for me, and Roger even paused to make me a cup of tea before we left. I immediately got my second wind, and we were off to fly peregrines at grouse.

We drove the Land Rover to the fence at the edge of a forty-thousand-acre grouse moor and loaded the peregrines, two tiercels and two falcons, onto a cadge — the traditional square-framed carrier that falconers have used for centuries to transport falcons in the field. From there, we trudged miles across spongy, tundra-like ground and through heather in a steady drizzle (this was Scotland, after all), taking turns carrying the cadge and holding the two pointers, Wag and Imp.

When we got our first point, Mark put up his seventeen-year-old tiercel, Oliver Twist, which took a moderate pitch, waiting on steadily overhead. On the flush, he came down smartly, clipping a grouse and sending it down hard into cover, but the bird escaped when Oliver crashed down after it.

Oliver has had a remarkable career — both as a hunter and as a breeder. He is the parent or grandparent of an amazing number of the falcons I saw being flown during my stay in Scotland, and they were all excellent.

Next, Roger picked up his intermewed falcon Glorious (Oliver's daughter) from the cadge and removed her leash and swivel. By this time, the drizzle had turned into a steady downpour. Roger gave a wry smile as he removed his falcon's hood and said, "Mad dogs and Englishmen."

Glorious took off without hesitation and fought her way upward into position above him. Roger charged in after the grouse, but it was no good — a false point. This was a rare occurrence — the dog may have been scenting a clump of feathers that Oliver had knocked from the other grouse.

On the next point, Mark put up his other tiercel, the Artful Dodger — Oliver's eight-year-old son. (Clearly Mark likes to name his falcons after Charles Dickens characters — he also has a female peregrine named Peggotty.) Dodger went up nicely in spite of the rain, circling high and steady above us, pumping his wings constantly. On the flush, at least a dozen grouse burst from the heather beneath him, providing an irresistible target. Dodger turned over and with a few powerful strokes of his wings came streaking down in a sizzling vertical stoop, finally folding up completely. He cut down a grouse in a puff of feathers, threw up high, then plummeted down after another one, hammering it in beautiful style and taking it to the ground. Dodger was absolutely exhausted, with bill agape, after this performance. But it was completely understandable. This was only his third or fourth day in the field this season. Mark gave him a well-deserved feed on the grouse.

ROGER IS A tall man with thick gray hair and a beard. A former horseman in the Queen's Household Cavalry, he cuts a dashing figure in the field, often wearing a tweed cap and sport coat, sometimes with a red handkerchief stuffed in the front pocket as an accent. Roger was a good friend of the Queen Mother and often ran his pointers on her Scottish estate when she had grouse shoots. For her hundredth birthday, he gave her a collection of his poetry that he had handwritten in a leather-bound journal. It was one of her favorite gifts, and she kept it on her bedside table to read in the evening.

Roger has become the chief chronicler and historian of British falconry, authoring a series of books — *A Bird in the Hand: Celebrated Falconers of the Past; O for a Falconer's Voice: Memories of the Old Hawking Club; Hood, Leash, and Lure: Falconry in the Twentieth Century*. He also wrote an excellent book on hawking in the Middle East, called *Arab Falconry*. Roger has gone hawking many times with Arabs over the years, ever since the early 1960s when he received a serendipitous telephone call from the British Home Office. They told him that several Arab dignitaries were visiting Britain and had asked if they could go hawking with a British falconer. Roger was the first one who came to mind.

The Arabs had a wonderful time with Roger. They had felt out of place in London and had little in common with the British diplomats they met. With Roger, it was different. They all spoke the common language of falconry and became instant friends. At the end of their visit with Roger, they invited him to come hawking in Arabia — an offer he couldn't pass up. When Roger's wife asked how long he'd be gone, he said probably a couple of weeks. He ended up staying for ten weeks, and he's returned regularly ever since.

Being interested in the history of falconry myself it was great to spend time with Roger, staying up late into the night, listening to stories about the old days and all the great falconers who hawked at Caithness over the years. Grouse hawkers came to the area because it was much flatter than other parts of the Highlands, making it more suitable for flying longwings, particularly in the years before telemetry.

Caithness is beautiful. The land is wild, almost like the Alaskan tundra in places. On the rugged coast near the grouse moor where we were flying, the great castle at Dunbeath seems to hang at the edge of a cliff overlooking the sea, stark and breathtaking.

Gilbert Blaine, who began hawking grouse at Caithness just after the turn of the twentieth century, is a particular favorite of mine as a falconer. He was an avid member of the Old Hawking Club, which thrived in Britain from the late nineteenth through early twentieth century. Caithness was quite remote in those days, requiring a long, arduous journey on unpaved roads to reach. The bridges across the firths (or estuaries) had not yet been built, and people had to ride a horse or wagon — or later drive a car — far inland to get around every firth. Sometimes Blaine had his falcons shipped by boat to spare them the rough ride.

Blaine was one of those legendary figures who seems to come along every so often in falconry, raising the standards of the sport as well as pushing the envelope of what can be accomplished. Part of this was spurred, no doubt, by his boundless enthusiasm for the sight of falcons in action. Even after decades of flying falcons, Blaine would go into a near-apoplectic state whenever he watched a falcon stoop on a grouse, going red in the face with his eyes bulging. I've spoken with people who met Blaine in the 1950s (or who spoke to his assistant, Leonard Potter, who later worked for Jack Mavrogordato), and he was a colorful character.

Potter often told the story of how Blaine would grumble whenever a falcon had flown poorly and say that the bird would go hungry that night. But he always relented. Potter slept in a loft above the falcon quarters and would invariably hear Blaine sneak in during the night and feed the misbehaving falcon. Potter also loved to tell about his wedding day. He had asked Blaine if he could have the day off to get married. A confirmed bachelor, Blaine asked him what time the ceremony would take place. He told him two o'clock in the afternoon. "All right," said Blaine, grumpily. "Be back here at three."

In addition to being a falconer, Blaine was an avid big-game hunter who went on safari in Africa and India. Some people called him "the Eagle," both because of his fierceness as a hunter and the size and shape of his nose, which resembled the beak of a great raptor. Blaine stayed in Caithness for years, long after he had given up flying falcons, and he is buried there, although I wasn't able to find his grave.

Other members of the famed Old Hawking Club also used to fly falcons in Caithness. John Frost, one of the best professional falconers ever employed by the club, took sick with pneumonia one season and died there. One morning, Roger and I visited Frost's grave, not far from Dunbeath.

❧

ROGER'S SON, MARK, is a gifted falconer, and his peregrines made some of the best flights I saw during my stay in Scotland. He is an artist who most often paints scenes of hawks, horses, dogs, and various other country field sports. He's also done some excellent illustrations of Arabian falconry, based on hawking trips he has taken to the Middle East with Roger. Mark is an excellent cook and prepared most of the meals, especially the evening dinners, which were often memorable.

Mark tended to rise late while I was there and kept to himself most mornings, working on paintings. I would go off hiking with Roger and a couple of the dogs, up along the stream in the gorge below the cottage.

The streams there are not what you would call gin-clear. Far from it, they are the dark amber color of good Scotch, stained from the rich peat they flow through.

Sometimes peregrines nest on the cliffs just upriver of the cottage. On our walks, we would pass a gorge called Gunn's Leap, where an earlier member of the Gunn Clan (one of the most important local clans) supposedly escaped from some enemies by leaping to the other side of the river at this spot. I've always been pretty good at the long jump, but this chasm looked easily ten times wider than anything I could ever have jumped across.

Another illustrious member of this clan was Neill Gunn, a popular author who spent his life in the Dunbeath area and set most of his novels there. Some of the place names around the grouse moor Roger leases are mentioned in Gunn's books.

॰

I STAYED WITH Roger and Mark for several days, watching their falcons improve vastly each day as they got back into shape after being taken up from the molt. The tiercels had become fit quickly and were hammering grouse like old pros in just three or four days. It took a little longer with the falcons, but the last time I saw Roger fly Glorious, she fought her way up to a good pitch in a driving rain, clobbered a grouse back into the heather, and remounted a couple of times for reflushes.

Unfortunately, Caithness does not have as many grouse as it did in its falconry heyday, and the Uptons have to work hard to find enough slips (flushes). Some of the best areas — such as the grouse moors hawked for years by Gilbert Blaine and later by Geoffrey Pollard and others — have been largely ruined for grouse by pine plantations, which the government has subsidized. Many falconers have stopped coming to Caithness and now fly in more productive areas south of Inverness.

After leaving Mark and Roger, I drove to an area near Grantown-on-Spey to visit some Italian falconers — Umberto Caproni, Fulco Tosti, and Ferrante "Frikky" Pratesi. They had been going to Scotland for decades and were leasing two enormous grouse moors: one at Lochindorb, a pretty Scottish lake (or loch) surrounded by picturesque hills clad in purple heather; the other nearly an hour's drive away in an area with steep, rugged hills. Both places were crawling with grouse. Sometimes as we moved in on a point with a peregrine above us, we'd flush a different grouse at our feet and get a colossal stoop from straight overhead. If we were lucky, we'd get a chance to put another falcon up and fly the original point.

Although she tended to be headstrong, Frikky's pointer, Vodka, was excellent at finding grouse and incredibly steady on a point. I remember her once being on point for nearly an hour on an adjacent hillside as we flew a peregrine on a different covey of grouse. We then flew Vodka's point with Frikky's excellent intermewed falcon, Carpe Diem, which went incredibly high on the updraft of the wind blowing against the hillside and whacked a grouse stone dead in a classic stoop. Of course, we spent a lot of time trying to get Vodka to obey us. One day Frikky told me, "People probably think we're all heavy drinkers, because we're always walking around the moor, shouting, 'Vodka!'"

Umberto, Fulco, and Frikky had leased the lodge at Lochindorb for a couple of months, and several nonfalconer friends from Italy joined them while I was there. Most of them tended to wake up late, have a fantastic brunch in the late morning, then head off for a tough afternoon, trudging up and down steep hills in wind, rain, and sometimes-frigid temperatures to watch the falcons fly. We'd often get back well after dark, then partake in a sumptuous meal of grouse, salmon, and other local specialties, washed down with fine wine. I always enjoyed going hawking with the Italians. They were fun to be with and avid about falconry. Sometimes the three of them would get into little disputes about the best tactics to use in a given situation. Should we hawk on the east side of the hills or the west? Should we flush from this direction or that? We would always pull off and park on the way to the most distant grouse moor to figure out the direction the wind was blowing — which would determine where we should fly the falcons. Frikky and Fulco would argue about the wind direction. They'd both stand there tossing clumps of grass in the air, and then point this way and that to indicate which way the wind was blowing. They rarely agreed. At this point Umberto invariably stepped from his car with his little plastic bottle of soap bubble liquid and waved the tiny children's bubble wand through the air. This was the court of last appeal. The delicate, weightless soap bubbles invariably sailed straight downwind.

The Italians were all gourmands, relishing fine food and wine. They were particularly enamored of the huge wild mushrooms growing in the woods alongside the road in Scotland and were aghast that none of the locals ate them. (I suspect all the Scottish and English children have it drilled into their brains at an early age never to eat wild mushrooms.) We'd be speeding down the road when Umberto would suddenly spot a good stand of mushrooms and slam on the brakes. "Mamma Mia!" he'd shout. "Porcini!" And he and the entire entourage following behind would get out and pick mushrooms. By the time I left, we were eating them with almost every meal and had dozens of them drying out in the kitchen.

After dinner most days we'd finish the evening in the game room, staying up late shooting billiards or playing ferocious Ping-Pong games. They were lively company, although, because I speak no Italian, I sometimes felt like I was in a Federico Fellini film without subtitles. Umberto would often key in on this and give me a thumbnail sketch of the conversation. But after a couple of glasses of wine, I was usually laughing right along with everyone else anyway, even though I had no idea what they were saying.

❧

AFTER STAYING SEVERAL days with Umberto, Fulco, Frikky, and their friends, I decided to hit the road again, this time heading southward from the hills near Inverness all the way past the Scottish border to the north of England, nearly a six-hour drive away. I'd made arrangements to meet John Loft there and go crow hawking for a couple of days with Nick Fox.

Although I hadn't met either of them before, John seemed like an old friend. We'd been corresponding with each other for several years, since he authored the book *A Merlin for Me* and I got in touch with him.

I had always intended to write a book about merlins myself — ever since the spring of 1970, a few months after my release from prison, when Hollis and I trained two female merlins and flew them together as a cast. At that time, few American falconers had flown merlins successfully, and it felt like we were pioneering an unknown world. What kind of game could we hunt with them? What were they capable of doing? No one really knew. In Britain, merlins had always been flown at skylarks, which fly up high into the sky in great airy circles when pursued — a classic "ringing flight." As far as we knew, there was no comparable game to hunt with them in America.

But one day Hollis and I released our merlins at several cowbirds feeding in a big chili pepper patch surrounded by plowed earth, and a small flock of them circled into the sky with our birds ringing up after them, fighting for an altitude advantage. When the tiny falcons finally got above them, they stooped through the flock, causing panic in the cowbirds, two or three of which plummeted back to the pepper patch, with the merlins in hot pursuit. They each caught one, and that was the start of a wonderful couple of months of hawking cowbirds until the pepper crop was plowed under.

I wrote my first published article — which appeared in the inaugural issue of *The Journal of the California Hawking Club* in 1971 — about the ringing cowbird flights we had experienced with our merlins. But what about training merlins to wait on like a peregrine and stoop at game flushed by a falconer while they circled above? As far as I was able to find out, no one in the history of the sport had ever attempted that, and most falconers thought it was impossible.

The next young merlin I flew, Hannah, took to waiting on flights like a natural almost from the start. And it was so easy. I released her directly from my fist one day at some mourning doves I flushed in a corn stubble field. She went right after them as they flew straight away, gaining altitude and scattering as they went. It was a futile chase; she didn't even come close. But when she broke off the pursuit and turned back toward me, she was nearly a hundred feet in the air. I knew that dove flocks almost always have stragglers that don't take off in the initial flush, so I ran at full speed through the stubble field toward Hannah — clapping my hands all the way as she continued flying in my direction. Several more doves flushed as Hannah was right above me, and she made a beautiful vertical stoop right through them, hitting one solidly, knocking out a cloud of feathers. This had a demoralizing effect on the dove, and Hannah chased it all the way to some shrubs, where she smashed in right behind the bird and caught it.

This was just the beginning. Hannah started waiting on higher and higher each day as she quickly learned her craft. I would let her go as soon as I stepped out of my car in the field and then sprint to the best game areas as she circled above me, quickly gaining altitude. We were a great team, and we both came to have incredible endurance.

As any avid hawk watcher will attest, merlins are remarkable raptors: so tiny — barely larger than a kestrel — and yet such powerful, aggressive flyers. At migration hot spots such as Cape May, New Jersey, and Hawk Mountain, Pennsylvania, merlins are always the ones that come tearing across the sky, stooping wildly at every other hawk in sight, no matter how large. Hannah was an exemplar of all things merlin, full of the vigor, exuberance, and speed her species is known for. She caught forty doves that season — as well as many other birds such as starlings and sparrows — and she is still one of my favorite falcons I've ever flown.

I lost Hannah overnight several times as she tore away across the horizon chasing game (this was long before the age of merlin telemetry). And then I finally lost her for good. But there were no regrets. She was simply ready to move on. I wrote about teaching her to wait on and catch doves for the journals of both the California Hawking Club and the North American Falconers' Association.

Another of my all-time favorite falcons was a tiny wild-trapped male merlin I flew while I was in college. I called him The Corporal. In some rural regions of America, merlins have long been nicknamed "little blue corporals," which is part of the reason I gave him that name. But another, more important reason was because Napoleon had often been called "The Little Corporal," and this merlin certainly had the most Napoleonic attitude of any bird I've ever flown. He'd attack anything, and in the four years I flew him, he caught birds ranging from sparrows to starlings and doves — and almost always from a waiting on position.

The Corporal was funny. He would circle above me, flying hard constantly for maybe ten minutes as I tried to flush birds. If he didn't catch anything, he'd fly to a tree and rest for ten or fifteen minutes while I sat on the ground in the field. As soon as he was ready, he'd fly back to me, make a quick dive past my head as if to say, "Hey, it's time to get going again," and then ring up above me, ready to hunt. Looking back, I'm amazed at the endurance I used to have. Sometimes I'd work an entire field, then run across an open plowed area for nearly a mile to get to another field and start flushing. He knew just what I was doing and would follow me.

I remember the day I finally lost The Corporal. I had moved to Santa Cruz to work at the University of California's Predatory Bird Research Group, an affiliate of the Peregrine Fund that was trying to boost the number of nesting peregrines in California. It was early fall, right in the middle of migration, and I heard songbirds calling each night as they flew southward. I flew him at a flock of cowbirds in some fields near the campus and lost sight of him as he went stooping through them. I never saw him again. I'm sure he gorged on the bird he caught and just continued on the migration I had interrupted four years earlier.

These are but a few of the many memories I have of hunting with merlins. I flew several more in addition to Hannah and The Corporal, and they were all spectacular hunters. I came to think that I'd carved a special niche for myself in falconry with these birds — which is why I had a momentary twinge of regret when I heard about John Loft's merlin book. I remember thinking: *that should have been me; I should have written that book.* But I got over it quickly, especially after reading Loft's book, which was full of fascinating lore about the history of merlin hawking, including some great material about E. B. Michell, another of my childhood heroes. So, I wrote a fan letter to John, and we've been pen pals ever since. But until that summer, we had never met. He lived quite a distance south of Scotland, in Lincolnshire, but he suggested that we meet halfway and go hawking with Nick Fox in the vast area along Hadrian's Wall in Northumberland. The idea was appealing. I really wanted to meet John after all the years we'd been corresponding.

I said goodbye to my Italian friends one morning and headed southward, driving hard for several hours, stopping only for coffee and gasoline. I was amazed to see the new highway rest stops along the way, featuring Starbucks-like coffee bars where young Scottish women with names like Fiona actually made great coffee — a new concept for the United Kingdom. But John Loft's road directions fell far short of Mark Upton's. The directions included things like: Look for an old, disused public house, which may or may not have a pair of buffalo horns on the wall. (I saw nothing like that.) You might find a left turn that is probably signposted.

I drove up, up, up into the stony green hills — and got completely lost. But I did know the place was somewhere close to Hadrian's Wall, and I was somewhat familiar with the area. I'd explored the wall and the ancient ruins of Vindalonda a couple of times years earlier. I knew there was an excellent museum there, so I went straight to it and asked directions. Fortunately, a woman who worked there knew the exact farm I was looking for and gave me some improved directions.

On the way, I spotted a man standing beside a small red Renault at the side of the road. He was thin and wiry with a neatly trimmed gray beard. I stopped and rolled down my window.

"You wouldn't be John Loft, would you?" I asked.

Beaming, he walked over to me as I got out of the car, and we shook hands. It was wonderful to finally meet him, and we stood in the road for ten minutes or more, having a conversation. John is a retired schoolmaster who now spends much of his time writing and also working on translations of early falconry texts. He told me he had recently turned eighty years old and no longer trained falcons.

"Why not?" I asked. "You must have all kinds of free time now that you're retired."

"Yes, but at my age, you never know when you might hop the twig," he said.

"Hop the twig?" I said, laughing. "I've never heard that one before."

We finally got back into our cars. John told me to follow close behind and he'd take me to Nick's cottage. As we traveled along the tiny roads, I thought that I never would have found this place in a million years.

Meeting Nick was great. He has the charisma of a born showman and a wry sense of humor. Well known as a raptor biologist and falconer, Nick has produced several films and books about the sport. He introduced me to his Swedish wife, Barbro, and John Lawson, a young man from Finland who had signed on as an apprentice with him, working with the birds and learning the ropes of falcon handling.

Lawson looked a bit like a younger, leaner Sylvester Stallone, and he spoke nearly flawless English. His father was originally from England, so he had a good person from whom to learn the language. Nick worked Lawson hard. When we went out hawking that afternoon, Nick would give him instructions like: "See those crows in that tree a half mile out in that open field? As soon as I put up the falcon, run over there to head the crows off if they try to hide in them." And he was off sprinting full out. And if the crows went somewhere else, Nick would get on the walkie-talkie and send Lawson to the crows' new location, but he always took it good-naturedly.

The first afternoon, we headed up to the high ground along Hadrian's Wall and actually slipped the falcon (a peregrine/saker falcon hybrid) from the ancient Roman stone works, which had been erected only fifty years or so after the birth of Christ. This is one of the windiest places I've been in my life. Years earlier, my wife and I had taken our eldest daughter, Railey, here when she was seven years old, and she had been terrified by the velocity of the wind and walked along holding on to the wall. It's an exciting and beautiful place. It seemed as though I could see a hundred miles on either side, and it was all green, open, and magnificent — perhaps not that much different from how it looked in Roman times.

Flying there was effortless for the falcon, which went up like a kite on a string above us. When some crows took off in the distance, she went off chasing them. But the flights seemed as if they were in slow motion in all that wind. The falcon would chase a crow into a small, sparsely foliaged tree and go right in after it, sometimes hopping from branch to branch, trying to either catch the crow or put it to flight again so the chase could resume.

After perhaps forty-five minutes of this, we saw a storm blowing in from miles away. Nick brought out his lure, which he swung on the end of a long fishing rod blank with a piece of surgical rubber tubing on the end, and gave the bird a fast series of stoops. Nick seemed very good at timing the arrival of the storm. He took his time stooping the bird, then fed and hooded her and started down the hill just as the clouds were about to burst. We sprinted from Hadrian's Wall and then down the steep hill all the way to the Land Cruiser and got there just as the rains began pelting down in one of the most powerful thunderstorms I've ever seen. We all huddled in the car until it passed and the sun came out again.

One day recently Nick had been out here with this same bird at Hadrian's Wall, when a group of Hasidic Jews came walking along, sightseeing along the wall, clad in black hats and robes, with dark beards and long side-locks of hair blowing wildly in the wind — looking remarkably similar to the clump of black feathers Nick uses as a lure to exercise his birds. The falcon made several nice stoops at the men as they ran along the wall, ducking each time the bird shot past. Nick finally got the falcon interested in the real lure, called her back, and beat a hasty retreat down the hill.

Unlike some of the other falcon flights I've written about, crow hawking is generally not done from a waiting on position above the falconer. Instead, the falcon is flown directly from the fist as the crows flush. In the best flights, the crows ring up high above the spectators below, fighting to maintain an altitude advantage over the falcon — just as skylarks do when they're chased by merlins. Later that day, we got just such a flight, and it was fabulous. At one point, both birds — the falcon and the crow — were right above us, hundreds of feet up, battling for aerial supremacy. The falcon actually bound to the crow and went almost all the way to the ground with it before it broke away. And this time, the crow out-flew the falcon and disappeared in a clear blue sky.

This part of England has a centuries-old tradition of falconry. There's actually a stone carving on a cross (the Bewcastle Cross) not far from there depicting a man with a trained falcon dating to around 600 A.D. More recently, in the late nineteenth century, famed falconer Major Hawkins Fisher hawked ferociously in this area, flying peregrine falcons at rooks — a close relative of the crow — in spectacularly high ringing flights.

ᘓ

THE NEXT DAY would be the main event for us. Instead of driving around in a Land Cruiser to fly the falcons, Nick would do his specialty — releasing his falcon from horseback and galloping along to keep up with the flight and reflush the crows. We gathered up the horses and drove to a rendezvous to meet the other members of the Northumberland Crow Falcons — a group Nick had founded years earlier. Nick and Barbro wore green hunting coats with the group's initials, NCF, engraved on the brass buttons. Some of the others wore tweed coats, but they all wore ties, and the event had all the pomp of fox hunting.

Nick was a fabulous rider and cut quite a figure galloping up on his Arabian horse, holding a falcon on his left fist. He was skillful enough to hold the bird perfectly steady as he rode. He ran the show like a general, handing each person a walkie-talkie and giving them their marching orders — telling them which clumps of trees to ride to so they could try to head off any crows that tried to escape there. Still, every time a falcon was slipped at crows, things quickly broke down into a wild melee, with people riding this way and that, sometimes getting stuck in the mud or unhorsed in ditches, but that was all part of the fun. And the crows were completely unpredictable.

After several great flights, Nick's peregrine/saker falcon, Rainbow — the same one that had made the spectacular ringing flight the day before — finally caught a crow. I went in on the kill and took several pictures of Rainbow with her crow. Then Nick let me feed her on my fist as John stood beside me feeding another falcon.

"Are you sure you're ready to give up hawking?" I said. We both laughed.

As we stood around, we spoke with Michael, one of the other riders. He was in his sixties — an ex-British officer, and he looked the part, with a steady bearing, an upright stance, and a clipped accent. In the early 1960s, he had been stationed in Oman — a country bordering southeastern Saudi Arabia — training the country's military, and he had taken up falconry there, learning the art directly from the local people whose ancestors had trained falcons for thousands of years. Michael spoke with great fondness of the old days, camping in the desert with the Arab tribesmen and galloping after falcons as they chased houbara bustards across the barren desert sands.

"It's a different world now," John lamented.

"Yes, but not, I fear, a better one," said Michael.

THE NEXT MORNING I bid a farewell to everyone and thanked Nick and Barbro for their hospitality. As we walked out to our cars, I shook John's hand and gave him a hug. I only regretted that our visit together had been so brief. I drove behind him as he left, following him back to the main road that cut horizontally across this narrow part of Britain. I waved goodbye as we turned in opposite directions. I took off fast, driving hard all the way back to Caithness. I was eager to spend a little more time with the Uptons and also to meet a few more falconers before flying back home.

ONE OF THE most interesting parts of my trip to Britain was driving to the Dornach Firth area, south of Caithness, to visit Stephen Frank. Steve is one of a handful of legendary British falconers who, like Geoffrey Pollard, kept the sport of falconry alive in the years after World War II, maintaining a quality of grouse hawking as great as that of Gilbert Blaine in his heyday.

Although they were good friends, Geoffrey Pollard and Stephen Frank could not have been more different. Geoff brought all of the dignity of a barrister into the hawking field, walking slowly and quietly across the grouse moor, solemn and serious — lacking only the powdered wig and black robes to complete the picture.

Steve cut quite a different image in his youth, racing full speed over the moors like a wild stag, clad in sneakers and a bright-red sweater (which he hoped his falcons would key in on), his voice echoing across the valley as he shouted at his dog and his falcon, rejoicing in a cracking good stoop or a kill. He was a picture of vigor, exuberance, and boundless optimism.

I had gone to Geoff Pollard's cottage in Dunbeath for tea a couple of times when I was staying with the Uptons, and the place was immaculate — clean, tidy, tastefully furnished, with paintings of falcons and hunting scenes on the walls. We ate cake and biscuits and drank tea from fine china cups. Steve's cottage was, well . . . different. He lives in an old stone crofter's cottage that he bought years ago for next to nothing. He likes to say that the place is "a bit undusted." It's the ultimate bachelor falconer pad: worn old chairs; a battered sofa covered with dog hair (with an aging pointer asleep on it); dishes piled high; damp wool socks steaming on the heater; stacks of books and picture albums; cards and pictures stuck everywhere — basically the detritus of a long lifetime of falconry. A pair of barn swallows had taken up residence in the bathroom. Getting in and out through a broken windowpane, they built a nest on top of the mirror and were raising young. (Steve advises visitors to use nature's bathroom outside.)

When I dropped by Steve's cottage, Christian Saar — the famed German falconer and raptor biologist — was visiting, as he has done nearly every grouse season since 1970. The two are great friends and share the same optimistic outlook toward life. They are in their seventies and have both had hip replacements, but they are in no way ready to give up the sport they love. (I think it's significant that both of them are training young peregrines, and Steve has a new puppy.)

We all sat together in front of Steve's cottage, basking in one of those rare Scottish days when the sun is shining. His old pointer, Handel, lay curled nearby on a battered easy chair with foam rubber stuffing sticking out of torn seams in the tweedlike material. We spoke about hawking and about dogs. He is as much (or possibly even more) of a dog person than a falconer, and the dogs he has bred, the bloodlines he has developed, have become popular with field-trial enthusiasts and falconers alike.

A while later, we moved inside to look at some of Steve's picture albums and so I could show them, on my laptop computer screen, some of the pictures I had already taken during my trip to Scotland. Steve apologized for not having any decent food to offer me, but then whipped up a great meal of sausage, eggs, and coffee, with a beer chaser.

As we ate, Steve told me about his long friendship with actor James Robertson Justice, who was an avid falconer and spent many seasons hawking there at Steve's place, called Londernaich. Justice appeared in numerous films and was an unforgettable presence with his deep voice and bushy beard. I particularly enjoyed his work in the film *Captain Horatio Hornblower*, in which he played Quist, a burly English seaman who helped Hornblower (Gregory Peck) escape from the French. When Justice passed away in 1975, Steve helped fulfill the actor's dying wish. He and a group of Justice's friends brought his ashes in a leather falconry bag and placed them under a small stone cairn on a hill overlooking Steve's grouse moor. A bagpiper played as they toasted the life of James Robertson Justice — using his favorite single-malt Scotch.

I saw the spot later in the afternoon, when we drove to Steve's grouse moor, which was just over the hill behind his cottage. Steve and Christian now try to drive as close as possible to the hawking areas, to avoid stressing their arthritic joints. We chugged up a steep, rocky path in Steve's small red station wagon, with Christian's VW van lurching and bouncing behind us. When we got high enough on the hillside, we let out Handel, along with Christian's dog, Jette, and worked the moor with them, searching for grouse. Unfortunately, grouse were scarce, so it took a long walk before Handel went on point and Steve put up his eyas peregrine. The young tiercel went up decently and was well positioned for a stoop, but we weren't able to flush any grouse. Perhaps they had run ahead of the point.

A short time later, Jette came on point, and Christian slipped his eyas tiercel. By this time, it was starting to drizzle, but the peregrine waited on well above us. An old cock grouse broke first, drawing the tiercel's fire. And as soon as he was committed to the stoop, all the young, inexperienced grouse blew out the back door and escaped, as did the cock. But there were no regrets. Christian called down his tiercel and fed him, just before the weather fell apart. As the rains came down, we sat in Steve's car, passing around a flask of Scotch and talking about great flights and falcons and dogs long past.

At perhaps that same moment, a ceremony was taking place on a different grouse moor about an hour-and-a-half's drive north. Geoffrey Pollard was with Roger Upton and several other friends, scattering the ashes of his wife, Diana. I think with this symbolic act, he was saying goodbye to life.

I had noticed in my conversations with Geoff that he had a wry, witty sense of humor, but his comments were almost always tinged with melancholy. Down deep, he obviously was not a happy man. "It's so hard to give up all of this," he told me one day, nodding toward his three falcons, which were sitting on block perches in the garden. "I've only been good at two things in my life," he said later, "falconry and the law, and now they're both finished for me."

One of Geoff's sons took him back to England shortly after he scattered his wife's ashes. Roger Upton remarked sadly to me, "He won't be back in Scotland again." He was right. Less than two months later, on a quiet Sunday morning in mid-October, Geoffrey Pollard passed away, just a few days shy of his eightieth birthday. I was grateful to have met him.

13

A BORN-AGAIN
FALCONER

I COULDN'T WAIT to get home from Britain and start flying Macduff again. Seeing all the great peregrines stooping at grouse — especially Mark Upton's two tiercels, Oliver and Dodger — had built my excitement to a fever pitch. The only thing missing from my journey to Scotland was having my own tiercel perched on my fist. I knew Macduff would have done well on red grouse. But the season was still young. If I started working him hard now, he would be in fabulous shape by the time the ducks arrived in force in late October. I hoped to have him ready for a peak performance by the time of the North American Falconers' Association (NAFA) annual field meet during Thanksgiving week. This year it would take place in Kearney, Nebraska, so greater prairie chickens — a species of grouse — were a possible quarry for him, along with numerous ducks.

This would be my eighth season flying Macduff — the longest I've ever kept a single bird. In my early falconry days, I released most of my birds after a season of hawking, but it's nice to keep a falcon for several years — the bird and the falconer gain such a deep understanding of each other and much of the interactions between them become intuitive.

I'm glad I've had such a long time to fly Macduff. I enjoy the way he flies, his energy, and his ferocity as a hunter.

Most falconers tend to associate me with flying tiercel peregrines and merlins — fast, agile, stylish flyers but significantly smaller than the female peregrines and gyrfalcons that others swear by. And this is not entirely incorrect, especially when it comes to merlins. But I've actually flown only three tiercel peregrines, including Macduff.

First there was Odysseus, a first-year tundra peregrine I trapped on the Gulf Coast many years ago with Hollis. He had been born somewhere in the Arctic that spring and was on his first migration to South America when I met up with him in early October. What a delight he was right from the start. Most of these young Arctic falcons have had little or no experience with people and tend to be remarkably tame. I'll never forget when I finished putting leather jesses on his legs and lifted him onto my fist for the first time; he sat calmly without even having his beak agape. And a minute later when I set him on the headboard of the bed in our motel, he shook his feathers, a sign of ease and contentment in a raptor.

On the drive home to California, I let him sit unhooded on my fist as Hollis drove. He was so calm, the only times he tried to fly were when a mourning dove or other small bird would flush along the highway. I knew right then how fabulous he would be.

I named him Odysseus after the tiercel peregrine the Craighead brothers had flown in the 1930s. They had called their bird Ulysses, so I decided to use the original Greek version of that name from Homer's epic poem *The Odyssey* for my tiercel.

He was great from the first time I flew him free, rising high above me in tight corkscrews as he gained altitude. And he would make the prettiest vertical stoops as I flushed mourning doves, pigeons, and other game beneath him, swinging straight up if he missed and stooping again and again and again. In terms of style and elegance, I've never had a falcon his equal, and he caught several birds in short order. Unfortunately, my time with him was far too brief. One day when I got to the field, an hour's drive from home, it was full of dove hunters, walking in a line with shotguns.

I didn't want to fly him anywhere near the shooters, so I drove ten miles away searching for a safer place. I wanted him to get some exercise that day even if I couldn't find any game. The place I chose was hillier than I would have liked, but Odysseus had always been completely reliable, so I slipped him and watched him circle up powerfully as he always did.

And then I saw her, a big female peregrine blasting across the sky toward him. I put my binoculars on her as she got right behind Odysseus and chased him away. I saw him zigzag a few times with her behind and then start to pull away from her in the distance. The female finally broke off the chase and started circling. But Odysseus had already blinked out in the clear-blue sky. This was in the days before telemetry, when having a wild-caught peregrine blast away like that usually meant it was gone for good. The birds quickly revert to the wild. I spent days looking for Odysseus, but he was long gone — perhaps continuing his interrupted journey to Argentina or some other faraway place.

And then there was Silver — the beautiful blue-backed adult tiercel who broke my heart and caused me to stop flying falcons for a decade. He was a tundra peregrine, too, but he had been taken as a nestling years earlier to use in a captive-breeding project. The only problem was, he didn't work out as a breeder. After spending several years in a breeding chamber with a variety of different females, he was given to me to fly so the chamber could be used for a more productive pair.

Silver was a fierce little monster at first, almost like Krag but smaller. He was nothing like tundra peregrines are supposed to be — good-natured and easy to tame like Odysseus. Silver had been loose in a chamber for too many years; he didn't want anyone touching him. I was working at the Predatory Bird Research Group at UC Santa Cruz at the time, and I would walk him around in the evening for hours in the dimly lit hallways of the falcon-breeding facility. He was wild. The most depressing thing was the way he would let other people walk past when I had him perched out, but the instant he saw me, he would fly away to the end of his leash, screaming and trying to escape. He was intelligent and recognized me instantly as the only one who would pick him up.

But gradually, after countless hours of patient work, Silver came around and eventually became one of the most perfectly tamed birds

I've ever had, a complete joy to be around. It took a lot of work to get him ready to hunt. After being kept in flight chambers all his life, he was flabby and became winded quickly. But he enjoyed stooping to the lure, so I would make him dive at it repeatedly each day until he was tired out. His endurance improved quickly, and I began working on his pitch — encouraging him to wait on higher and higher above me. Silver was a game little bird in everything he did, and he was soon flying with all the vigor and skill of a wild adult peregrine. One day he even drove off a wild prairie falcon that tried to attack him.

I flew Silver for a couple of wonderful years, hunting him at doves and pigeons and other small game. At the time, I also had a wild-caught female merlin named Scout, after Tonto's horse — I figured since Silver was named after the Lone Ranger's horse, I should continue the theme and name my other falcon after Tonto's horse.

They were both remarkable falcons. Scout would wait on high above me, making blistering stoops at mourning doves, just as Hannah had done a few years earlier. And it was great. Everything was going well in my falconry, my life, and my career. I received an excellent job offer to be associate editor of *Western Outdoors*, a glossy hunting and fishing magazine based in Orange County. This would be my first job in the publishing field after college. But it meant moving back from Santa Cruz to Southern California.

I was amazed how rapidly the area was changing as more and more land was being developed. Most of the fields where I used to fly hawks were gone, replaced by massive housing developments, malls, and highways. Falconers had to go farther and farther to hunt with their birds, sometimes driving sixty miles or more each way to get a single daily flight at game. And sometimes they found nothing.

For me, it was heartbreaking. So many of the places I loved as a teenager had been destroyed. To think that as a junior in high school I had two white-tailed kite nests within walking distance of my home and a golden eagle nest I could ride my bike to in less than two hours was staggering. The places had all vanished without a trace.

I quickly became a falconry commuter, taking my birds with me to my job at *Western Outdoors*, keeping them in my truck as I worked on the magazine. I flew them whenever it was convenient before, after, or during my workday, doing my best to keep them fit. It was tough. Then I started taking advantage of the development projects underway nearby in the vast ranching empires of Orange County. Entire ready-made communities were being carved out of these huge properties, which had always seemed immune to development. These were places that had been barred to the public for decades, where trespassers were dealt with severely — like the place where Mac and I had been shot at during the 1960s. But as hordes of construction workers flooded into these areas to create the new communities, it suddenly became easy to slip inside in a truck, just like one of the workers, only with a couple of falcons stashed in the back. But it was sad. These places were good only for a couple of months and were then lost forever. I started feeling like a vulture, searching constantly for wonderful pieces of habitat that were about to be ruined — just to be able to give my birds another few weeks of flying, just to make it through one more season.

There was one huge field in Huntington Beach where I started flying my falcons two or three days a week. It was close to where Jeff Sipple and his family lived, so I could perch my birds on his back lawn during the day, and his wife would keep an eye on them. Although the field was bordered by housing developments, it was amazingly vast with a tall bluff rising above it that had another big field on top. A small road ran through the far side of the upper field, and there was a golf course on the other side, which made the area seem spacious and excellent for flying a falcon. A stiff breeze often blew in from the ocean, so it was pleasant to fly there most days. I would often release Silver on top of the bluff and wait for him to reach a nice pitch above me. Then I'd run down to the field below. Huge waves of mourning doves would burst from the low cover as I raced through, clapping my hands. With a shout, I'd alert Silver, but he'd usually already be on his way down, stooping wildly at the doves.

Occasionally, feral pigeons would be feeding just over the bluff, and he'd stoop after them. One day I lost him chasing a pigeon into the field below and didn't see which way the flight had gone. Although by this time I did have a telemetry transmitter on him, I did not yet own a receiver, so I had to drive around searching for one to borrow. I finally got one from the girlfriend of a falconer who lived nearby. She didn't even know me, but I guess I looked too frantic to be making up a story, so she let me have it.

I tracked Silver down quickly in a tall stand of bamboo, sitting in a pile of pigeon feathers, completely gorged on his kill. He looked for an instant like he might fly away as I approached through the stalks of bamboo, but I knelt down and slowly moved my gloved fist closer, and he stepped onto it, looking pleased to be taken back home.

Another time, in a flight at another pigeon, I wasn't so lucky. It was Christmas Eve morning, and I had rushed to the Huntington Beach field to fly Silver so I could get back and celebrate with my family. It was a nice morning for flying, clear and crisp but sunny, with a pleasant ocean breeze blowing across the field. Silver went up well like he always did, and I rushed over the bluff, hoping to flush some doves. Instead, several pigeons got up. He stooped hard at one that flew behind me in the direction of the golf course. After three or four stoops, I could see Silver starting to break off the attack. He almost turned and came back to me, but then he read something in the way the pigeon was flying — the way the trajectory of its flight suddenly bent lower as it started heading for cover instead of toward the open sky. Silver turned and redoubled his efforts, flying harder than ever after the pigeon.

I put my binoculars on the birds and tried to follow the flight. I saw the pigeon heading toward some low trees beside the road with Silver right behind but then lost sight of both of them. I sprinted all the way to the edge of the road but didn't see anything. I paused, listening intently, and then spotted Silver sitting on the ground a couple of hundred feet away. He didn't have the pigeon. I was relieved to see him and started walking quickly there to pick him up, when the pigeon suddenly burst out of the trees, flying madly back in the direction from which it had come. I turned and saw Silver launch himself from the ground and go after the pigeon.

Looking back now, I can still see the rest of the flight unfolding in slow motion — the pigeon fighting to gain altitude, then suddenly turning back in my direction, dipping low toward the road. Silver stooping down after it, just as several cars start flowing past. The pigeon exploding in a cloud of feathers as it's struck by a pickup truck. Silver swooping up, looking back over his shoulder, then stooping again toward the pigeon, which lies dead just below the curb on the other side of the road. And Silver vanishing as quickly and completely as if a magician had waved a magic wand over him. Then a gray Volvo station wagon slowing down and pulling to the side, and something falling from the car's front grill onto the road below.

Silver looked so perfect as he lay there — not a drop of blood showing, barely a feather ruffled. Only he was dead. I picked him up and gently folded his wings closed and held him in my hands as I knelt beside the road. The woman driving the car got out and walked back to me. She looked horrified.

"What happened?" she asked. "What is it?"

"He's a peregrine falcon," I said.

"Was he yours?"

I nodded.

"I'm so sorry," she said, close to tears.

"It wasn't your fault," I said. "There's nothing you could have done."

⁓

THIS IS THE ultimate horror for a falconer, to have a bird killed in the field. Of course, wild raptors face this every day — the risk of being hit by a car, electrocuted by a power line, shot by a hunter, crashing into a fence or building, or being killed by another predator. But it doesn't make it any easier. I felt like a zombie as I made my way back to my mother's house that day. I spent the rest of Christmas Eve in shock, barely able to speak with my relatives and friends.

And that's when I decided. I can no longer do this. I can no longer fly falcons in the horrible messed-up place Southern California had become. I gorged Scout on rich meat for the next few days and then cut her jesses off and set her free. I gave most of my equipment away, even the leather I used for making hoods and jesses. After twenty solid years of training birds of prey, I was finished. And I didn't train another falcon for more than a decade.

⁓

THE WAY I got back into falconry was pretty much an accident. It was in the early 1990s, and I was living in upstate New York, editing *Living Bird*, a bird-watching magazine published by the Cornell Lab of Ornithology. Someone brought in a young kestrel that had fallen from her nest. The person at the front desk advised him to take the bird to the Cornell vet school, which was the standard response when anyone brought any kind of helpless or injured wildlife to us. But in this case, it seemed like a bad idea. There was nothing wrong with the kestrel; she just needed to learn how to hunt. I decided to take her home and work with her. I arranged to get a subpermit under a local wildlife rehabilitator and started training her.

I didn't have great ambitions for the bird. I only wanted her to start catching appropriate kestrel prey so I could release her. I went tromping around the grassy fields, kicking up grasshoppers, and she would fly off after them, often snatching them in midair and carrying them back to my fist to eat. She'd take ten or twelve grasshoppers in a row as I strolled through the field. Then I started kicking bushes and turning over various pieces of junk in the field, sometimes uncovering a mouse, which would run off to cover with my kestrel in hot pursuit. She caught several and even chased a few sparrows. I did release her and she spent two or three weeks in the wild until the weather turned cold and she got hungry. Then she flew right down to someone to beg for food. She became an education bird and was taken to classrooms to teach students about birds of prey.

The next step in my rehabilitation as a falconer occurred when an injured merlin showed up at the Cornell Veterinary Clinic. She was a wild first-year bird that had been hit by a car somewhere near Syracuse. Her wing was broken and her beak had been injured in such a way that the upper and lower mandibles were no longer aligned correctly. The bird was given to me when she had recovered sufficiently to be trained. In the meantime, I had applied for and received both state and federal falconry permits. I was classified as a master falconer because of my extensive previous experience.

I've always loved merlins, and it was great to have another one after all those years. I worked hard with her, stooping her to the lure to build up the muscles in her injured wing. Unfortunately, she never recovered entirely from her injury and could never again fly as well as a wild merlin. There seemed to be a hitch in her wing, and she tired easily. She would chase game, but she just never had the speed she needed to catch up with a bird. And because her upper and lower mandibles didn't line up correctly, her beak was constantly getting overgrown and I had to trim it frequently, so she could never be released. She is now more than ten years old, and I still fly her to the lure, but she's never been a serious game hawk.

Macduff was the falcon that finally pushed me over the edge, taking me back to my crazy days when flying a falcon meant more to me than anything else. Gary Boberg, an old friend in California, was breeding peregrine falcons, and he told me he wanted to give me a beautiful young tiercel his birds had produced that spring. I would just have to pay for the air transport costs to have him delivered to me. How could I say no to that?

Macduff arrived at the airport in a medium-sized pet carrier. The airline personnel were gathered around, peeking through the air holes at him as he sat on some Astroturf covering the bottom of the box. He was wearing a leather hood and was oblivious to everyone. As soon as I got home, I attached a leash and swivel to his jesses, lifted him up to my gloved left hand, and finally removed the hood. He immediately reared up, hissing at me with beak agape. He'd been raised by his parents and then turned loose in a large flight chamber with a couple of other young male peregrines. He hadn't been handled at all and was on the spooky side. But he was beautiful, with a dark back, a vividly streaked breast, and one of the fullest caps (the dark area on the head of a peregrine) I've ever seen on a young peregrine.

I didn't know what kind of game I was going to hunt with Macduff. The area where I lived was so new to me. I still had to go exploring, searching for fields and checking out hunting opportunities. He was attacked a couple of times by flocks of crows in the early stage of his training, and he seemed to take a strong dislike to them. He was always taking off after them and chasing them around the sky, so I started deliberately looking for places where I could get good slips at crows. Crows are difficult to catch in the kind of habitat available around Ithaca. They are intelligent, crafty birds, and to catch them consistently requires wide-open country — like where Nick Fox flies in Northumberland. Here in upstate New York, crows can usually drop into the forest canopy and escape whenever they're hard-pressed by a pursuing falcon. Macduff made some spectacular flights at crows, fighting his way upward until he got above them, then hurtling down in roller-coaster stoops, twisting and turning behind the bird he had singled out. But he rarely caught them.

In one memorable crow flight, Macduff flew off someplace shortly after I released him. I was trying to ambush some crows feeding in some deep furrows in a wide-open agricultural field. They were a long way off and hidden from Macduff's view, but I knew if I had tried to release him closer, they would have flown away instantly. I took out my telemetry receiver and tried to figure out which way he had flown. I discovered he was circling somewhere right above me, too high to see.

I dropped the receiver and antenna on the ground at once and sprinted to the plowed area where the crows were feeding. For a second when I got there, I couldn't spot them, but then I noticed them hugging the ground, trying to slither away down the furrows. I ran through them, clapping my hands and shouting, flushing several, one of which turned right and flew off across a flat grassy field just past the furrows. I heard Macduff before I spotted him, the wind whistling loudly through his flight feathers as he stooped. He cut the crow down in an explosion of black feathers, sending it tumbling to the ground, and was on it instantly.

That was the best crow flight I've ever had with him. More often the flights ended up in stubble fields, with the crow running along on the ground, ducking behind cornstalks each time Macduff stooped at it and gradually working its way to the safety of the forest. After one flight like this, Macduff was still full of energy, and he rang up to a spectacular altitude above me. On a whim, I decided to sprint to a pond on the other side of the field and see if it might have some ducks he could chase. I was hoping there might be something small such as a ring-necked duck or a green-winged teal, but when I got up on the dike at the pond's edge, a flock of six huge mallards burst from the water. Macduff absolutely hammered a beautiful drake, with a great *whack* that echoed across the field. I was shocked to see the duck tumble and even more amazed when

Macduff crashed into cover where the duck had fallen. Peregrines hardly ever go into cover; they're far too dainty. But here he was, behaving like a rough-and-tumble prairie falcon, and it was great. He had killed the drake mallard.

That was just the beginning. The following season when he was in his beautiful blue adult plumage, I began flying him exclusively at ducks, and we've been doing that ever since. Although he occasionally takes smaller ducks when they're available, it turns out that most of my local ponds hold only mallards in the fall, with perhaps a few black ducks — which are close relatives of mallards and just as large — in winter. This limits the number of ducks he can catch, because they're so big and strong, but I have fabulous flights for most of the season, until the ponds and streams freeze over with thick ice.

I'VE ALWAYS HATED the first day of flying a falcon free after the molt. The bird has been loose in a flight chamber or "mews" for months, getting flabby and aloof, and suddenly it's time to get the falcon in shape and return to the field. Falconers have molted their birds for centuries in this way — leaving them alone to get on with the process of growing new feathers — and it is probably the best way. If the birds were flown during the summer, they would be handicapped by the gaps in their wings where the feathers are missing and the growing feathers would run an increased risk of breaking. And besides, most game seasons are closed in summer.

I took Macduff out of the mews at the end of September and, as always at the beginning, he was bad tempered and hissed at me as I picked him up on my fist. I ignore it now and get on with training him, walking him around the yard with me, hooding and unhooding him to get him back into the routine. I never bother to put him back on a creance. I just handle him for a few days, reduce his food intake a little to get him more interested in eating, and take him out flying. This time I flew him for the first time on October 3, a mild Tuesday morning. He didn't do much, just buzzed around low, circling the field, never getting above thirty feet high. When he got up to his highest point, I finally swung the lure, tossing it out to him as he flew toward me. There was a time when it would have really bothered me to have a bird fly this poorly. I take it in stride now. It's a temporary condition at the start of a new season. I knew in a few days he'd start getting fitter, flying higher and longer, and in two weeks he'd be scorching the sky with his stoops. I couldn't imagine any reason why he wouldn't be in great shape in time for the falconry meet in late November.

A few days later, the season turned distinctly autumnal, with a cool breeze sweeping the field and the surrounding forest ablaze in a stunning tableau of red, orange, and golden leaves. Mornings like these are when I feel most alive. And I can see the change of attitude in Macduff — his restlessness, his intense eagerness to be out in the field hunting. In his exuberance, he took off high and wide, barely in my view with 10x binoculars as he circled up. Some wood ducks I hadn't seen flushed from a small wooded creek as I was making my way to a pond across an open field. Macduff was completely out of position for the flush, but he streaked across the sky, eagerly pursuing the ducks until they dropped into the safety of the forest. I called him back to the lure then fed him on my fist. I walked around the field for half an hour as we both enjoyed the beautiful autumn morning. He was beginning to fly wonderfully. I knew it wouldn't be long now.

Less than a week later it all came together for him. It was a perfect morning for hawking — cool and crisp with a stiff wind sweeping across the sky. Macduff felt the strong urge to fly. He pumped his wings as he stared up at the big white clouds moving across the sky then took off to the west, rowing his powerful wings as he gained altitude. But he was all business. He turned left and started going up in tight circles, fighting to get above the wind. He had chased some more wood ducks the day before and come within an inch of catching one, tapping it lightly in a stoop as it dodged at the last second and doubled back to the nearby forest. Wyoming this is not. If a falcon doesn't take care of a duck quickly here, it always escapes to the trees.

Miraculously, the wood ducks were here again on the same pond. (It's rare for me to get more than one try at wood ducks per season in the Ithaca area, but this was my third chance in a week.) This time he was in perfect position as I charged the pond, throwing rocks and shouting. The ducks flushed cleanly out the north side of the pond, and Macduff folded up into a breathtaking vertical stoop. He hammered a female wood duck as she flew sixty or seventy feet in the air, and that was it: she tumbled to the ground. He swooped back up and then went straight down. When I reached him, he had already killed the duck. I gave him a good feed on the duck as a reward. It was mid-October, and he was already almost at the top of his game. And I still had more than a month to go before the falconry meet in Nebraska.

It's funny how easy it is to get cocky and overconfident when you have a bird flying this well — when everything looks so promising. Less than a week later, my life was turned upside down again.

It was one of those blustery autumn days, with a cold wind blowing from the north. A storm front had moved through in the night, bringing heavy rain as well as numerous newly arrived ducks. It was just the kind of situation I'd been waiting for. Taking a quick peek at the first pond, I spotted at least three common mergansers and several mallards, the first decent group of ducks in a hawkable place I'd found all season. My heart raced as I got Macduff ready, taking off his leash and swivel and attaching his telemetry transmitter.

Macduff knows his business well. As soon as I released him, he quickly fought his way up above the turbulent air and made his way toward the pond. When he got above it, I saw him perk up and instantly begin climbing higher and higher — something he always does when he sees a large flock of ducks. I knew there must be many more ducks than I had seen. I waited for him to swing around to the far side of the pond, and then I raced up to the rim on my side. I saw more than twenty-five mallards, in addition to the mergansers. I threw a rock and shouted, flushing most of the ducks. Macduff went into a powerful stoop as they swung out over dry land, perhaps sixty feet in the air, and turned downwind. He slammed into a hen mallard, which went down hard in the field about eighty feet past the pond. He swooped up, did another stoop at the duck on the ground, then went down. I ran to the place where I had lost sight of him but didn't hear any bells at first. Then I spotted him, just at the edge of some cover, standing without the duck. He didn't look right. His wings were spread as if to hold himself steady. I carefully picked him up, and he almost fell over. He couldn't put any weight on his left leg. As I stood there, the duck suddenly burst from cover nearby and flew away strongly. Macduff didn't even pay any attention to it.

I did my best to feed him as he lay on my fist with his left leg dangling limply behind. Tearing up the meat with my right hand and my thumbnail, I fed him bite-sized pieces that he could eat without using his feet. I could see he was in bad shape. As soon as he'd had a decent meal, I hooded him and carried him back to the car.

When I got Macduff home, I wrapped him in a towel and held him steady so I could feel along the length of his leg, trying to see if there was an obvious fracture. I couldn't find one. Later I had him x-rayed by a veterinarian, and no bones were broken, but his leg was obviously sprained or had some kind of soft-tissue damage. There was no way to determine how long it would take to heal and how well Macduff would be able to use it in the future. This might even be the end of his career as a hunter. It was a disaster.

I put Macduff in a warm, dimly lit room at home and kept him well fed. It was important to minimize his stress and give him time to recover properly. It was a discouraging time for me, seeing him lying like a nestling on the soft carpet I put down for him. After two weeks, he was beginning to improve noticeably. He would sit on his block perch with his left foot pulled up, looking almost normal. He even started using that foot to scratch his head. But he limped badly whenever he tried to walk.

I decided to pull the plug on my dreams of taking Macduff to the NAFA meet. It was only three weeks away, and I knew there was no way he would be able to whack mallards and prairie chickens in that amount of time. Perhaps he'd never be able to do that again. I was already committed to attending the meet, but I'd be going without a bird, so I didn't need to drive. The good part was, my wife was flying there, and I had planned to meet her with my car. Instead, I bought a last-minute airline ticket and would be traveling with her. At least we would have a nice vacation together.

14

FORTY YEARS AFTER

RACHEL AND I got up early and headed to Syracuse Airport well before much traffic was on the highway. It was the Sunday before Thanksgiving and once again we were on the road together. (Traveling together twice in one year was a new record for us.) Rachel had just driven to Northampton, Massachusetts, and back — a solid ten hours of driving — the day before to pick up Railey from college so she could take care of the kids again.

This time we were on our way to the 2006 North American Falconers' Association meet in Kearney, Nebraska. It was a special trip for both of us. Rachel would have another chance to spend time hawking with Steve Chindgren and meeting other falconers from around the world. And I would be celebrating an anniversary. It was exactly forty years earlier that I went to Centerville, South Dakota, with my friend Rich to take part in NAFA's 1966 falconry meet.

Our journey to Nebraska went surprisingly smoothly. Rachel and I blasted from Syracuse to Chicago, dashed to our connecting flight, and arrived in Lincoln before noon. We decided to fly to Lincoln instead of going directly to Kearney, because it was actually faster (even though we would have to rent a car and drive for an hour and a half) and much less expensive.

The hotel was easy to find. As we drove through the parking lot we saw the usual falconry meet scene: various hawks and falcons perched out on a big lawn surrounded by a makeshift fence; falconers standing around here and there talking enthusiastically about great flights they'd seen. Occasionally we'd see someone using his arm to describe a flight, raising his right hand high, letting it hang in the air for an instant and then come stooping down on some imaginary prey.

I didn't notice anyone I knew, so we went inside to check in and get our room. The first person we ran into was Tony Huston, walking briskly down the hallway. He was barely recognizable with his hair neatly trimmed and his face clean-shaven, wearing a sport coat and a turtleneck. Without his graying beard, he looked a good ten years younger than he had the previous January in Wyoming.

The three of us had one of those lightning-fast chats people have in passing, filling each other in on what we'd been doing for the past few months, and then Tony was off to make arrangements for the next day's hawking. He knew the area well from previous seasons and was helping to coordinate the hunting activities so the guests from the International Association for Falconry and Conservation of Birds of Prey would be able to experience the best of American falconry.

After checking in, we had a quick meal then started wandering around, looking for familiar faces. Steve Chindgren pulled up in his truck a short time later with Jomo, his other falcons, and Tucker in the back. Tucker had developed a limp, and Steve wasn't sure if he'd be able to run him at the meet. He let him out and tied him to a tree outside the hawking area.

I ran into a falconer I had known years ago in California — Dave Cherry, who was with his wife, Lisa. Dave is someone who stands out from the crowd at a falconry meet. He's tall, with straight, somewhat overgrown gray hair and a beard. And he has a wild-eyed look as though his mind is perpetually focused on events going on a couple of thousand feet overhead — which it is; he's obsessed with training high-flying falcons. We had a long talk that afternoon as we stood beside the weathering yard, and he expounded his philosophy of life.

"I've found my ruling passion — falconry — and that's the only thing I want to do in life," he told me. He also stressed how important it was to find the right woman. She had to know that falcons come first.

"How would you feel if you were dating a woman who had children, and she told you: 'Let's go out and party; it doesn't matter about the kids'?" he said. "You wouldn't want to have anything to do with her, because she's a lousy mother, right? I feel the same way about my birds. If I'm not good to my falcons, what good am I?"

We also talked about Mike Connolly, one of the pioneer longwing falconers in Southern California during the 1960s and '70s, whom we had both known well. Although Mike no longer trained falcons, he had become an almost legendary figure in the intervening years. Dave was in awe of him.

"He was the best hunter," he said. "He could size up a situation instantly."

Dave had once crawled up to the edge of a pond with Connolly to check for ducks before flying. Dave had binoculars and scanned the pond carefully, trying to spot all the ducks. But Mike had already seen everything with his naked eyes. "He knew instantly where all the ducks were, what species they were, and what would make most sense in terms of the flush." And this is vitally important in falconry. Each duck species has particular escape strategies they tend to use when they flush, so a falconer needs to adapt tactics accordingly. Mike was a master strategist, which is what made him such an effective hunter.

I still receive e-mails from Mike Connolly once in a while. He is retired and living the good life, but is as tough as ever. He had always been a big-game hunter, going on safari in Africa or hunting bears in Alaska, and he still keeps that up. Mike is obviously cut from the same cloth as Gilbert Blaine and other famous falconers of old. He is the quintessential hunter/outdoorsman. He now has a home in Montana and spends days trekking up into the mountains after elk and other game. To recuperate, he comes back home and soaks in a hot tub.

Mike also has a place in Cabo San Lucas, at the tip of Baja California, and a boat named *The Falcon*, which he uses to pursue marlin and other big-game fish. I think the only reason he gave up falconry is because he knew it would be impossible for him to practice it at the same level he had before and in a place as excellent as the San Diego area had been in the 1960s and '70s. Back then it was a paradise for falconry. The weather was perfect most of the year. There were numerous excellent fields in which to fly a falcon safely. Game was abundant. The laws pertaining to falconry were less strict. And most important, the human population was much lower.

These days, Southern California is quickly becoming a hell on earth. Rampant development has destroyed most of the open land where we used to fly, and there's no end in sight. The falconers who remain now have so few places to fly that they have to fight over ponds and fields, and the whole experience is becoming unpleasant, which is why some California falconers like Dave Cherry now look for flying opportunities in faraway states, such as Kansas, Nebraska, Montana, and Wyoming.

℮

RACHEL AND I didn't go flying on the day we arrived. The next day would be the main event for us. We were part of an invited group who were being flown to Boise, Idaho, to tour the Peregrine Fund's World Center for Birds of Prey. I'd been there several times before, but not since 1999 when the center hosted a major event to celebrate the peregrine falcon being removed from the endangered species list. The peregrine had bounced back strongly from near extinction and was increasing in numbers by about 5 or 6 percent each year — far higher than the most optimistic projections when the Peregrine Fund was founded in 1970. And this had come about largely through the organization's efforts. It was a proud moment, especially for falconers, who had strongly supported the captive breeding and reintroduction effort from the start.

The World Center had recently constructed the new Sheikh Zayed bin Sultan Al Nahyan Falconry Heritage Wing to house an extensive Arab falconry exhibit. (This is the part of the building that houses the Archives of Falconry.) The centerpiece is a huge goat-hair Bedu tent and all its fittings — wall-to-wall oriental carpets; cushions; accoutrements for roasting, grinding, brewing, and serving Bedu coffee; and three life-like sculpted figures of Bedouins in traditional dress, clustered around a fire in the tent, drinking coffee. But this is just part of the exhibit. In addition there are numerous other artifacts, paintings, interactive kiosks, and signage to familiarize visitors with the centuries-old tradition of falconry on the Arabian Peninsula.

Sheikh Mohamed bin Zayed (son of the former president of the United Arab Emirates, the late Sheikh Zayed bin Sultan Al Nahyan) provided funds to erect the new wing, which was named after his father. He also chartered a commercial jetliner to fly nearly 300 international falconers from the Kearney meet to Boise free of charge so they could tour the World Center and see the exhibit.

Rachel and I were excited to be part of the group. We got up before dawn and went downstairs to the hotel lobby. Dozens of people were already gathered, including Kent Carnie from the Archives of Falconry, who was checking peoples' names against a list and giving them each a nametag to wear so they could board the plane. A retired military officer, Kent has become one of the elder statesmen of American falconry. He pushed for the creation of the Archives and was its founding curator and director. When I finally got to the front of the line, he gave us nametags to hang around our necks, then we went outside, climbed aboard one of the buses, and drove to the Kearney Airport.

The flight crew finally let us clamber aboard the chartered Miami Air Boeing 737, and our group almost completely filled the plane. We made up such an amazing mix of cultures and ethnic groups. Some were dressed in the traditional hunting garb of their countries — like the two Kazakhs with their exquisitely embroidered tunics, pants, and hats; the young Czech man with his collarless loden jacket; and the Japanese falconers clad in Samurai-like splendor. The airline crew was mostly Cuban.

The crew finally closed the airplane door, and we seemed to be about to take off, when they abruptly stopped and opened the door again. Three tardy German falconers climbed aboard and strode down the aisle looking for some vacant seats. And then, finally, we were off, soaring up high above the bleak brown farms and flatlands.

❧

FOUR BUSES WERE waiting to meet us when we arrived at Boise Airport. As we drove to the World Center, I was amazed at the number of new houses I saw. It had seemed much more remote the last time I visited. When we got there, we were divided into four groups. We were supposed to tour each area of the World Center separately, so that no single place would get too crowded.

Rachel and I began in the library and bird skin collection, where the curator showed us a remarkable assemblage of raptor specimens from around the world, plus other interesting birds, such as the extinct passenger pigeon. Then we moved on to the Archives of Falconry and the new Arab wing. It was wonderful — even better than I had imagined, featuring a huge mural depicting an Arabian desert with two houbara bustards mounted in front and an interactive kiosk where visitors could learn more about the traditions of Arab falconry. Several other kiosks stood nearby in front of inset windows where falconry equipment was displayed. The architectural details inside the new wing suggested Arabia. I especially enjoyed the Bedu tent and the three sculpted Arab men inside, which were like figures from a wax museum.

I ran into Christian Saar, whom I hadn't seen since the day in September when I went hawking with him and Stephen Frank in Scotland. He told me all about how the rest of their hawking season had gone. His two young tiercel peregrines had become spectacular flyers, one of them consistently going up so high he was difficult to see. Tony Huston came over while we were talking. He knew Christian well and had often gone grouse hawking in Scotland with him and the other people I had visited there.

I saw Bill Burnham's wife, Pat, and his son, Kurt, near the Arabian exhibit, and it was sad. This was the first time I'd seen them since Bill had passed away, just a few weeks earlier. Bill was one of the most determined, hard-driving people I'd ever known. He had been president of the Peregrine Fund for twenty years and, despite the ever-growing administrative duties of running the organization, he continued taking part in research projects, traveling each year to Greenland and other faraway places.

I had gone on two expeditions to Greenland with Bill and Kurt several years earlier. No one worked harder than Bill on these expeditions. He was an inspiration to all of us. I'll never forget standing below a tundra peregrine eyrie on a lofty cliff in northern Greenland, peering through a spotting scope and talking to Bill via walkie-talkie, helping him locate the nest ledge so he could band the young. He had carried the climbing gear to the top of the cliff from the other side and tied his rope to a boulder. Because it was a cold day, he wanted to get in and out quickly to avoid stressing the young falcons. He made three lightning-fast rappels, using ascenders to climb back up each time before finding the correct ledge, then banded the young and got out of there in a matter of minutes.

I still had a hard time accepting the fact that Bill was gone. He was such a strong individual and just fifty-nine years old when he died of a brain tumor. It had only been diagnosed in January. Peregrine Fund founder Tom Cade and his wife had stopped by my office in the summer when they were visiting Ithaca, and they told me the details about Bill's condition. I'd already heard he was seriously ill, but I didn't know it was terminal.

After being near death for weeks, Bill had surgery to give him temporary relief from some of the debilitating effects of his illness. Almost immediately, he was making plans, wanting to get back into action — like a human dynamo who could not be stopped. And that summer, he made one last trip to Greenland, a place that had meant so much to him for so many years. Although he was too ill to go into the field, he would wait eagerly for the researchers to get back so he could talk with them about what they had seen. But by October, his condition crashed, and he died a short time later.

Pat and Bill had been together since high school, and he had died far too young. She told me people had been trying to comfort her by saying how wonderful it was that he had accomplished so much in so few years — far more than most achieve in a long lifetime — as though that made it OK that he had died so young. She didn't buy it. "Just imagine how much he could have accomplished if he had lived another twenty or thirty years," she told me.

Kurt seemed to be holding up well, though it's sometimes difficult to tell with men — especially one like Kurt who may well have inherited Bill Burnham's tough, tight-lipped, stoic nature. He and Bill had been as close as any father and son I'd ever known, spending weeks at a time together in far-off places like Greenland. It had to be unimaginably painful to lose him like that, struck down by an illness.

I saw Tom Cade standing near the mounted houbaras in front of the desert mural, and we talked for a while. He and his wife had stayed in the Ithaca area for a few days during the summer, and we had gotten together a couple of times. I had told him about my plans to travel through Italy visiting Frederick II sites, and he was excited. Like me, he is a lifelong Frederick II enthusiast, and he joked that he'd love to come with me and carry my photography equipment.

As we talked, several International Association for Falconry and Conservation of Birds of Prey (IAF) members approached Tom and asked to have their picture taken with him. Tom is a legendary figure among falconers and raptor conservationists worldwide for his work in restoring peregrines to the areas from which they'd been extirpated in North America. Without his efforts, there would never have been a Peregrine Fund — and who knows what shape the falcons would be in now?

I introduced myself to Frank Bond, a longtime Peregrine Fund board member and also NAFA's general counsel. Frank is a tall man who often wears a gray Stetson. An attorney in Santa Fe, he is a former member of New Mexico's House of Representatives and once ran for governor. He is an avid falconer who flies gyrfalcons. I had seen him at other meets years earlier, but we had never spoken with each other. He had heard all about the ivory-billed woodpecker rediscovery and seemed fascinated by it, asking me many questions about the species and the search.

A SHORT TIME later, everyone went outside and posed for a group picture behind the new wing. After the picture taking, Frank stood in front of the group and made a short speech and introduced the sheik's representatives — a man and a woman — who had come from the United Arab Emirates to attend the meet and the tour. When that was finished, it was past three in the afternoon and time to herd everyone back into the buses for the return trip to Boise Airport.

After lunch the following day, we hooked up with a huge hawking party, maybe sixty people, and followed Tony Huston out to look for prairie chickens. We rode in a big white van driven by Bill Johnston, a falconer from Massachusetts. The van had been rented by NAFA to take meet participants out to see hawking, but it was practically empty. The only other passengers were Bill's wife, Pauline, and Peter Devers of the Archives of Falconry.

Someone had spotted a group of prairie chickens, so Tony quickly got Johnny out, rigged up his telemetry, unhooded him, and put him into the air. He went up well, just as he had done months earlier in Wyoming. Tony and a small group of beaters worked their way across the field to where they knew the prairie chickens were crouching. But before they got there, Johnny raked off, stooping after something in the distance. As soon as he was safely out of the airspace above them, prairie chickens burst out everywhere, flying to safety in the endless fields of low cover and stubble. Tony went striding off after Johnny, holding his telemetry antenna in the air to get a signal. We jumped into the van and drove up the road in the direction Johnny had vanished. We spotted him sitting in a low tree in a wide-open field, but Tony had already seen him. Ralph Rogers and several other people were leaving to fly somewhere else before it got dark. We got in line with the other cars and took off down the dusty road.

We managed to get separated from the longwing group; we turned right, following three or four cars that turned out to be shortwingers. Ralph and the other falcon men had turned left. We watched a man fly a big European goshawk for about ten minutes, then went off in search of the others. Bill got Ralph on the cell phone. He said Pete Widener was just about to fly his falcon at some prairie chickens, and he gave Bill rough directions for how to get there. We spotted the cars parked along the edge of the cornfield, but the hawking party was almost a mile in, up a long rise. We got out and started walking quickly toward them. People were spread out over the entire distance. It was like a scene from a sci-fi movie — all these people trudging slowly up a hill through a cornfield, babbling in a dozen different languages, there among the crop rings, perhaps hoping to meet an alien spaceship.

Widener's falcon had been drawn away by a hen mallard that flushed unexpectedly when they were moving toward the prairie chickens. The falcon had followed the duck all the way to a pond near us. We missed most of the flight, but the peregrine buzzed around near us, then went back to Pete. He then put up a very dark, first-year tiercel peregrine, which went up well. A group of falconers went to the pond and managed to flush the mallard a couple of times. The tiercel made some nice vertical stoops at the duck, but didn't seem eager to connect. Then a wild prairie falcon came in and crabbed with the peregrine, both birds screaming like a couple of rusty pumps — *creak, creak, creak, creak*. Pete called his bird down to the lure.

By then, it was well past dusk on a beautiful evening. The sunset was stunning, and I took numerous pictures of a hill to the west of us, with a windmill silhouetted against a purplish pinkish sky.

I saw Frank Bond feeding his gyrfalcon beside his truck. Like many of the falconers at the meet who had brought these striking arctic birds to fly, he was dismayed by the weather — perhaps warmer than anyone had ever experienced at a NAFA meet. Here it was at the end of November in Nebraska, and it was practically T-shirt weather. Gyrfalcons need to have a little cold weather to get serious. Was it global warming or just a weird year?

e⌒

I WAS HAPPY to run into my old friend Jamey Eddy the next day. He lives in western Wyoming now, and I hadn't seen him for years. He used to work at the Santa Cruz Predatory Bird Research Group shortly after I left there to work at *Western Outdoors* magazine. He was responsible for breeding all the quail to feed the falcons. I used to run into him every time I went back to Santa Cruz for a visit. Jamey is thin, with brown hair and glasses and usually wears a cotton visor to keep the sun from his eyes. Although he is probably only five or six years younger than I am, he has always looked like a kid to me. He has a subtle sense of humor, which I appreciate. He loves tiercel peregrines — which I also appreciate — and is currently flying an eight-year-old at ducks. From everything I've heard about his bird, I'm dying to see him in action. Jamey flies at first light every morning, so we had already missed that day's flight, but I told him definitely to include us the following morning.

I hooked up with a group led by Tony Huston heading out to search for prairie chickens that afternoon. I was a couple of trucks back with

Andrew Beske, the NAFA southeastern regional director, and a falconer from Denmark named Tage.

Andrew had a big white female gyrfalcon, a beautiful bird. I was looking forward to seeing her fly, as well as seeing Tony's peregrine, Clara, and his hybrid, Johnny, in action again. But when we got to a crossroad, Tony wanted to go one way and Andrew the other. Tage decided to get out of the car and go with Tony. I continued on with Andrew. He wanted to go back to the field where he had waited the previous evening. At four-eighteen sharp, a large flight of prairie chickens had come cruising in, and he wanted to see if history would repeat itself. Andrew had some misgivings, though — not about the grouse but about his falcon. It was so warm and sunny outside. How well would an Arctic gyrfalcon perform in such mild weather?

It didn't take long to find out. The game birds came in right on schedule, just one minute later than they had the day before. But when Andrew slipped his gyrfalcon, she flew right back to where he had parked and landed on top of his SUV. She sat there for a long time, relaxing in the balmy weather. We decided to start walking into the field, hoping she might get restless and come after us. She finally did take off at one point, but she just flew into the field and landed. Then prairie chickens started popping out everywhere. She followed them, but it was a futile effort, and she soon landed on a windmill. The next time she started flying, Andrew called her to the lure and took her back to the car.

It's not a good idea to call a falcon directly down (or to flush game) when it is perched, because it rewards negative behavior. The occasional times my peregrine has landed, I've always tried to wait him out, calling him back or flushing game only when he's already on the wing. The only exception is if there is some danger present in the field — such as a hunter or perhaps another predator of some kind — and I need to get my bird safely back on my fist as quickly as possible.

After botching the flush on the prairie chickens, we made our way back to the place where Tony had gone flying, but he was already finished, and it was nearly dark. Things had not gone well for him either. Clara flew poorly, he told us, buzzing around low in the field. Although Johnny had gone up well again, they weren't able to flush any prairie chickens until he had finally drifted well out of position — then the elusive game birds were bursting out everywhere.

I've always thought that chicken is an unfortunate name for these birds. The greater prairie chicken is a spectacular grouse, in many ways as challenging to catch as a sage grouse. Certainly none had been caught yet at this meet — even though many had been chased by falcons — and time was quickly running out.

The evening program was starting when we got back, led by NAFA president Darryl Perkin's presentation. Darryl is a middle-aged African American whose looks remind me a little of B.B. King. His talk was hilarious — especially when he showed a computer-altered video of himself chasing down an antelope on foot. Steve Chindgren showed a well-produced DVD he had made, featuring his falcons flying at sage grouse, with accompanying music. Shawn Hayes finished the evening with some films of his gyrfalcon/peregrine hybrids in action.

I had met Shawn several years earlier at a California Hawking Club meet. He's a good friend of Jamey Eddy, and we made arrangements to go flying with the two of them early the next morning.

Shawn cuts a striking figure in the white-bread hinterlands of Nebraska. A stocky, muscular African American, he sports a mass of tightly woven, shoulder-length braids, held out of his face by a tan cotton visor like the ones golfers wear. He is a born athlete who went to high school with basketball legend Reggie Miller, and the two are still good friends. (Although he played with Miller in an intramural league as a kid, Shawn wasn't tall enough to be a serious basketball player.)

Besides being one of the most avid falconers I know, Shawn is a professional rodeo clown — one of the guys who jumps into the ring to distract a bull after it has thrown a rider, encouraging the raging beast to chase him instead of stomping or goring the cowboy. (Shawn and others engaged in this activity prefer to be called bullfighters, not clowns.) It's a highly physical, extremely dangerous occupation, perhaps becoming more so as Shawn ages — he is now in his midforties. But the pay is decent and, because he is self-employed, Shawn can live the life of a falconry bum during hawking season, traveling across the West and Midwest in search of grouse, ducks, and other prey for his two excellent falcons.

In his travels, Shawn has seen the best and the worst America has to offer. When hawking in faraway places, it's impossible to avoid having close encounters with local residents, and you never know how things will go. It often involves driving out long dirt roads to lonely farmhouses to get permission to fly at game or to search for a lost falcon on a land-owner's property. And Shawn sometimes travels to parts of the country where black people are rarely seen. People tend to fear what they don't know and can sometimes lash out in frightening ways.

But Shawn is one of the most amiable and outgoing individuals I know and is a master at putting people at ease. He's so open in his demeanor and genuinely enthusiastic when he meets new people it's hard not to like him. I've frequently observed him as he's walked up to strangers and struck up a conversation. As he approached, they would seem fearful, but in a minute or two he would have them laughing at his jokes, joining him in conversation, and very often offering to help him find game for his falcons.

Shawn is the kind of person who will always take time to stop and talk with someone, even if he's in a hurry. He's incredibly patient with children, carefully explaining how hawks are trained, what kind of game they take, and how to use various hawking equipment.

He has a way of fitting in easily with the small-town communities he encounters. A few years ago, Shawn spent several weeks in Kansas, flying a wild-trapped prairie falcon at game. He made friends with an elderly farmer named Harmon McCabe, and the two of them would eat at a local café together every day. At first, the locals in the café were standoffish — they'd never seen anyone quite like Shawn — but it didn't take long for him to win them over. He was soon just like one of the locals, even running a tab at the diner. He became even more popular after he gave a talk at the local high school. He showed the students his falcon and explained the sport of falconry to them — but he also told them how important it was not to start experimenting with drugs. The kids accepted him and thought he was cool, so what he said made a much deeper impression on them than it would have coming from their parents or teachers. The townspeople appreciated that. But even in this idyllic setting, Shawn had an ugly encounter.

One day he lost his falcon a short time before dusk and tracked her telemetry signal to a clump of trees out a long dirt road, not far from a farmhouse. It was dark by then, and he knew he wouldn't be able to get his falcon until the next morning. He wanted to let the property owners know what was happening and that he would return shortly before dawn.

When he went to the house, the only people at home were a couple of elementary-school-age children. Their mother had driven to town to get pizza for dinner. He talked with them about his lost falcon, and just as he was about to leave, their mother came home. He explained the situation and showed her his telemetry receiver. She and the kids walked out to the trees with him and saw how the beeping signal became louder and stronger as he pointed it up into the tree where his falcon had gone to roost. He said he would be back at five o'clock the next morning, so he could be there waiting at first light when his falcon woke up. She said it was fine, so he drove back to his room and slept for a few hours.

When he got there the next morning, Shawn found that his falcon had flown during the night, but the telemetry signal showed she was still nearby, perhaps sitting on a low fencepost. He drove to an adjacent field then started walking across it, swinging his lure, hoping his falcon would see it and fly to him. By this time, it was light out, and he noticed a cowboy in a pickup truck who drove past again and again. The man finally stopped and called to him. It was the woman's boyfriend. Although the man had already heard about the lost falcon, he was furious Shawn was out there.

"I thought you was just going to get your bird from the tree and get out of here," he said.

"I was," said Shawn. "But when I got here, she'd already flown out here somewhere. I'm picking up her signal in that direction."

"Yeah, well I don't care about that. I want you to get the hell out of here now," he said, suddenly brandishing a handgun at Shawn. "And I don't want to see you coming around those kids anymore. I see you anywhere around here again, you're a dead man."

"Look, I just want to get my bird back," said Shawn, and then he walked quickly away from the man and started swinging his lure. A minute later, his falcon slammed into the lure and took it to the ground. He picked her up and started feeding her on his fist, ignoring the cowboy. He finally heard him start up the truck and drive away, leaving a cloud of dust blowing in the breeze behind him.

But Shawn was badly shaken. He immediately drove back to his room to pack up his belongings. He ran into Harmon briefly and told him what had happened. Shawn said he'd decided to move on and find a different area to hawk. The old man nodded sadly, then shook his hand and left.

A short time later, Shawn stopped at the café to pay off his tab. A lot of people were gathered there, and they seemed particularly effusive and happy to see Shawn. Then one of the farmers took him aside and said he didn't have to worry about anything; he was welcome to stay around as long as he wanted. The cowboy with the gun had worked for him, but he had just fired him and told him to clear out of town.

Shawn has had several other racist encounters in his life. He shrugs it off. "Sometimes I feel like I have a big bull's-eye painted on my back," he told me, laughing.

⌒

WE ALL GOT together the next morning, but there was a snag. Rob Bagley of Marshall Radio — a company that produces falconry telemetry units — had gone up in a plane the previous day and located several excellent duck ponds nearby. He was supposed to lead us to them so Jamey and Shawn could fly their falcons, but first he had to give the opening remarks at the International Association for Falconry's official meeting, taking place in one of the hotel's ballrooms. Shawn walked in there briefly to talk with Rob and was amazed by what he saw — an assemblage like a mini United Nations, with delegates from all over the world. Rob assured him it would take only twenty minutes at most to complete his talk, so we stood around the lobby, impatiently waiting to go flying.

It was almost eight-thirty by the time we left, and the crowd wanting to watch the falcons had grown considerably. Half a dozen vehicles pulled out of the parking lot headed south, with Rob Bagley's truck in the lead. We drove well out of town, along the road that goes by Fort Kearney. We passed some feedlots and eventually came to a close-cropped, fenced-in field with beef cattle grazing inside. Rob told us there were three ponds about a half-mile into the field, near a small line of trees. Although he had gotten permission to fly there, he cautioned that only a handful of people should go inside. He didn't want to risk spooking the cattle, so most people would have to stay at the fence. Shawn and Jamey took Rachel and me inside with them to help flush. As we were going through the gate, Shawn looked at a freckle-faced kid in a baseball cap standing at the edge of the group. "You can come, too," he said. The boy ran over to us, beaming to have been included.

Jamey flew his tiercel first, and he went high and wide, quickly becoming a tiny speck moving in and out of our vision. As we carefully made our way toward the first pond, we could hear the ducks quacking — probably all mallards, I thought. But before we got to the rise blocking our view of the pond, Jamey's peregrine went streaking off to the east in a long, angular stoop. As often happens in open farm country, a pheasant walking along in the field caught the tiercel's attention, and he went off after it, launching a lightning-fast sneak attack. The pheasant had other ideas. It flushed early and made it easily to the safety of cover. So our duck slip had been ruined for nothing. Jamey called his bird back and fed him.

Shawn was up next. He quickly unhooded his tiercel gyrfalcon/peregrine hybrid and launched him into the clear blue sky. Although his bird didn't go quite as high as Jamey's tiercel peregrine, he reached a nice pitch and waited on steadily. We got three or four flushes on the mallards, but they would just fly from one pond to another, splashing down into the safety of the water as soon as the falcon came close. Still, the kid who went out with us couldn't get over how great the stoops were, and he kept asking us how to train the falcons to fly like that. He owned a red-tailed hawk he was hunting at rabbits, but I think from that morning onward, high-flying longwings would fill his dreams.

Shawn called the tiercel down and got out his other hybrid. This bird didn't fire. He landed on the crossbar of a huge double-power-line pole where a prairie falcon was perched. The two had a little scuffle, then Shawn called his bird back and we quit flying for the morning.

He planned to go out again in the evening to search for slips on prairie chickens.

Unlike hunting red grouse, sage grouse, sharp-tailed grouse, and many other game birds, for which a good pointing dog is essential, a falconer can usually get by without a dog when flying at prairie chickens. The technique is to park near a flat, wide-open stubble field and wait for the chickens to fly down and start foraging near dusk. When the falconer releases his falcon, the game birds will crouch down and hide. But it is vital to remember exactly where they are and try to flush them when the falcon is in a good position above them for a stoop. It works well in theory, though in practice it's often much more complicated. It takes hard work, a good falcon, and a lot of luck to take a greater prairie chicken. And so far, no one had succeeded at the entire meet. Shawn hoped to change that.

WHEN WE RETURNED to the hotel, we took part in a Thanksgiving lunch that had been set up for falconry-meet participants. Rachel and I sat at a table with Kent Carnie, John Swift, and Peter Devers, all from the Archives of Falconry, and Christian Saar, so we ended up talking mostly about the history of falconry. Later, Rachel decided to spend the rest of the day working on a writing project, so I strode aimlessly around the weathering yard, looking for other falconers to hang out with.

Dave Cherry was getting ready to fly, so I started walking back to my car to get in line behind the other vehicles. I saw Eckart Schormair — who for many years was president of Germany's national falconry organization, the Deutscher Falkenorden — and offered to give him a ride to the field. Before we reached my car, though, we ran into Steve Martin (the well-known professional bird trainer who has designed bird shows around the world, not the comedian), and he offered to drive both of us, along with Steve Chindgren.

We followed Dave and Lisa Cherry and another falconer's truck for nearly an hour, traveling far from town; we finally stopped beside a field that had been productive earlier in the meet. The other two trucks continued on up the road to wait at other spots for prairie chickens to show up. They were supposed to call us if they saw anything. It seemed like we sat next to the field forever. We finally got a call from Dave. He had seen a single chicken fly across in front of them and land on a hilltop. It seemed like a long shot, but because it was so late he decided to try for a flight at the lone bird.

As we got there, Dave had already let his dog out and was getting his hybrid tiercel ready to fly. He walked to the edge of the fence and held his bird into the wind. And he waited ... and waited ... and waited. Steve Martin took a few pictures of Dave standing there waiting for his bird to take off. He used one of the pictures the following evening in his talk as an example of how important it is to be patient with a bird and not try to rush it. Dave had waited nearly ten minutes, even though the sky was quickly darkening.

Dave's falcon finally took off, and then the bird was all business, rocketing up to a lofty pitch, high above the field. We had a long walk ahead of us up the hill, and very little time. When we got to the crest of the hill, the prairie chicken miraculously flushed, right beneath the waiting on falcon, and the chase was on. The falcon clipped the chicken in a beautiful stoop, knocking out a fistful of feathers, but it was a glancing blow, and the grouse went streaking away, vanishing in the dim light. But his falcon was still in the air, remounting nearly all the way to his original pitch. We could see him silhouetted against the sky, although where we were, at ground level, it was nearly pitch black. Suddenly a small flock of grouse came shooting past, and Dave's bird made another fabulous stoop, this time knocking one down and going into the grassy cover after it. We had to use telemetry to find his bird, but when we got to the falcon, he didn't have the grouse.

A few us went searching for the prairie chicken, in case it was injured. But it blasted away unscathed. The falcon was already being fed. Ekhardt complimented Dave on what a great flight his falcon had made, but Dave wouldn't hear of it.

"No, it was awful," he said. "He usually goes up twice as high." Dave is the consummate purist and probably rarely sees a flight he considers adequate.

෴

AS WE WERE hawking with Dave Cherry, Shawn was having quite a different falconry experience. He took a large group of international falconers with him, perhaps fifty or sixty in all, following behind in several vehicles. They broke up into a handful of smaller groups and staked out some fields, watching intently for prairie chickens to come flying in low over the cornfields and land to feed. Representatives from the North American Falconers' Association had already visited all the farmers in the area in advance to explain what would be going on at the meet and to get permission to fly hawks on their land, and they printed handouts for falconers to give to landowners. Although everything had been set up well in advance, NAFA still wanted people to stop at houses before hawking on private property. It was working well, and the local people seemed to enjoy the falconers being there.

Shawn had a long wait, but he finally spotted a group of prairie chickens cruising into the field and landing. It was getting late, but he decided to gather together as many of the visiting falconers as possible to see the flight. Many of them hadn't been able to see a falcon fly yet. At American falconry meets, it often seems as though people hang around all day with nothing happening, and then everyone jumps into cars and dashes away in a brief flurry of activity. People who are not ready for that tend to get left behind. Then at dawn or earlier, groups form again and go. This is the exact opposite of European falconry meets, at which everything is planned to the smallest detail, and people who want to see hawking just have to be there at the correct time and place.

Shawn wanted to make sure everyone got to see a good flight. He left someone at the other field to make sure the chickens didn't leave and then hurried to round everyone up. Suddenly it seemed as though dozens of falconers started gathering at the edge of the field, waiting to see a wonderful flight. But although dusk was quickly descending, Shawn still felt he should stop at the farmhouse and tell the people what he was doing. He chatted with the elderly couple there, and they said it was fine to fly his falcon on their land. Walking out past their house, he strode quickly into the field, taking off his falcon's equipment as he walked. He already had the telemetry transmitter rigged up. When he removed his falcon's hood, it was obvious the bird was excited and ready for a peak performance. He pumped his wings eagerly then took off, ringing up in tight circles, less than a hundred yards in diameter, corkscrewing up above Shawn. His rate of ascent was astounding. Shawn's tiercel quickly became a tiny speck and still he climbed. A murmur went through the crowd. Everyone knew something awesome was going to take place. The excitement was palpable. Shawn walked carefully onward, probably now less than forty yards away from the prairie chickens. No need to rush it. The falcon was still climbing.

But suddenly a truck came driving into the field honking. Shawn barely noticed at first; his concentration was total. He had permission; there should be no problem. And a couple of falconers who had spoken with most of the landowners before the meet were back in the crowd. They could take care of it.

"Get the hell out of here, you hear me?" a man shouted from the truck. Shawn glanced back briefly and saw a falconer walking toward the truck. He looked back up at his falcon, nearly impossible to see at his altitude, and continued walking toward the chickens, now crouched down less than twenty yards away.

"Damn it, get out of here!" the man screamed. "I got a gun and I'm going to shoot your bird if you don't leave right now."

A falconer called out to Shawn. "You better call your bird down," he said.

Shawn looked back, stunned. "You're kidding," he said.

"No. He's got a gun, and he's mad. Better just get your bird down."

Shawn was in shock, as were all the falconers watching, particularly the ones from other countries, most of whom had never seen American falconry. They all had wanted to see the stoop, which everyone knew would be colossal. Instead, Shawn walked out of the field onto the edge of the road and called his bird to the lure. Even his falcon must have been astounded to be called down without a flush.

As Shawn walked back through the crowd, people milled around him offering condolences for the spoiled flight. One woman wept. Christian Saar told Shawn that in all his years as a falconer he had never seen a bird fly as well as that and was so sorry that he didn't get to flush game for his falcon. Christian later told me he was sure the man in the truck had done this because Shawn is black. And we later found out that the man didn't even own the property; he was a brother-in-law or some other relation of the landowners, and he'd had a few too many drinks at Thanksgiving dinner.

e⁓

IT WAS INTERNATIONAL night that evening, and all of the programs dealt with hawking overseas. Gilles Nortier from France showed pictures of his annual hawking vacations in Scotland, where he and Patrick Morel of Belgium lease a fine grouse moor not far from Lochindorb. The pictures filled me with regret that I hadn't taken time to visit Gilles and Patrick the previous September in Scotland.

A young man from the Czech Republic, wearing a traditional loden jacket with detailed embroidery, had numerous still photographs and a five-minute film taken at a falconry meet in his home country. The films were particularly graphic and astounding, goshawks attacking and being knocked around by huge nine-pound European hares and golden eagles catching everything from hares to roe deer and even foxes. In a castle yard at the end of the day, the hunters displayed the game their birds had caught, with pine boughs arrayed colorfully around them. Everyone was impressed.

e⁓

WE MET IN the hotel lobby promptly at six-thirty the next morning, and this time everyone was there and ready to go. Jamey would fly his tiercel again. Shawn was going along, too, but wasn't going to fly until the evening. After the night before, he was absolutely determined to catch a prairie chicken. Several other falconers showed up before we left.

When we got to the field — a different one from where we had flown the day before — I sneaked out to the high rim of the pond and peeked over to see if any ducks were around. This was right at dawn and the sky was just lightening — Jamey's favorite time to fly. The pond was fairly long and had a decent-sized flock of teal on it. I ducked down instantly and hurried away from the edge. This was all Jamey needed to know. He walked back well away from the pond and the small crowd of falconers and held up his tiercel. His bird didn't mess around. He went roaring up to a staggeringly high pitch, and we all began walking quickly to the pond, picking up rocks as we went along to throw into the water.

There's something about the explosion of a flock of ducks bursting from a pond that makes a falconer's heart race. I heard the air whistling through the tiercel's flight feathers as he plummeted down in a steep vertical stoop — which made the denouement all the more anticlimactic as the teal sidestepped his stoop. We all dropped to the ground, hoping to avoid prematurely flushing any ducks that might remain on the pond. Jamey's bird seemed eager to fly and quickly remounted once again to a lofty pitch. On the reflush, he repeated the fine stoop and this time knocked a teal down, threw up vertically at the spot, and went right back down. But the duck escaped — not an uncommon occurrence with a green-winged teal, one of the quickest and slipperiest waterfowl around. Jamey called his bird down and gave him a well-deserved feed. Rachel and I went back to town and had breakfast with Jamey and Shawn.

Later that day would be the last chance to take game at the meet. The banquet was set for that evening, and the next morning most people would start scattering across the country — and the world — to return home. I definitely wanted to go hawking with Shawn and see if the state of Nebraska would make amends for his terrible experience the day before.

As people gathered that afternoon, the word was out. All of the falconers who had gone with Shawn the day before were there, plus one or two dozen more, all intent on seeing if his bird would repeat its astonishing performance — only this time with a flock of grouse flushing beneath him.

I hitched a ride with Frank Bond, and we joined the lengthy line of cars. We drove to the same general area of yesterday's little misadventure and hoped for the best. Apparently everything had been smoothed over and nothing like that was supposed to happen again.

Most people parked in one area beside a farm where they could sit and wait while a few of us drove away and stationed ourselves in strategic places to watch for incoming prairie chickens. We sat for forty-five minutes or more and then got a call from Shawn. This was it: Some chickens had flown into the field not far from where everyone was parked. When we got there, Shawn and Jamey were walking into the field with a falconer from Spain, and a minute later Shawn's tiercel was in the air.

And it was good. He circled higher and higher and higher, pumping constantly as he rose up in a tight circle above the three falconers. I put my 10x binoculars on Shawn, who was already well out into the field, and I had a perfect view of the prairie chickens bursting into the air. I quickly looked up, straining to find the tiercel, and there he was, a streak against the blue prairie sky, hurtling down, gaining speed with every pump of his wings until he folded up completely into a strange silver projectile, unlike anything else in nature. And then prairie chicken feathers exploded everywhere and Shawn's bird was going right back up in a vertical arc from his stoop, letting his momentum carry him all the way. The prairie chicken seemed unfazed, flying away strongly toward a distant fence line with brush at the bottom. But the tiercel never gave up. He tail-chased the chicken all the way to cover, crashing in right behind it. And this time he had it: a beautiful greater prairie chicken cock.

And it was such a proud moment. Shawn with his prairie chicken — the only one taken at the meet — and caught in full view of all the foreign falconers, many of whom now rushed out to greet him. But than an astonishing thing happened. From out of nowhere a man in hunting clothes came racing across the field driving an all-terrain vehicle. When he got close, he jumped off his four-wheeler and raced up to Shawn, who suddenly looked sick.

"Did you get one?" the man yelled before noticing the chicken Shawn held in his right hand. And this was the most amazing thing — he threw his arms around Shawn in a great bear hug and picked him up off the ground. It turned out that this was the friendly farmer who had been helping everyone find game to hunt. He was so excited about Shawn catching a prairie chicken he couldn't contain his glee. But something about the way he had looked racing up on that four-wheeler — particularly after what had happened the night before — had given everyone chills.

Shawn got over it quickly. He was walking on air as he strode back up the road to his truck, feeding his tiercel as he went. But he still took time to have a five-minute talk with three farm kids who came running out of their house to see what was going on. He finally apologized to them. "I'd like to stay here talking with you longer, but you see all those people up there?" he said, nodding toward the huge group of falconers gathered by their cars and trucks a hundred and fifty yards away, eagerly awaiting him. "They came from all over the world, and they want to see the prairie chicken my falcon caught. But I'm sure I'll see you again out here sometime, and I'll tell you all about falconry." It was the perfect end to a remarkable falconry meet.

15

THE SARACEN
CITADEL

AFTER A LONG rainy night, the morning broke clear and sunny. I was excited to be waking up in Lucera and eager to start exploring the heart of Frederick II's realm, in one of his favorite cities — a place rich in history. I'd already been in Italy for several days, spending the first night in Rome and having dinner with Frikky and his wife and some of the people I'd met in Scotland. Then I traveled to several Frederick II sites, but there wasn't much to see at them.

I had started by blasting east to the Adriatic coast of Italy and then north to Ancona and west about twenty miles to Jesi — a pretty town with an imposing buttressed medieval wall. It was here in a pavilion tent in the market square that Frederick was born on the day after Christmas in 1194. His mother, Constance of Sicily, had been rushing south to attend her husband's coronation in Palermo. Henry IV was already Holy Roman Emperor but was now to become King of Sicily, adding greatly to his empire.

Constance was forty years old when Frederick was born — at that time considered quite old to be giving birth. To allay suspicions that Frederick was not really her son, she had the tent set up in the public square and allowed the matrons of the town to come and go freely, witnessing the birth and seeing her breast-feed him for a couple of days after. (Despite this precaution, rumors spread that Frederick was actually the child of a butcher, not the son of Henry IV and Constance.)

The square where this remarkable event took place is still there and is now called the Piazzo Federico II. A large stone monolith and a plaque commemorate Frederick's birth, and several local businesses are named after him.

It was nice visiting Frederick's birthplace, but Jesi did not figure largely in his later life. I knew I needed to head south and explore the cities and villages of Apulia, where Frederick spent much of his life. My next stop was Foggia — a city Frederick loved and where his heart was kept in a casket for several centuries. Unfortunately, a powerful earthquake devastated the city in the eighteenth century. (Frederick's heart was lost in the quake.) And later, during World War II, Foggia was absolutely hammered by Allied bombers. I was disappointed. The city is now a shabby, ugly place with nothing to suggest its rich history. All that remains of Frederick II's great imperial palace is part of an archway with two stone eagles that is inset into the outer wall of the civic museum.

Frederick rode from Foggia in early December 1250, on the last hawking excursion of his life. He took ill with a recurring intestinal infection, so he and his entourage headed for Lucera, home of his beloved Saracens. But his symptoms became so severe he had to stop short at Castel Fiorentino, a few miles north of Lucera. According to the lore of Frederick II, a prophecy told that he would die beside an iron gate in a place with a name associated with flowers. For this reason, he always avoided the city of Florence. While he lay abed at Castel Fiorentino, Frederick asked the name of his resting place. He blanched when he heard it and commanded that the stucco be removed from the wall beside his bed. When the workmen smashed through it with huge hammers, the falling plaster revealed an old iron doorway leading up to the keep. That's when Frederick knew the prophecy would be fulfilled, and he would die here — or at least that's how the story goes.

I found little left of Castel Fiorentino and the surrounding town —just quiet, windswept ruins near present-day Torremaggiore. Five years after Frederick II's death, Pope Alexander IV sent troops to destroy Fiorentino, and the residents had to flee for their lives.

So, in just a couple of days I had traveled from Frederick's birthplace to the place where he died, stopping in between at the city where he left his heart. But I still felt I knew little about the man. Nothing really remained that had been there in his day. I hoped that would change as I explored more of Apulia. I was glad finally to be in Lucera, which had figured so prominently in the Frederick saga. It was here on the site of an ancient Roman stronghold that Frederick solved the dilemma of the rebellious Saracens on the island of Sicily. He uprooted thousands of them and brought them to Lucera, establishing a thriving Arab colony, where they could continue their cultural traditions and practice their religion without restriction. Though it sounds cruel to move a people en masse, a lesser medieval monarch would probably have exterminated them. Instead Frederick embraced them. He employed thousands of Saracen archers in the Imperial Army, and he always traveled with a Saracen guard. He felt they were his most trustworthy soldiers because the Pope could never coerce them with threats of excommunication or promises of heavenly favors.

The first stop in my explorations of Lucera was the great castle I had walked around just before dark the night before. This time the gates were open, and I strolled around the grassy inner courtyard, gazing at the ruins. I saw two middle-aged women working at a small tourist building — a shack, really — inside the castle walls, and I tried to ask them about the history of the place. They didn't speak a word of English, but they handed me some maps, brochures, and other literature, some of which were understandable enough to be useful.

The castle walls and towers were impressive — the only problem was they were not built by Frederick but by Charles of Anjou, who had conquered Frederick's kingdom in southern Italy after his death and destroyed the Hohenstaufen dynasty at the bidding of the Pope. All that remained of Frederick II's fabulous palace was a foundation of stone blocks that had been excavated from the lawn in the interior of the castle. The original building blocks that formed the walls of Frederick's palace had no doubt been plundered centuries ago to erect other structures in Lucera — just as Frederick had used Roman blocks to build his palace.

A short time later, I decided to look around the old medieval section of the city. The roads there were hopelessly narrow and winding, so I didn't want to attempt driving. I parked on a main road, as close as I could get. I should admit here that I am directionally challenged at times. (One girlfriend years ago used to call me "Wrong Way Gallagher.") And nothing is more confusing than trying to find your way around an ancient town or city. But I've managed over the years to develop coping mechanisms, such as taking elaborate mental notes, forcing myself to remember key directions and landmarks whenever I'm going through unknown terrain.

Whenever I feel as though I really need an outside aid, I reach for a compass. This was one of those times. I approached that medieval town like it was an orienteering course, taking compass headings everywhere I went and jotting them down in my notebook, along with any street names or descriptions of landmarks I passed. I was determined not to get lost. I followed the tiny yellow metal signs pointing the way to the cathedral. It was a wonderful walk. The narrow streets were charming, paved with flat stones, exquisite buildings rising vertically on both sides. And suddenly I came out into a picturesque square with the cathedral on one side. More than a dozen men loitered in the square, lazing quietly in the pleasant morning sunlight or talking in small groups here and there. One man leaned against the side of a car, holding two live red chickens upside down by their legs. He was in the middle of a conversation and seemed indifferent to the chickens.

Although it was Friday, it seemed to be a church day, and people were starting to congregate on the steps of the cathedral. I slipped inside, hoping to take some pictures of the interior. The bells began ringing and people streamed inside, kneeling and crossing themselves before making their way to the pews. A couple of very short nuns scuttled past. One of them, who clipped along using short metal crutches with arm clamps, seemed barely more than waist high compared to me.

It was a beautiful cathedral, built by Charles II in the early fourteenth century. I wondered what the mosque that had originally stood on this spot had looked like. The presence of the Saracens and their mosque in the heart of Christendom had always been a thorn in the side of the popes who fought against Frederick II. After Charles of Anjou wrenched control of the Kingdom of Sicily from the Hohenstaufens, he laid siege to the city of Lucera and ultimately defeated the Saracens. Any who refused to convert to Christianity were put to the sword, and their mosque was later razed to the ground. Such was the end of Arab culture in Lucera. As I stood in the cathedral, I wondered how many people had been cut down right here.

I walked outside and went looking for the local museum, which was supposed to be nearby. I had seen several small yellow metal signs pointing the way to the museum, similar to the ones I had followed to the cathedral, but I just couldn't find it. I would see a sign and follow it until I found another sign and then another, but invariably, I always came to a sign pointing me back in the direction from which I had just come. It was frustrating.

I went back to the square in front of the cathedral and saw several policemen in black uniforms hanging around, smoking cigarettes and enjoying the sunshine, pausing occasionally to stare as a pretty woman strode past. I went up to one of them and asked, "Parla inglese?" He did not. I showed him the museum's name, which I had written on my pad. He shrugged, then walked over to talk with another policeman. He seemed clueless, too. The policeman came back and waved his arms in a large circular motion in front of me, as though describing a zero. I had no idea what he was trying to tell me, but I thanked him and went on my way. I tried going down several more streets before giving up and making my way back to my car.

I decided to look for the first century B.C. coliseum, which, according to a popular tourist book, lay just at the eastern edge of the city limits. I pulled my compass out again and tried to find the place. I finally reached a spot where the road was blocked, and I could go no farther. Then I noticed it, down the road in a trash-strewn field past a chainlink fence. Although it was covered with scaffolding and obviously being repaired, I could plainly see the imposing gateway of the coliseum, with a Latin inscription above the twin columns, too faint and damaged to be legible from this distance. I only wish I could have gotten inside and looked around.

❧

AROUND MIDDAY, I decided to embark for the next stop on my Frederick II odyssey — the town of Melfi. After a long search for a gas station, I fueled up and headed cross-country through fields and farmland. This was really flat country. It made Kansas look positively mountainous. Places like Lucera are an anomaly, rising several hundred feet on a hill above the endless flatlands in this part of Apulia. These are the true hinterlands of Italy — the least touristy part of the country, and few people speak English. It is the breadbasket of Italy, beloved of Mussolini, who had big plans for the region, but not much came of those plans. The height of Apulia's power and glory came during the reign of Frederick and not much has happened there since.

❧

MELFI IS THE market town of an extensive olive-growing area. It is much hillier than the Tavoliere, where I had been. The city stands on a hill on the foothills of Mount Vulture, an extinct volcano. As I got off the highway and drove the short distance to Melfi, I spotted the castle at once, an immense stone edifice looming high on a steep hill. The medieval city stands beside it on the same hill. A ditch is still visible, along with ten towers and almost two miles of defensive walls. It's easy to see why the site was chosen. No army in those days, no matter how large, could have taken Melfi through a direct assault, without an enormous loss of life. That's why the siege was such an important military tactic in the Middle Ages. The attackers would surround a city, not allowing any supplies to get through, and attempt to starve the defenders into submission. It took enormous willpower on both sides to succeed.

I drove out on a road that ran along the bottom of the hill, below the castle, and stopped to take a few pictures. But I was eager to get inside the castle and look around. Since the 1970s, it has housed the Museo Nazionale Archeologico, a well-regarded museum. Getting there was not easy. Like many of these medieval hilltop Italian cities, it was a maze of tight little streets winding here and there, with numerous one-way streets that invariably seem to be leading in the opposite direction from where I needed to go. But I was stubborn — and I had my compass. I didn't care if I had to go in the wrong direction for a while, as long as I kept the correct compass bearing in my head and ultimately pushed myself slowly in that direction. I finally reached the entrance to the castle and found a place to park on the road leading up to it.

A curious thing happened when I went to buy a ticket to enter the castle and museum. As always, the person working there spoke no English, but I indicated to her through sign language (actually pointing at the admission sign) that I wanted to go inside. I held out a twenty-euro note. It was always my strategy to hand people more than enough money and then get change, so I didn't have to count out the various coins. She took out two tickets, imprinted them with her official stamp, and handed them to me with my change. I started to walk away and realized that she had charged me for two admissions. I went back and told her, "No, No. Just me." I held up a single finger and pointed to myself. This happened a couple of more times during the trip, as though no one could believe I was traveling alone.

I spent quite a bit of time walking through the museum and looking at the many exhibits. The ancient relics of the Romans and Etruscans were wonderful. The most magnificent piece was a sarcophagus from Rapolla with a carving of a Roman lady. But I was disappointed by how little the museum had about Frederick II. I found only a single panel about him, and it was written in Italian. I thought they would have at least a room devoted to him, perhaps with information on the Constitutions at Melfi (also called the Liber Augustales) of 1231 — arguably the finest example of modern written law since Roman times and one of the highest achievements of Frederick II's reign. The legal system of the kingdom had largely broken down after the death of Frederick's father, and this was his attempt to create order from the chaos and also to promulgate a fairer judicial system. Before this time, no uniform law of the land existed — almost every city had its own set of rules and regulations and tax codes. Frederick eliminated trial by combat, which he said did not prove who was in the right but only who was the stronger or better fighter. He created a bureaucracy of paid officials who were not local feudal rulers or churchmen. And he created an early form of free-trade zone, eliminating internal tariffs within the Kingdom of Sicily.

AS I LEFT the castle, I decided to stroll along the grassy area below the outer walls and take some pictures from a different perspective. I hadn't gone far when a feral dog dashed out with bared teeth, snarling and lunging at me. I grabbed a stick and tried to keep him at bay. The joke was, it was tiny — a rat dog, barely the size of a fox — but it was crazy and came at me all teeth like a piranha. I figured I could intimidate the dog if I were aggressive, so I ran at him shouting. This only infuriated the little beast, which suddenly shot through the air at me. I fended him off with my stick, like a fencer parrying an attack, and backed away carefully, never taking my eyes from him. After a few more parries, he grabbed the end of the stick in frustration, flinging his body around this way and that, growling in a frenzied, Lilliputian rage.

Then I got lucky. As I backed farther and farther away, he started losing interest in me. Maybe I had gotten off his turf. Maybe he thought he had beaten me. Whatever. He eventually broke off the attack and strode proudly back to the little ditch he had burst from when I first saw him. But what was I to do now? It was too far and the hillside was too steep to walk around the entire castle and make my way to the first passage through the city walls. I started thinking about my options — what it might be like to be bitten by a strange, possibly rabid dog in a foreign country. Then I remembered: you have about a month after being bitten by a rabid animal to complete the series of anti-rabies injections. I'd be home in a couple of weeks, so maybe everything would be OK. Maybe I wouldn't even have to go to the doctor until I got back home.

I decided to make my way back to the car. I started sneaking slowly and quietly along the bottom of the castle wall and got amazingly far before the dog noticed me. Then I burst like a sprinter, running full out, leaping a low fence and racing, racing, racing down the cobbled street. I had my key fob out and pressed down on the unlock button right before I reached the car. I dove inside and slammed the door behind me just as the little shark smashed into the side of the car. I rolled the window partway down and barked and snarled at him while firing up the engine. He was biting at the tires in a rage when I pulled away.

As I left Melfi, a huge fire burned on the far side of Mount Vulture. Was it deliberately set, perhaps an agricultural burn of some kind? Or was it a forest fire raging out of control? I don't know, but the smoke billowed up as if from a volcano (which Mount Vulture had been thousands of years earlier) and filled the sky.

According to my calculations, Lagopasole Castle wasn't much farther down the highway, so I started racing toward it, trying to fit in one more Frederick site before settling down for the night. Of course, it wasn't on any of the maps I had. This became a constant problem during my entire trip. Many of the roads, towns, and villages I encountered were not on my maps. So if I had a route planned in which I was supposed to turn right at the third road past a certain town there could be a problem — there might be several roads going right that were not on the map. So how could I figure out which was the third road? They certainly were not marked well. I took the wrong road several times. Eventually I might run into a village with its name stated plainly on a sign as I drove through and would think: *Good — now I can find it on the map and figure out where I am.* But when I checked the map, the village wouldn't be there. This was the case with Lagopasole, which has a decent-sized town of the same name below it. What I really needed was something like a Delorme guide, with every possible detail included.

I wondered if I would recognize Lagopasole. All I knew was that it was on a prominent hill twenty miles or so north of the city of Potenza. But it turned out I saw the castle looming ahead in the distance, beautifully lit by the afternoon sun, long before I got there. This was a place commanding a magnificent view of the surrounding area. No armies could possibly sneak up here unseen. Frederick spent his summers at Lagopasole toward the end of his life. It was far cooler up there than in the blazing flatlands of the Tavoliere.

I wound through the town of Lagopasole and made my way up to the castle, at the highest point of the hill. It was still open when I arrived. I walked across the open courtyard inside the castle walls and went into a small bookstore. A woman in the back talked animatedly on a telephone as I glanced around at the various books and DVDs. Nothing was in English. I kept hoping she would get off the phone and let me know if I had to pay anything to look around the inside of the castle. I finally stood very near her for a few minutes. She still ignored me, so I decided to walk past her and enter the inner castle. This got her attention instantly, and she told me in Italian that I would have to pay to go inside. I handed her a five-euro bill, and she tried to give me two tickets.

Lagopasole is an interesting place, but like many of Frederick's castles I was to visit, it had been entirely renovated. It had modern glass windows and was comfortably heated. I wished I could find a castle someplace that was maintained exactly as it had been in the Middle Ages. I wanted to see exactly the kind of rugs and wall hangings they used. I wanted to experience what the heating and lighting were like. The way this castle was renovated gave me very little feeling for what it must have been like to live there.

The castle did have one interesting exhibit — a gleaming steel column in which falcon images from below were reflected: a peregrine, a gyrfalcon, a saker, and a lanner. They appeared to move as I circled around the column.

Lagopasole had been one of Frederick's favorite castles, built to his own design. I took a hike along the hill behind the castle before I left. It was so quiet. I sat for a time, soaking up the atmosphere. I could hear the tinkle of the bell on a sheepdog's collar and the words of the shepherd as he spoke to his dog far below.

I could have sat there for hours, but it was already getting late. I knew I should try to find a place to stay for the night. I figured I had only thirty-five minutes or so until it was dark, and I had no idea where to go. The town of Lagopasole was pretty and quaint, but I didn't see anything that looked like a hotel. As I drove past a few shops, heading northeast, the town petered out, and I was suddenly in the land of mad dogs again, as two huge brutes charged my car, putting their massive paws right on the hood and barking in my face. I just shook them off and drove on.

That was the start of an awful night. I could see it unfolding, but there was nothing I could do about it. I saw a small sign just outside of town that seemed to indicate there was a place to sleep up ahead. But after following the direction a few miles, I found a similar sign pointing back the other way. Of course, my big problem was that I badly needed advice, but I was unable to communicate effectively with anyone. I was like a person with severe disabilities: I couldn't hear, speak, or read. I was cut off in almost every way from humanity. As nightfall finally took hold over the land, I decided to head to Potenza. Surely a city of that size would have a hotel. The only question was would I be able to find it?

I blasted to Potenza and got off the highway on what looked like a main thoroughfare, but all I could find were huge financial buildings, then various industrial plants. I was clearly in the wrong part of town, but where to go? I pulled over near a factory and started looking through my maps and my tour guidebook with a flashlight. I found the name of a hotel in Potenza, but how would I ever locate it? The street address meant nothing to me. I didn't have a map of Potenza. And I hadn't been able to find a SIM card for my cell phone, so I had no way of calling anyone.

As I sat there, a car pulled up behind me with a couple of tough-looking teenagers inside. Maybe they were harmless. I don't know. When they stepped out of their car and were walking up behind mine, I fired up the engine and raced away. No reason to take a chance.

It was getting late now, and the temperature was plummeting. This was, after all, mid-December in the Apennines. I began to imagine what it would be like to sleep in that tiny Fiat Panda, and it was not a pleasant thought. I stopped at a gas station and tried to explain my predicament. Neither of the men understood what I needed. One of them pulled a pack of cigarettes from the rack behind him and held it out to see if that might be what I wanted.

I drove back to Lagopasole to see if I might have missed something. I still didn't see anything that looked like a hotel. By this time I really was considering just sitting up in the front seat of the car all night, depressed and shivering, but I wanted to find a place where I wasn't likely to be hassled by the police — or worse, by young thugs who might want to rob me. I started driving around on the roads outside of town. I spotted a place that looked like a restaurant up a steep driveway on the left and decided to check out. Walking inside, I didn't see anyone at first.

It looked brand new. It definitely was an eating establishment but the tables and chairs lay in darkness. Maybe it hadn't opened for the night yet. Or maybe it hadn't even opened up for business. I was hoping I could at least talk to someone.

A dark-haired middle-aged woman suddenly stepped into the room through a back door and gasped as she saw me standing there. "Sorry," I said, smiling. "Parla inglese?" She shook her head. "Um, um . . . hotel?" I asked. She stared blankly. "Albergo? Albergo?" I said, laying my head to one side on my hands like I was sleeping. She shook her head, indicating that they did not take boarders there. It looked like they were planning to do that at some point, but the upstairs was still under construction. I communicated as best I could, pulling out my cheap phrase book and reading it to her — asking if I could eat dinner there; asking if she knew of any place where I could stay.

A few minutes later, her husband came roaring up on the back of a four-wheel all-terrain vehicle driven by his chubby ten-year-old son. The man had his foot in a cast, which is why his son was driving the four-wheeler. We tried to talk to each other. Italian and English were hopeless. We both knew some Spanish, but it was French that worked best. I'd studied the language in high school and college and could get by passably well if people spoke slowly. He did not know the language well, but understood enough words to know basically what I wanted. He said his name was Salvatore. He tried to show me how he had been injured. As near as I could figure, he had fallen off the roof or some other high place during the building of the restaurant, hotel, or whatever it was. As we struggled along in our conversation, neither of us speaking in our native language, I came to understand that he was creating a place where people could stay and go trail riding on horseback in the surrounding hills. But it was nowhere near finished. They did not have a room for me, but I was welcome to eat dinner there, and his wife would make some phone calls, trying to find lodgings for me. Great. Things were starting to look up.

About this time, five or six other men — most of them in their sixties or older — came inside. They looked like peasants from an old Italian movie — short, stocky, most of them wearing Greek fishermen caps. He introduced them to me enthusiastically, like I was an old friend. I don't know what he said — maybe something like: "This is a poor deaf mute who stumbled in here this evening. He doesn't know who he is or where he's going. Please humor him while we figure out what to do with him." They all took turns shaking my hand, but none of us knew what to say.

They went out to the large room with the dinner tables and sat down. Salvatore motioned me to sit at a different table nearby, beside the fireplace. I had no idea what food was available, and I more or less told him to bring me whatever he had that he thought I'd like. The other men were having a huge meal, so he brought me plates of the same things they were having, beginning with prosciutto, bread, cheese, and various other appetizers. He also brought a small ceramic pitcher full of dark red wine, and it was good — or so it seemed, but maybe I was easy to please that night. Just being in a warm, dry place, eating piles of food and drinking wine, was enough to make me happy no matter what they served me.

Salvatore came in a few minutes later carrying some enormous pieces of split wood and piled them high in the fireplace. He overdid his enthusiasm for my well-being, though, because it soon became unbearably hot and smoky. And then the smoke alarm went off, emitting an ear-splitting, high-pitched sound that had me ripping chunks of Kleenex off and stuffing them in my ears. It didn't help. The other men seemed oblivious to the sound. They just talked and laughed louder.

Salvatore tried his best to fix the problem. He fooled around with a thermostat-like device beside the fireplace, then went outside on the other side of the wall behind the fireplace and started banging on something with a hammer. The sound continued. When he came back in, he apparently touched a reset button on the thermostat, and the noise abruptly quit, and it was the most amazing relief not to have to bear that horrid sound. But it was short-lived. A minute later, it was back on. He touched the button again and then tried to explain what was wrong — something about a broken pump that usually circulates water or air or something and keeps this from happening. And then the alarm came on again, and this time he gave up. He went back to the kitchen to get more food. I sat there feasting, eating every single scrap of food he gave me — until he brought what looked like a couple of raw lamb chops soaked in olive oil. He seemed disappointed when I turned my nose up at them, but they looked so unappetizing.

I tried to ask Salvatore a couple of times what was going to happen — where would I be spending the night? He just kept saying more or less don't worry about it, everything is taken care of, so I drank a little more wine and sat quietly enjoying the ambiance of the scorching-hot fire and the smoke alarm screaming in my ear. I still felt nervous about my fate for the evening, so I decided to settle up my bill and leave. It was a great bargain: he only charged me the equivalent of ten or twelve dollars, and I was stuffed and pleasantly high from the wine. I tried to leave a tip, but he wouldn't hear of it.

Salvatore and his wife attempted to explain what they had set up for me in terms of lodging. By this time, it was late and my mind was dulled from a combination of exhaustion, Apulian wine, and smoke-detector-induced deafness. I was clueless. They took me outside and pointed off in the distance into the darkness, trying to describe various left and right turns that would take me to some destination about twenty kilometers away, but it wasn't clear whether it was a hotel, a house, or a farm. I stared blankly at him. He finally shook his head and smiled, beckoning me to follow him. Despite his injured right foot, he was going to drive his tiny pickup truck to the place. He motioned me to follow him in my car. *This is great*, I thought. *Nothing can go wrong now.*

It was pitch dark out as we drove the winding road off the hill where Salvatore lived, so I stayed close behind. I finally saw a gas station up ahead on the right with some kind of tavern behind it. He turned in but drove beyond to another large building well behind it. I kept looking around for a sign of some kind indicating that this was a hotel or inn but saw nothing. The building was two stories high, and the entire lower level had floor-to-ceiling windows, revealing a huge, brightly lit dance floor to the right and a semidarkened restaurant area to the left. A wild party raged inside — perhaps a wedding or other large family event. The people were well dressed, varying in age from children to elderly people, but they all danced with reckless abandon to the rhythm of the rock band playing loudly at one side of the room. There was a folk-dance aspect to their movements, like some kind of reel with a frenetic, wholly Italian quality. I couldn't see anything that looked like a hotel entrance.

I ran to Salvatore's pickup truck before he could leave and pointed toward the party. "Hotel ... albergo?" I asked. He nodded, laughing. "Thank you for everything," I said. And then he was gone, driving off into the darkness. I took a deep breath and exhaled, then walked on the sidewalk toward the glass door leading into the party. It was the only door I could see. A man who looked unnervingly like Tony Soprano stood just outside the glass door, drawing deep breaths from a cigarette. Was he a guard of some kind — a bouncer? Or had he just come out to cool off and have a quick smoke? I don't know. "Albergo?" I asked. He shook his head and motioned his right arm toward another part of the building. I walked all the way around to the other side, but the only other door I saw led into the dimly lit dining area. I went inside, looking for someone to help me, and eventually found a waitress. "Albergo?" I asked. She looked perplexed at first but then led me to a small room in the back where a woman sat at a desk. She was clearly a manager of some kind.

She didn't speak English, so I went through my sign-language routine to let her know I needed a room for the night. I could see she was groping for the right words to use.

"Is problem," she said. "No ... um ... no heat."

"Is OK," I said. "No problem."

She clearly still had something else on her mind.

"Other problem," she said. She then went through an elaborate pantomime like she was turning on a faucet, having water splash down over her from an imaginary showerhead, and then shivering uncontrollably.

"Oh," I said. "No hot water?"

She nodded.

"Is no problem," I said. She could see there was no getting rid of me, so she finally opened a cabinet and pulled out a key, which was attached to a round brass ornament heavy enough to use as a blackjack. She got a blanket, sheets, and a pillow plus a towel and washcloth for me and had a busboy lead me upstairs to my room.

It looked like a dormitory room in a rundown, tenth-rate college, as charming as a prison cell. And the room was freezing. It was all starting to make sense now. This was the off-season in a place that doesn't even have an on-season for tourism. The hotel section was obviously closed for the winter and was being renovated. I was too tired to worry about it. I was happy I'd be able to stretch out in a full-length bed — as soon as I put the sheets and blanket on the mattress. It would be much better than trying to sleep huddled in the tiny blue Panda. This would be fine. I'd just brush my teeth and go to bed. As I turned on the faucet, rusty red water burst out, splashing all over the sink and me. I finally gave up, crawled into bed, and spent the rest of the night shivering. *Maybe this is what sleeping in a real medieval castle was like*, I thought.

16

THE EYE OF APULIA

I'M A MORNING person. No matter how bad the night before was, I'm usually OK when the sun comes up and the birds start singing. I wake up feeling like I can do anything. And this day was no different, even though I'd gotten only a couple of hours of miserably cold, shivering sleep.

A remarkable scene greeted my eyes as I went downstairs and stepped into the big room with the dance floor — the detritus of a wild night of partying. Streamers, crushed party hats, and empty wine bottles lay strewn underfoot. And the place was full of workers, pushing brooms, scrubbing walls and counters, climbing up ladders here and there to make various repairs.

"Excuse me," I said to one man. "Parla inglese?" He shook his head and left the room. A woman came out a minute later, but she couldn't speak English either. "Last night . . . albergo," I said, pointing upward in the direction of my room. I held out my wallet. She motioned for me to wait, and she went into the other room to make a phone call. When she came back, she was accompanied by three or four other women, all wearing rubber gloves. I guess this was the most exciting thing that would happen there all day. She told me I would have to pay twenty euros for my accommodations, but when I pulled out my credit card, she shook her head — I could only pay with cash. This might be a problem.

I hadn't seen an ATM machine since I left the autostrada a couple of days earlier, and I was running low on cash. I pulled my last five-euro bill from my wallet, then started digging through a small zippered pocket in my backpack where I'd been stashing my pocket change. I laid the five-euro bill on the bar and started stacking one- and two-euro coins beside it. Twelve euros ... thirteen euros. By the time I got to fifteen euros, I was already putting small change on the bar, even pennies. She stopped me when I reached seventeen-and-a-half euros.

"OK ... OK. Have a nice day," she said, using her one line of English.

"Thank you," I said. "I appreciate it. Have a nice day."

"Have a nice day," the other women repeated, giggling.

⁓

I GASSED UP at the filling station in front of the tavern and drove off, taking a secondary road cross-country toward Spinazzola, which would line me up in the general direction of Castel del Monte. I was hoping when I got that close I might be able to spot the castle. For centuries, superstitious peasants had called Castel del Monte the "Eye of Apulia," because it could be seen from so far away — a perpetual reminder of imperial oversight.

I had come to dread driving through the old medieval hill cities of Apulia, with their tight, mazelike streets, packed with traffic. But I needed these towns. They were like lodestars in my travel, letting me know I was headed the right way and providing another place where I could check the map and take a compass reading for my next destination, and so I set my sights on Spinazzola.

I've already confessed to being an idiot when it comes to finding my way around. And this is confounded by the fact that I am often distracted by birds — especially when I'm traveling in a foreign country where all of the birds seem so fresh and different. I'm particularly susceptible to raptors, and there were plenty of them on the open plains and rolling hills of Apulia: common buzzards (large soaring hawks, somewhat similar to American red-tailed hawks, though wimpier); red kites (spectacular fork-tailed scavengers that often hang high in the air like the child's toy named after them); and kestrels, everywhere kestrels, engaged in their characteristic flight, hovering stationary in the wind as they try to spot mice and insects below.

The vegetation was remarkably lush and green — contrary to what I'd heard about Apulia. But it was winter, a time few people travel there. I'm sure it must be parched brown in summer by the pitiless southern sun and swept by the scorching African winds, filling the air with choking dust that gets into everything.

As always, I tried to imagine what it was like for Frederick. Why did he like this place so much? Clearly, for someone hunting with wide-ranging, hard-flying raptors like gyrfalcons (long before the age of telemetry), the flatness and openness of the landscape was a great asset. Falconers could see a flight from a long distance away and ride along on horseback at a full gallop to keep the birds in view — without having to worry about being brought up short by a barbed-wire fence. And even now, in the twenty-first century, I saw few fences. The settlement patterns established centuries ago still held true there. The people built their settlements on the hilltops because they were defensible. In the Medieval Age and much earlier, the peasants would trudge miles or ride in ox-drawn carts each morning to the fields they tended, then return to their homes on the hilltops at night. Had they lived on the flatlands, they would have been vulnerable to any raiders — and there were many — sweeping across the land. But only a determined foe could harm them if they drew up into their walled hill towns and waited (with huge rocks in hand and hot cauldrons of oil to drop on their attackers).

I wondered what kind of game Frederick hunted here. There were certainly plenty of magpies around, which can provide a fun flight in an open place like this where they can't escape instantly to the safety of trees and dense cover, but that hardly seemed like the grand spectacle Frederick would have been after. And I saw plenty of hooded crows — like those that Nick Fox pursued with his peregrine/saker falcon hybrids in northern England — which sometimes ring up nicely in classic style when pressed by a falcon. He may even have been interested in hunting red kites. According to eighteenth-century falconers, these birds were a great quarry for gyrfalcons, ringing up superbly to escape the determined falcons, which were usually flown in a same-sex pair, called a cast. But what Frederick really loved to hunt were cranes and herons. The flights would cover miles, with the spectators galloping their horses to watch the falcons as they chased their quarry ever higher, sometimes into the clouds. The invention of barbed wire in the nineteenth century put an end to this kind of hunting in many places — it's just too dangerous for horse and rider. But I think a falconer could have good sport on crows here even now.

Frederick also wrote about hunting ducks with peregrines — what he called "hawking at the brook." This was done in the same style in which I fly Macduff, encouraging the falcon to wait on high above the falconer as he flushes game.

e⌢

I FINALLY SPOTTED an old train station, standing in a vast open field a couple of hundred feet from the highway. A white sign with bold black lettering stated simply "Spinazzola." I got off the highway as soon as possible and went back to the station. It was quaint but looked like it had been closed for years. The town was a couple of miles farther on, but at least I could see it now.

Like many of the towns and cities I encountered in Apulia, this one had an ugly industrial zone I had to drive through before reaching the town proper. It's almost as if they do everything they can think of to make a place uninviting, so you're already turned off to a city before you get to the main part, which might be lovely. But, of course, the traffic is so awful once you get inside these hill towns it's impossible to enjoy them — at least if you're driving. My shoulders and neck would lock up instantly as I headed uphill into yet another dense traffic jam, with cars honking all around me, trying to push their way in from every side road, while scooters blasted through everywhere. And invariably, little detours would appear, taking me away from the road I needed to be on but not providing any follow-up signs to get me back on the right track.

Spinazzola was like that. That day turned out to be a market day, and the road I needed to be on was blocked off to provide space for the vast street market. (I started popping ibuprofen tablets the minute my shoulder and neck muscles began seizing up, hoping to avoid a full-blown spasm in my back.) If I had looked at my maps a little more closely I'd have seen that I could easily have skirted Spinazzola, which is what I did the next time I passed through the area. But who cares? I was out of the maze. I escaped from the town and went blasting through the hills of Le Murge, moving ever closer to Castel del Monte. I made sure not to take the road to Minervino Murge, a significantly larger city than Spinazzola. Although this route would also have taken me to Castel del Monte, I had no wish to thread my way through another urban area. I wanted wide-open country roads and clear sailing.

↩

SEVERAL FRIENDS HAVE asked me why I chose to do this journey the hard way — renting a car and driving off into the unknown with no place to stay, no knowledge of the language, and no one to help me if I got into trouble. The simple answer is there was no other way. I tried again and again to find an easier way to explore Apulia (or Puglia, as it's often called now). I contacted the tourism bureau, hoping they might help set up an itinerary for me, but got nowhere. I visited libraries and bookstores. Despite having three shelves full of travel books devoted to Italy, the local chain bookstore didn't have anything on this part of the country. They all covered either popular cities such as Rome and Florence, or glamour regions such as Tuscany and the Amalfi Coast. I found nothing about Apulia, beyond a tiny section here and there in books about Italy. This was clearly the least touristy part of the country, for better or worse. I read that many Italians in the more cosmopolitan areas spurned Apulia and viewed it as a bleak land of peasants and vast agricultural fields. And some tourist guides warned of dangers — carjackings and robberies in Brindisi and other places I planned to visit. Even the *Lonely Planet Guide to Italy* (which is aimed at more adventurous travelers) cautioned that visiting Apulia would entail going well "beyond the comfort zone" of most American tourists — you actually have to interact face-to-face with the people.

I did extensive Internet searches but didn't find much — just a few hotel phone numbers, but when I called them, the people couldn't speak English. One semi-official tourism website said of the Apulian coast, "not many tourists make it this far and those who do probably do it to take the boat to Greece" — hardly a ringing endorsement.

At first I'd hoped that I could do some combination of riding trains and buses and walking to get around in Apulia. I really didn't want the responsibility of driving a rental car. But everything I read about the area indicated that renting a car was the only way to get around. Even Castel del Monte — one of the hottest tourist destinations in the area — was miles off the beaten track, especially in winter when few if any buses travel there.

⁊

I KNEW I was getting closer when I started seeing *trulli* in the fields alongside the road. These odd dwellings — which look almost like huge stone igloos — are found nowhere else. Rocks have never been in short supply in the region, so peasants were able to clear a field of stones and gather building materials at the same time. Many of these unique buildings were inhabited well into the twentieth century. Some have been modernized and are rented out to visitors as cottages. But most are either abandoned or are now used as farm outbuildings or shelters for sheep.

Castel del Monte emerged suddenly up ahead, unmistakable as it loomed up through the mist, high on a distant hill. Seeing it made me push the gas pedal down harder, and I raced toward it. I decided to get a hotel before visiting the castle. The weather had turned rainy and blustery, and after the tough time I'd had the night before, I really wanted to sleep in a comfortable place and eat a great meal. Just past the turnoff leading the last mile or so to the castle, I saw the entrance to the Castel del Monte Park Hotel, which was just what I was looking for. It had warm, comfortable rooms in some one-story buildings, plenty of free parking, and a restaurant. And the price was reasonable. I asked the woman at the desk if she could speak English. "Of course," she snapped back, almost insulted that I might think she didn't.

I noticed on the walls of the lobby as well as in the rooms they had nice prints of the artwork in the Vatican Library's copy of *De Arte Venandi cum Avibus*. They were printed on parchment, and an artist had dripped blotches of molten gold leaf on them, giving them a rich, distinctive look. I asked the desk clerk about them, and she said they were just some typical medieval art pieces. "No," I told her. "These are from Frederick

II's book on falconry." She shrugged and seemed unimpressed. She said she didn't know where they had come from.

I decided to take a room for two nights, so I could explore all day long and come back late, not having to worry about finding a place to stay before dark. It was a great relief. I locked my luggage safely in my room and headed to the castle, taking only my camera with me. I had to park well below Castel del Monte and walk the last hundred yards or so up the hill to reach it. There were more feral dogs here than at any other place I visited in Italy. And they were big. A massive white Great Pyrenees seemed to rule the pack, and I saw several pups that looked like him. Fortunately, these dogs were not vicious toward people. I think they lived on the handouts given to them by castle visitors. But I did see a dog fight there, with much snarling and snapping, as I sat in my car in the dirt parking lot, studying my map.

Before I went inside Castel del Monte, I walked around the entire building, taking pictures. It is a magnificent structure. Designed entirely by Frederick, it was built between 1229 and 1249, completed not long before his death. It is one of those places, like Stonehenge, that holds a special fascination for many people, who wonder if its design has a special, hidden significance. It's so unlike any other medieval building in Europe. The entire design is based on eights. It has an octagonal court-yard surrounded by eight trapezoidal rooms on both the top and the bottom floors, and eight towers (perhaps seventy-five feet high) — one at each corner of the octagon. Many articles and books have been written speculating on what this all means. Does it have some kind of astronom-ical significance, perhaps lining up perfectly with the sun or various con-stellations at particular times of the year? Is there some kind of strange mathematical symbolism about the castle's shape and the repetition of the number eight in every aspect of its design? Had Frederick II been influenced by the octagonal design of the spectacular seventh-century Muslim shrine, the Dome of the Rock (built over the sacred stone where Muhammad was said to have ascended into heaven), which Frederick had visited during his Crusade?

Did Castel del Monte have a military purpose? Many historians point out that it is too small, not really strategically placed, and does not have many of the effective defensive features typical of most military fortresses. Or was it just a curiosity — like a Victorian folly? I think there was a bit of the latter in Frederick's design. He was an artist as well as a scientist, a mathematician, and a poet. Perhaps he wanted to create something interesting, original, and enduring. It appears that he succeeded. In 1996, the United Nations Educational, Scientific, and Cultural Organization (UNESCO) declared Castel del Monte a World Heritage Site.

I spent a couple of hours inside the castle, exploring the lower rooms, the staircases leading to the second floor, the towers, and the upper rooms with their exquisite vaulted ceilings. The windows were larger in the upper rooms than those down below and provided spectacular views of the countryside for miles around. I sat in one window for a time, gazing out at the vast green landscape as the rains poured endlessly down. To me, as I thought more about it, this place was a falconer's lodge — similar in purpose to Steve Chindgren's hideaway in western Wyoming, but on a grander scale: a perfect place to stay with the falcons and dogs on a journey through the area. I didn't buy the wild speculation about Castel del Monte's deep mysterious symbolism. It was just a great place for a falconer to keep his birds. As I sat there, I pictured what it must have been like when the massive fireplaces were still intact in each of these upper rooms, when thick oriental rugs covered the floors and ornate wall hangings adorned the rooms and hallways. It is now stark and bare.

Castel del Monte lay abandoned for centuries, sometimes serving as a place to corral sheep, sometimes as a hideout for bandits. It was stripped bare of its marble and its sculptures long ago and stood quietly decaying almost to the present time. But a few years ago it underwent a major renovation. Again, I have mixed feelings about that. I'm glad they have stopped the deterioration of this magnificent edifice — but at the same time, I'm very sorry I didn't get to see it before it was renovated. Seeing it now as you walk up the hill, it looks like it could have been built last year: everything is so crisp and clean. I remember seeing pictures of it in the early 1970s, when I was first thinking about traveling there. It was a wild-looking place then, with bleak gray walls and dark shrubs growing on top, giving the castle a crazed feral look like the pack of dogs roaming outside its walls. And it had a peregrine nest on one of the towers, which is a symbol Frederick certainly would have appreciated. I didn't see any falcons there this time.

It was dark by the time I left the castle grounds and headed back to the hotel. I was feeling good about my journey again. There had been some sad parts; I often choked up as I visited these Frederick II sites. And I usually felt tense and physically exhausted by the late afternoon from the strain of driving in such difficult situations. But it was exciting to be visiting these places after so many years of dreaming about this trip, and I had already amassed a great collection of photographs that I downloaded from my camera to my laptop computer every night.

I decided to splurge on a great dinner that night, complete with wine and appetizers. Apulia was supposed to be famous for its cuisine, and I wanted to sample it more fully. I took a hot shower, dressed in clean clothes, and walked over to the restaurant. The woman who was working the front desk when I checked in was not there anymore, and no one could speak English, so I was thrust back into my verbally impaired state. I had no idea what to order, but I did see the word *pesce* in one of the entrée names, which looked similar to the Spanish name for fish, *pescado*. I pointed at it when the waiter came by. "Seafood?" I asked. He nodded.

I sat there blissfully waiting, sipping at my wine and munching on wonderful bread and appetizers. Then he came marching out, bearing my dinner proudly on a big platter. I hope I didn't blanch noticeably as he set it down in front of me. I looked at it for a moment then said thank you. I hardly knew where to begin. I just stared at it, a strange cartoon-like octopus plopped in the center of the platter with its long purple tentacles pointing outward around it, each one curled up, exposing its many suction cups. In place of its head, they had created a big round object out of thinly sliced, marinated squash, with a single large shrimp stuck on top so that it resembled the big red crest on a Roman helmet. I was so hungry, I just stared at it for a few seconds and then dove right in, cutting up each tentacle into bite-sized pieces and wolfing them down, followed by the squash, the shrimp, and everything else that looked half-way edible on my table. Then I washed it all down with the rest of my wine and walked back to my room, ready to face another day.

17

JEWEL OF THE HILL

I WOKE UP the next morning aglow with confidence, ready to take on Apulia and visit a few more castles. Maybe it was the octopus I ate the night before, maybe it was the wine, but the skies had cleared, the sun was shining, and I was ready to go. Frederick's castle at Gravina di Puglia turned out to be the easiest one to find on the whole trip. I just turned left out of the hotel parking lot, drove a few miles through the magical land of the *trulli* houses until the road ended at a T intersection, then turned left again and continued on the highway until I reached my destination.

In the old cities I'd been visiting, I usually headed to the central district or the historical section of the town, hoping I would run into the castle or church I was looking for — or at least find a sign pointing me in the right direction. But Frederick's castle at Gravina di Puglia was impossible to miss, high on a hill overlooking the western edge of the medieval city. I turned left off the highway and drove a short distance up the hill to a small, broken-glass-and-trash-strewn parking lot.

On this pleasant Sunday morning, I had the whole place to myself. I could hear church bells tolling across the town, summoning worshippers, as I stood on the breezy hill, gazing at a different kind of church — this one dedicated to falcons. Frederick named the castle Parco per Uccella-gione — "Park for the Birds" — and he had clearly built it as a base for his falconry activities in the area. You could say that my wish had finally come true: I was visiting a Frederick castle that had not been renovated. But it was sad. The place was utterly neglected — just one more throw-away ruin in a country filthy rich in archaeological sites from countless ancient cultures.

The castle had been an elaborate two-story structure enclosing an open rectangular courtyard, but now it stands a crumbling ruin, completely exposed to the wind and rain. The excellent craftsmanship is still evident in the cut stonework, especially in the gateway and in the high section of outer wall at the far end of the castle. But the courtyard is strewn with rubble, with bushes and shrubs growing up everywhere, even on top of the walls. I made a complete circuit of the outside of the castle, strolling along below the walls and through the trees growing on one side. The place reeked of urine. The walls were badly marred with graffiti, both old and modern: some of it carved into stone, some of it spray-painted on. Garbage lay strewn everywhere: plastic grocery bags hanging from trees; beer and wine bottles, papers, Styrofoam cups, and used condoms on the ground — the detritus of a lost empire.

I stood quietly for a time, taking in the view of the surrounding countryside. As I watched, a kestrel blasted past, trying to sneak up on some prey that was invisible to me. I watched the small falcon with my binoculars until I lost sight of it behind some trees. I could feel a sense of melancholy descending over me as I hung around the bleak shell of Frederick's castle. I decided to go exploring in town.

Gravina di Puglia has a long and interesting history and has been conquered many times. Like many areas near the Adriatic coast of southern Italy, it was once part of Magna Graecia — Greater Greece. But the Romans conquered the city in 305 B.C. (A well-preserved Roman bridge still stands nearby.) Gravina stood right on Rome's most important ancient road, the Appian Way, leading from the port of Brindisium (now called Brindisi) all the way to Rome — more than 350 miles away. In later years, the city was ruled by the Byzantines, Lombards, and even for a time by North African Arabs. It was subsequently conquered by the Normans and became part of the Kingdom of Sicily, which Frederick inherited as a child.

I've heard two stories about how the city got its name. According to one, Gravina is a shortened version of the motto Frederick II gave to the city: *Grana dat at vina* ("It gives grain and wine") — not an inappropriate motto for anywhere in Apulia, the breadbasket of Italy and a major wine producer. Others claim it was named after the ravine that cuts through it, and this seems more likely — *gravina* is the Italian word for "ravine." The medieval section of the city balances right at the edge of the ravine, which has some amazing cave dwellings carved into it, including an entire church.

❧

MY NEXT TARGET was Frederick's castle at Gioia del Colle, due east on the road to Brindisi. I liked the name, which means, "Jewel of the Hill," and I was eager to get there. On the map, it looked like a snap — an hour's drive at most in America. But I was getting much better at reading between the lines when looking at Italian maps. I saw I'd have to make my way through the cities of Altamura and Santeramo in Colle to get there, and right away my mind conjured images of steep hills, tight medieval streets, and packed traffic. It could take hours. But maybe Altamura was worth seeing anyway. After all, Frederick II himself founded the city. Although an ancient city had previously existed there, it had long ago fallen into decay. Frederick revitalized the place and erected medieval defensive walls right on top of the ancient megalithic walls. He also ordered the construction of the Altamura Cathedral in 1232 — perhaps the only church he ever commissioned. This could be a great place to explore. And besides, the most famous bread in Italy comes from Altamura, and I was starving again.

Unfortunately, I hit a snag right away when I drove into Altamura. Like Spinazzola the day before, the main road through town was blocked off, and I was funneled into a maze of one-way alleyways taking me away from the direction I needed to go. Only this city was much bigger than Spinazzola, and I quickly became lost. I had my compass handy in the glove compartment, so I pulled it out and tried to figure out the direction I needed to travel. Farther along, I did manage to get back up to the main road, but it was blocked off there, too, so I had to backtrack and try to find another way through. I finally reached a dead end right at the edge of the city, where I could look down the hill and see the countryside far below. I got out my map and laid it on the hood of the car. Then I used my compass and lined the map up perfectly on the north-south axis. I looked on the map at the highway I needed to get on and took a bearing with my compass. Looking down the hill in that exact direction, I could see a long, thin highway lined up perfectly with the compass heading.

That was where I needed to be — right there, driving straight toward Santeramo in Colle. But how could I get there? A chainlink fence with a field below it blocked my way. I backtracked and tried another road, which took me lower down on the hill, but I ended up in the fenced-in parking area of an apartment complex. I tried again, going back partway up the hill and taking another way down. On the fourth try, I hit pay dirt and finally made it to the correct road.

I was very sorry that I missed all the wonderful sights of Altamura (and didn't get to eat lunch). But as soon as I got trapped in that maze, I knew I had to get out of there and keep moving. By this time, I needed gas, so I stopped at a station not far from Altamura. As always, I asked the gas station attendant if he spoke English, and for the first time, this one said yes. In fact, he spoke English better than anyone I'd met in Italy. He was about nineteen or twenty years old, and it turned out he was an Arab, who had come here to work. We had a nice conversation for five or ten minutes. He told me how much he wanted to move to New York City. It made me realize how much I was starved for conversation — just to be fully understood by someone and to completely understand what he was saying: such a simple, basic human need.

Before I drove away, he encouraged me to visit nearby Matera and see the Sassi — a huge complex of cave houses dug into the soft tufa rock formations along an ancient river channel. Like a human anthill, these dwellings have been lived in since prehistoric times and were still occupied in the 1950s, until the government forcibly evicted most of the inhabitants. The problem was the low life expectancy and high child-mortality rate among the people living in them. These are similar to the cave dwellings in Gravina di Puglia, but there are many more of them and they are more elaborate. They have become a tourist attraction — especially since Mel Gibson used them as the setting for his film

The Passion of the Christ. I told the gas station attendant I would visit them a day or two later, but for now I had only one thing on my mind: Frederick's castle at Gioia del Colle.

It turned out to be hard to find. The streets of Gioia del Colle were even more choked with traffic than the other towns I'd driven through, and I had no idea where to go. I just followed the signs leading to the center of the city hoping I would see something. At one point, I glanced to the left to look at the street vendors up a small side road and caught a glimpse of a castle tower looming above the surrounding buildings. I saw it for only an instant before the traffic pushed me along, but I had seen a picture of the castle once, and the tower was unmistakable. But now what to do? There were no open parking spaces on this road. After driving a couple of blocks, I decided to turn left on a narrow street and see if I could find a place to leave my car. Miraculously, I spotted a car pulling away from the side of the street up ahead, leaving an open space. And it was right across from the Federico II — a tavern or eatery of some kind. It was a common thing throughout Apulia to see businesses named after Frederick: restaurants, stores, even laundromats. There is even a small airline named Federico II Airways. One of its advertisements features a gold Augustales coin, which was minted by Frederick and has his likeness on one side and an eagle on the other.

I made my way through the heavy pedestrian traffic, making sure to take note of every turn so I could find my way back to my car. The area with the street vendors was completely jammed with people trying to barter for various trinkets and flea-market items on the tables lined up there. I paused at a table where a man was selling a variety of Benito Mussolini memorabilia, including numerous photographs of Il Duce (looking bullet-headed in some pictures wearing a gleaming, oddly shaped metal army helmet), a variety of fascist insignia, and even one of the original fascist hats with the tassel. Quite a few older people in this region still look back fondly on the Mussolini era. He put a lot of money into this area, launching building projects and creating schools. This had been — and still is — a neglected part of Italy.

It was interesting to see how the city has grown to the very walls of the castle, butting right up against it in places. (This had been one of

Frederick's great hunting spots; now it is in the middle of a congested urban mess.) The castle is in good shape overall, although only two of the original four towers remain. I read that when Count Resta — who owned the castle in the late nineteenth and early twentieth centuries — was carrying out restorations, he found many of Frederick II's original furnishings and decorations, including the pieces of his imperial throne, piled up in a huge heap.

This castle is special for a number of reasons. First, it was here that Frederick's mistress, Bianca di Lancia, gave birth to his favorite son, Manfred, who looked the most like the emperor of any of his children and followed in his footsteps as an avid falconer. (It was he who put together the stunning illuminated manuscript of *De Arte Venandi cum Avibus* now housed at the Vatican Library.) Manfred was with Frederick at Castel Fiorentino when he died, and he later succeeded him as King of Sicily.

A ghastly legend exists about Frederick, Bianca, and the castle at Gioia del Colle. As the story goes, Frederick became jealous and suspected Bianca of infidelity, so he kept her imprisoned at Gioia del Colle, guarded by eunuchs. One day, sometime after Manfred's birth, Bianca supposedly cut off both her breasts with a sword, then put them in a covered silver platter and had them delivered to Frederick with his breakfast. It makes for a great yarn, but I find it hard to believe for a number of reasons. First there's the pain involved in such self-mutilation. Then you have to wonder if someone could survive the loss of blood and the risk of infection, particularly in the Middle Ages. And last, is it even remotely conceivable that after committing an act of this kind that a woman would go back and have more children with the man who had driven her to such a horrible act of desperation?

I paid a couple of euros to enter the castle and look at the museum on the ground floor, then walked around the courtyard inside. It seemed so quiet and peaceful it was hard to believe that a thriving city was bustling right outside. After I looked through every place in the castle that seemed open to the public, I realized something was missing. Where was his throne? I knew it had been reassembled back in the time of Count Resta. Where was it now?

I returned to the museum downstairs and tried to find out about it, but no one understood what I was saying. I was not ready to give up yet, so I went back to the courtyard, walked upstairs, and started trying to open every door I came upon to see if I could get into another part of the castle. The first three doors were locked tightly. Then I tried one more door, and it swung open before me revealing a large, bare room. The light streaming in through an upper window was the only illumination, but I spotted Frederick's throne immediately, at the far end of the room. The throne was large, made of pale marble with unusual engraved Persian patterns in front, but what was most interesting was the row of carved falcons high on its back. That was the unmistakable mark of Frederick. I walked to his throne and stood there gazing in awe. Here, for the first time, I was looking at something that he had actually touched — a throne he had sat upon nearly eight hundred years earlier. I reached up and traced the abstract falcon motif with my fingertips. And then — seeing that no one else was around — I sat down on his throne, closing my eyes and soaking in the ambiance of the place.

This was Frederick's throne room — the place where he would receive the various dignitaries and visitors who came before him. But it was far more than that. It was here, in this very room — shortly after his death at Castel Fiorentino — that Frederick lay in state for the last time on the Italian mainland, guarded as always by his loyal Saracens. From here his body was taken to Taranto and carried on a ship to his last resting place in Palermo.

I stayed in that room alone for perhaps half an hour, deep in thought. I had such an intense and eerie feeling. I'd been immersed in the lore of Frederick II for such a long time. I'd read so many books about him, including the one he wrote himself about falconry, the passion we both share. And now I was traveling through his realm, digging into his past, and it was a sad story: one of thwarted ambitions, of dreams unfulfilled.

I wondered why I came. What good would come of any of this? I was just an intruder. Maybe Frederick should be left to slumber alone and undisturbed. What right did I have to be there? The deep sense of melancholy I'd felt earlier in the day at Parco per Uccellagione came

back strongly as I sat on Frederick's throne, and it v
was all the more powerful because I was so cut off
no one to talk with about any of this. I thought abo
sorry childhood. I looked back to those days as a twelv
first became acquainted with Frederick II and read his
an escape from my own situation? I remembered all th
on my fist and flown at game. Where were they now? I
falconers I'd known over the years — many had vanishe
my life or were dead. And looming above it all, envelopi
I saw the gray prison walls that once surrounded me. W
mean? How could I even keep going in this life, putting one
of another?

This was a low point in my journey — a low point in my
it was all I could do to make myself stand up, walk out of
and make my way back to the car. I got back to my hotel late t
and didn't even bother to eat dinner.

18

ON TO SICILY

EVEN MY INNATE morning optimism wasn't enough to raise me from the despair I was still wallowing in from the night before, but I forced myself to get up, eat a big breakfast, and hit the road again. Taking action is the only way I've found to fight melancholy — seizing the initiative and pushing through the gloom. My next stop would be the city of Bari, the capital of Apulia. It is another of those notorious coastal cities like Brindisi that tourist guidebooks advise people against visiting. Most of the books have scary warnings advising tourists not to wear anything valuable or to leave anything in your car, even in the trunk. One of them said simply that it is best just to avoid Bari altogether.

I have to admit, the dire pronouncements in the guidebooks did cause me some concern, but I was determined to explore Frederick's castle in Bari, one of the largest in his realm. I thought if I could just go there first thing in the morning and get in and out early, everything would be OK. Of course, in Italy, going anywhere quickly can be a challenge, but this proved to be even more difficult than usual. I ran into a major traffic jam when I was still ten miles from Bari, near Bitonto, which I planned to visit later in the day. *If it's this bad here*, I thought, *how will it be when I get closer to Bari?* As it turned out, a traffic accident up ahead was causing the slowdown. I could hear the awful *hee-haw-hee-haw* wail of an ambulance, trying to fight its way through to the accident site.

When I finally drove past the accident, I saw a big transport truck on its side near a couple of dented cars. To avoid hitting the cars, the truck driver had apparently swerved his narrow, top-heavy vehicle and toppled over. A policeman stood in the road, frantically trying to direct traffic around the wreckage while the truck driver and another man stood off to the side, shouting in each others' faces, only inches apart, gesticulating wildly with their hands, Italian style. Some other people sat on the curb nearby, crying. One of them held a bloody cloth against his head. I could still hear the ambulance wailing away, stuck in traffic somewhere.

I rolled up my window and drove on as the policeman waved me through. I could already tell it was going to be a long day. The cars in front of me finally started moving as I got past the wreckage, but it was still slow going until I left the Bitonto area.

I didn't know what to expect in Bari. It was obviously a big, sprawling city, but I knew nothing about the topography of the place. I was pleasantly surprised — at least from a driving standpoint — to find that it was almost completely flat, and the roads leading into it were much wider than those I'd seen in other Italian cities. As always, I didn't have a city map and wasn't exactly sure where to go, but I did know that the castle is near the old town — the Bari Vecchia — which is on a peninsula near the port, so I headed through town toward the Adriatic shore.

A nice wide road ran right along the coast, with buildings on the left and boat docks on the right. As soon as I spotted a castle-like structure up ahead, I pulled into the first available parking spot and walked toward it. A brisk ocean breeze blew in my face, and the sky was clear and bright. It took me a while to figure out how to get around the wall and up to the building I had seen, but when I finally got there, it turned out to be a church.

I decided to go strolling through the old town. I knew the castle was on the other side, if I could just negotiate the confusing warren of streets in the Bari Vecchia. I figured I could ask people where to find the Castello Svevo (or Swabian Castle — the Hohenstaufens were from Swabia in Germany).

Although it was tough to get around in, the old town was like another world, with pastel-colored buildings, narrow stone streets, arched alleyways, and medieval churches. I loved it. And during my travels through it I stumbled upon the final resting place of Santa Claus — the Basilica di San Nicola. Turns out that the bones of Saint Nicholas are buried under the altar of this beautiful Norman church — not someplace in the North Pole. They were stolen from Turkey and brought here in 1087 by some fishermen from Bari, and the basilica was erected to house them. Santa's bones are said to have miraculous powers, so the basilica has been a pilgrimage site for centuries.

I finally stumbled out of the old town and into the Piazza Federico II di Svevia, right below the castle. I walked along outside the walls until I found the entrance, then paid my admission and went inside. The castle is huge, and in some ways a hodgepodge of constructions carried on through the centuries. The structure is mostly Norman, built on top of an ancient Roman fort. But Frederick II completely remodeled it and added two towers, which are still standing. The Spanish added some more features — the corner towers over the moat — when they ruled in the sixteenth century.

As I strolled through the castle, a thought struck me that had nothing to do with this place in particular. I had been thinking about all the castles I had visited during the past few days and the many, many more — far too numerous to visit on a short trip — spread throughout Frederick II's realm. I suddenly realized that this man had no home. He had no single place like London, Paris, or Rome that was strongly associated with his rule — no place where someone could go to view the heart of his kingdom, where he spent the bulk of his years. He was a vagabond monarch, a transient who spent much of his life on the road, traveling with his entire court in tow, basically conducting the day-to-day business of a vast empire from his mobile kit bag. For that I felt sad for him.

It also brought home to me how difficult it would be to truly experience the life of Frederick II. To do it at all adequately would require visiting the seat of the Hohenstaufen dynasty in Germany; the town of Jesi, where he was born; Fiorentino, where he died; and Palermo, where he lived as a boy and where his body still lay. But that would be just the start. There were so many significant places in his life — the many castles and hunting lodges he built, some of which I had visited; Rome, where he was crowned Holy Roman Emperor; and the Holy Land, where he achieved perhaps his greatest triumph, succeeding in a bloodless Crusade. I had barely scratched the surface of Frederick II. It would take more than the rest of my life to even begin to unwrap the mystery of this enigmatic man. What made him tick? What kept him going so doggedly against all odds for so many years? His strength, his will and fortitude, are almost unimaginable to me.

I was just beginning to understand why Frederick had put such a major effort into building new castles as well as rebuilding existing ones to put his own stamp on them. He had far more of them than he could ever use, spread everywhere across his realm. Clearly a public relations ploy, the castles were physical symbols of the power and might of the Emperor. Like "the Eye of Apulia," they stood as a constant reminder of Frederick II's presence. But to make them more effective in this purpose, he traveled constantly throughout his realm, using his great charisma and the color and excitement of his huge entourage to build his popularity among his subjects. He brought a traveling menagerie with him wherever he went, including an elephant, giraffes, and other exotic creatures, and also his falcons. He sought to give the impression that he could be everywhere at all times, but because of this, he was spread incredibly thin.

Frederick II was a great innovator. He may have been the father of political "spin." Centuries before newspapers, telegraphs, radio, television, and other mass media, he had mastered the art of disseminating his viewpoint quickly and effectively to his subjects and was able to respond quickly — and sometimes proactively — to the broadsides hurled at him by the Pope. Working closely with his talented chief minister, Piero della Vigna, and a team of scribes, he would jump on every rumor, every piece of misinformation, drafting lengthy messages, which were transcribed in multiple copies by the scribes and carried by couriers immediately to the towns and cities throughout the realm. This is how he stayed in power for so long, despite all the powerful forces lined up against him. He was tireless and absolutely determined to succeed.

I FINALLY MADE my way back to my little blue Fiat Panda and was grateful no one had broken in and taken my belongings. It was a constant worry. But the alternative of dragging my suitcase and backpack everywhere I went may have been just as bad, attracting the attention of thieves. I tried to limit what I carried to my camera, which I slung bandolier-style across my body, and my passport, driver's license, and a credit card, which were zipped securely in a front pocket of my shirt.

Bitonto was my next destination. I'd already crossed the outskirts earlier that day, but this would be my first foray into the center of town. I was looking for the cathedral, but there didn't seem to be any signs pointing to where it was. It had recently gone through major renovations, and apparently they didn't want to encourage visitors to come until the repairs were completed. I drove around and around through the narrow streets, filled with honking cars and jaywalking pedestrians, and finally found a piazza with metered parking right next to the gateway of the old medieval city.

Bitonto has an interesting history. The ancient Greek settlers referred to the indigenous people as the Butontinoi, from which the city name derives. It was enclosed with defensive walls as early as the fifth century B.C., and the walls came in handy. The townspeople stood off a Saracen siege in the ninth century.

I'd heard that the Cattedrale di Bitonto was the largest and most exquisite medieval cathedral in all of Apulia. Built in the thirteenth century, it stands upon the foundations of a much earlier structure. I was not disappointed when I saw the cathedral emerge up ahead as I strolled along the narrow streets of the old town. I loved the main doorway, with pillars at its sides supported by monsters, and the magnificent rose window high above. But what I really wanted to see was the carved marble ambo, or pulpit, and I headed right for it when I went inside. On the side of the stairway leading up to the pulpit is a detailed sculpture in high relief depicting four of the sovereigns in the Hohenstaufen dynasty. Frederick II commissioned the sculpture in 1229, after he returned from the Crusade.

The first and lowest figure in the sculpture is Frederick II's grandfather, Frederick Barbarossa — first of his line to become Holy Roman Emperor. He is sitting on a throne, passing a cross to his son, Henry VI, who stands beside him and slightly elevated. Next comes Frederick II, wearing a crown, who is higher still and is reaching up to pluck a piece of fruit. Last in line is Frederick II's son, Conrad, who is highest, though shorter than the others, and is also plucking a piece of fruit. At the feet of Frederick II and Conrad stands a stylized figure of a raptor, which seems to be holding the two of them up higher than the others.

This sculpture may have been intended to represent the biblical Tree of Jessee from the Old Testament Book of Isaiah, which describes the descent of the Messiah: "And there shall come forth a shoot from the stump of Jessee, and a branch shall grow out of its roots . . ." Perhaps Frederick II and Conrad are shown to be the logical evolution, the fulfillment of history and of the Hohenstaufen dynasty.

Author Daniela Boccassini (who wrote *Il volo della mente: Falconeria e sofia nel mondo mediterraneo: Islam, Federico II, Dante*) has an interesting alternate take on the meaning of the Bitonto sculpture. She believes that Frederick II saw falconry as a way to enhance the qualities of leadership required to excel as an emperor or king — a means of "self-taming" that would engender wisdom and tolerance. She points out that the bird of prey beneath the feet of Frederick II and Conrad is what raises them above the other Hohenstaufen emperors and enables them to reach the fruit of the tree.

I spent more than an hour exploring the inside of the cathedral, gazing up at its lofty interior, taking pictures of the wonderful architectural details and finally exploring the crypt. When I went back outside, the day had warmed considerably, so I sat on the low wall overlooking the piazza, which seemed little altered since Frederick's time.

It was here in front of the cathedral where the chronicler Matteo Spinelli di Giovinazzo came on December 28, 1250, to watch Frederick II's funeral procession. Draped in crimson velvet, the funeral litter passed slowly through the piazza, surrounded by Frederick's Saracen guards, all weeping. Six companies of cavalry accompanied him as well as many barons, dressed in black, and various officials of the realm. Along the route, heralds proclaimed the death of Frederick II and the accession to the throne of Sicily of his young son, Conrad, who would be represented by his other son, Manfred, as Regent.

From Bitonto, Frederick's body was taken to Gioia del Colle — where I had been the day before — and he lay in state there until he was taken to the port of Taranto. He was carried by sea to Messina on the island of Sicily and then borne the rest of the way to Palermo, where his body still rests in the great cathedral, along with the bodies of his mother and father and his first wife, Constance of Aragon.

So once again — and only a day since my experience at Gioia del Colle — I found myself reliving a sad chapter in the saga of Frederick II. The warmth and the sunshine in this place made it much more bearable, and I felt better for having come there. But Sicily still loomed large for me. It was such a long drive, followed by a ferryboat ride to the island and another long drive to Palermo, and there were so many unknowns. It would take me at least a couple of days of hard work to get to and from Palermo. Would it be worth it? Was there an easier way? I had looked into parking my car at the airport in Bari or Brindisi, flying to Palermo for a day, and flying back — or possibly even driving back to Rome and flying from there roundtrip to Palermo — but these options turned out to be expensive and just as time-consuming as driving.

What should I do? Maybe I should just scratch my trip to Palermo. I could explore a few more Apulian castles and maybe spend some extra time in Rome. But what kind of pilgrimage is it if you don't even visit the bones of the saint? I had to go there. I had to drive to Sicily — and the sooner the better.

❧

BEFORE I LEFT Bitonto, I was sketching out my plan, sitting in my car and studying the map. I had two choices. I could cross the heel of Italy from Bari to Taranto and head south along the Golfo di Taranto, finally cutting across to catch the main autostrada at its closest point and following it all the way to the ferry at Reggio di Calabria. Or I could head cross-country back to Potenza, and then it would be nothing but autostrada all the way. It was a tough call. It would be a longer drive if I went by way of Potenza, but what if those little towns the road went through south of Taranto were all tangled little medieval mazes like some of the others I'd navigated? It could take hours to get through them all.

I chose Potenza, but it was a mistake. As always traveling through the countryside, it was difficult to be sure of where I was going. A few times, I turned prematurely on a road that wasn't on my map, because I thought it was another road. You know you've taken a wrong turn when you drive five or six miles down a paved road and it suddenly turns to gravel, or worse, mud. But I hate to turn back. I'd end up blasting through tiny farmyards with big killer dogs snarling at me and trying to bite my tires. Eventually, using my compass, I'd come out onto a paved road again.

My plan was to drive hard all the way to Reggio. I knew it would be very late by the time I got there, and I was a little worried about finding a place to sleep. But I reasoned that there would be good signage pointing the way to the Sicily ferries and that I might be able to find a decently priced room near the ferry terminal.

I had no idea what I was getting into. As soon as I reached the autostrada, my journey descended into chaos. There was massive road construction everywhere, and the weather turned ugly, with lead-gray skies and fog, and rain pouring down endlessly. The hills and mountains I drove through were spectacular — easily surpassing the Big Sur coastline of central California — but I could barely see them: just a glimpse of a magnificent chasm here and there, looming up through the fog like a mirage and quickly vanishing again.

I tried to keep blasting along, hoping to travel as far as possible while there was still daylight, but the traffic would suddenly back up, and I'd be locked in bumper-to-bumper traffic for miles. I wasn't even sure if I was on the right road for a good part of the journey, because I went so far without seeing a road sign. I thought about chickening out a few times and trying to get a hotel. I saw a few of them off the highway, but they didn't look promising. These were mostly beach hotels catering to summer vacationers, and this was in the dreary depths of winter. I could see that many of them were closed.

The road south was very much a commercial route, and I got little respect in my tiny car from the truck drivers racing to their destination. Either they came flying up behind me flashing their lights, or worse, they wouldn't let me pass when I tried to overtake them on an uphill stretch. Although we had two lanes on our side, one truck kept drifting back and forth over the dividing line every time I tried to get past. But still I blasted along, keeping my gas pedal pushed to the floor for hours.

It was past midnight when I finally dropped down from the highway and started making my way toward the harbor. I quickly spotted a hotel and parked my car illegally right outside the front door. I almost took the room. Even though it was expensive, I was tired and just wanted to fall asleep someplace. But when it became clear that I'd have to pay a good deal extra to keep my car in an underground parking garage someplace away from the hotel, I decided to keep looking. This time, I made a good choice. I found a nice hotel right beside the ferry terminal, and it had free parking right outside. (I could even see my car from my fifth-floor room.) I checked in as quickly as possible and went upstairs. Before I went to sleep, I opened the curtains and gazed across the Straits of Messina, where I could see the twinkling lights on the island of Sicily. I had almost made it. Just a ferry ride and a three-hour drive, and I would be in Palermo. I got into bed and fell into a deep, contented sleep.

19

PALERMO WITHOUT
A MAP

THE NEXT MORNING, I finally managed to find a SIM card for my cell phone and get it to work, though it wasn't easy. I talked to the hotel concierge, who spoke a little English, and he told me about a mall not far away where he thought I could get one of the cards. He gave me a brochure with a map of the area and drew the route I should take with a pen. It was about a mile away, but I felt ambitious and decided to walk.

I found the mall and the electronics store fairly easily, but then my troubles began. First, I couldn't get anyone to assist me. The young women who worked in the store were too busy talking to each other to help me, and when I did get their attention, we had the typical communication problem. I had to take my cell phone apart and point to the place where the SIM card should go. That was no problem, but how was I going to activate the phone? This required calling an Italian cell-phone company and giving them my personal details, but the people on the other end of the line didn't speak English.

I finally threw myself on the mercy of the young women working in the store. Three or four of them gathered around me and through sign language I let them know what I was trying to do. They finally got interested and took on the job of getting my phone working. I ended up handing them my passport and my credit card so they could give the information to the phone company. I also needed an address in Italy to open a telephone account. Luckily the name and address of my hotel — which I would be checking out of as soon as I was finished in the store — was printed on the map the concierge had given me, so I showed it to one of the women, and she relayed the information to the phone company representative. So I was set. I could call my friends in Rome later when I was driving north and perhaps arrange to meet them.

After leaving the hotel, I drove to the nearby ferry loading area. I bought a round-trip ticket from a man in a small glassed-in booth and got in line behind the rest of the cars and trucks. When my turn came, I drove up the ramp into the ferryboat's dimly lit interior and parked. Then I got out and walked upstairs to watch the crossing from the enclosed deck, which had numerous places to sit, and a small snack bar. With great shaking and rumbling, the huge ferryboat churned away from the dock and began crossing the famed Straits of Messina. The sea is always choppy there. According to ancient Greek legend, two mythical monsters — the Scylla (a six-headed monster) and the Charybdis (a whirlpool) — cause the strong clashing currents in the straits.

The crossing was quick and easy, and I was soon off the boat, trying to escape from the streets of Messina. It wasn't too bad. The road took me up above the city and I was soon on the autostrada blasting toward Palermo, a three-hour drive away. It was a clear, sunny day, and broad vistas opened up before me. To my left, emerald green hills loomed high above; to my right, a vast blue sea spread to the horizon. In the distance, I could see the wispy smoke of Stromboli, an island volcano, rising up like a mist.

The highway was excellent. Although I had to stop two or three times to pay tolls, it was well worth the money to drive on such a good road. I was eager to get to Palermo. It was December 12, 2006, and I would be celebrating an important anniversary — not the anniversary of Frederick II's death but of his last full day of life. I had no wish to celebrate his death. I was interested in the living Emperor. On this date seven hundred and fifty-six years earlier Frederick had seemed to rally. He had gotten out of bed and eaten some pears. For a few hours it seemed feasible he might bounce back. That was the date I wanted to celebrate; that was when I wanted to visit his grave. I even had a small gift for him — a brass falcon bell that Macduff had worn for a couple of seasons of duck hawking. It still had the thin leather strap (called a bewit) attached to it. I wanted to set it down in front of his sarcophagus — a token, one falconer to another, of the bond we shared.

I still felt some dread about driving in Palermo. From everything I'd read, it sounded like one of the worst places in the world to drive a car, with tight, congested streets and wicked traffic jams. And my guidebook warned that car theft was a real danger. But I wouldn't be in the city for long, so maybe my luck would hold.

It was midafternoon when I hit the crazy maelstrom of inner Palermo, and it didn't take me long to get lost. I kept stopping wherever I could find a place to pull over as I tried to get my bearings. The map in my guidebook was completely inadequate, with only a few major streets marked. It didn't help at all, so I just started probing the streets and alleyways near the Quattro Canti (four corners), right in the center of the oldest part of the city. I would run into a dead end then try another way. If that route failed, I would try still another way. Finally I had one of those miraculous visions, like the one at Gioia del Colle, and just for an instant spotted a great dome rising above the surrounding buildings. I knew it was the cathedral, but I still had a hard time working my way through the maze to find it. Then I had another problem — finding a parking space.

After driving a few blocks and winding up and down a couple of streets, I did find a spot, although I wasn't sure it was a legal parking space. It seemed too good to be true. I was so frantic about getting to the cathedral I decided to take a chance. I grabbed my camera, locked up the car, and strode quickly down the street. En route, I spotted a couple of signs pointing toward the cathedral and followed them until I got there.

The cathedral was magnificent. It stood well back from the street with a huge open plaza in front. What a marvelous structure the cathedral was, with its high dome, its wild geometric designs, its many arches, and its ziggurat crenelations, giving it a distinctly Middle Eastern look — in fact, the whole scene, the architecture as well as the palm trees, seemed like something from an ancient Arabian city.

I was surprised by how many people were milling about in front of the cathedral, especially at the main entrance. They were packed so tightly, I couldn't get anywhere near it. What could this mean? Was it closed today? Had I come all this way for nothing? It seemed clear that the doors were locked — otherwise the people would have gone inside. Dozens of them stood praying and chanting. They seemed to be doing some kind of rote prayer-and-response litany, but I had no idea what they were saying. I could hear a man's voice somewhere up ahead, chanting a Latin incantation in a deep monotone, while everyone around me replied with a unison response. At first I thought the other voice was that of a priest, speaking from deep within the cathedral — perhaps a crowded service was taking place inside and this was the overflow crowd, giving their prayer responses from outside the locked wooden doors, I thought. But finally I spotted a short, stocky man with a beard and a brown knitted skullcap, pushed right up against the locked doors of the cathedral, leading the prayers.

I couldn't figure out what was going on, and no one there could speak English. Here it was, a Tuesday afternoon, and something big was happening, but what was it? Various carabinieri and soldiers stood in the plaza, plus at least one television news crew with a big mobile satellite van. I walked up to them, figuring that broadcast journalist types would probably be able to speak English and let me know what was happening. I was wrong. "Non parlo inglese," they told me.

As I stood there, not knowing what to do next, buses began pulling up, spilling crowds of additional people into the square. Worshippers in their Sunday best, churchmen clad in fabulous vestments, soldiers with plumed hats and sabers, and monks in brown wool robes tied at the waist with rope all descended on the place. It was annoying. Here I was on my own personal pilgrimage, and these guys were horning in on it. I was so afraid that I wouldn't get to go inside the cathedral after all this. How could I explain to them what I wanted? I had come so far. I was so close now. Would I ever get to see Frederick's sarcophagus?

Yes, I would. If there was one thing I was sure of it was that no one could turn me back now. Even if I had to beg on bended knees, pay a bribe, or climb through a window, nothing could stop me — I was going to stand before Frederick's sarcophagus and give him my falcon bell.

Finally, at 3:06 P.M. sharp, the doors opened and the crowd crammed into the cathedral in a great crush of bodies. I slipped inside with the rest of them and stepped quickly into the shadows to look for Frederick's sarcophagus. I knew exactly what it looked like. I'd seen a black-and-white picture of the sarcophagus in an old book and had also read a wonderful passage describing it, written more than a century ago by Oscar Wilde in a letter to a friend: "I knelt before the huge porphyry sarcophagus in which Frederick the Second lies: it is a sublime bare monstrous thing — blood-coloured, and held up by lions who have caught some of the rage of the great Emperor's restless soul."

But where was it? I moved toward the front of the church first, checking every alcove along the closest side without any luck. They all looked pretty much the same, with a religious painting and a place for candles. Then I turned and walked against the flow of incoming people, working my way toward the back. Finally, in an alcove near the rear corner, I saw it — a massive red porphyry sarcophagus held up by four lions. I knew instantly that this was it, well before reading the small white sign inscribed with black lettering, which had Frederick II's name on it but not much else. I wished the original inscription Manfred had placed over his father were still there, but it was long gone. It had read:

Si probitas, sensus, virtutum gratia, census Nobilitas orti possent resistere morti, Non foret extinctus Fredericus, qui jacet intus.

If a noble nature, great goodness, many virtues, and high lineage were sufficient to defy the power of death, Frederick would not be sleeping in this grave, which encloses him.

Frederick II's father, Henry VI; his mother, Constance of Sicily; and his mother's father, Roger II of Sicily, were entombed in separate ornate sarcophagi in the same alcove, as was his first wife, Constance of Aragon. But Frederick's tomb was the only one with flowers — three bouquets of red roses, fresh that day. I later mentioned this to Frikky, and he told me he had noticed the same thing several years earlier when he visited

Palermo's cathedral. He asked someone about it and was told that Frederick II always had fresh flowers at his sarcophagus.

I glanced around to see if anyone was watching me, but most of the people were moving quickly into the pews, trying to get a seat before they filled up. I reached into my pocket to get the falcon bell, which I'd wrapped in tissue to muffle the sound. It jingled for an instant as I removed the paper, but the noise was lost in the great hubbub of people massing inside the cathedral. I bent over and placed it at the base of the sarcophagus, right behind the flowers, then glanced around again, but I was sure no one had seen me. I wondered what people would think when they saw the bell. Would they regard it with awe and hushed reverence like a great supernatural occurrence: the Miracle of the Bell? Perhaps it would stay there through the centuries — an eternal mystery. Or would the cathedral's custodian carelessly whisk it into a dustbin with the flowers when they dried up in a day or two? That seemed more likely. At that moment, I wished I'd brought more. A hood would have been nice (it was Frederick who introduced the falcon hood to Europe; he had learned about it from the Arabs) or a leather gauntlet, but that would have to wait for a future visit.

As I stood there, I thought about Frederick's body, lying a few feet away. At one point in the eighteenth century, the heavy lid of the sarcophagus had been lifted off, and an artist drew a sketch of Frederick, which I had seen once in a book. It was a ghastly image — his face withered from the centuries, the crown still resting firmly on his head, which lay upon a leather pillow — but he was remarkably well preserved. I read somewhere that his sarcophagus was opened again in the 1990s, and some DNA was extracted from his corpse. I wondered, to what end? Were they still wondering if Frederick was actually the son of a butcher and not of Henry VI and Constance?

A few minutes later, I felt a hush descend over the cathedral and realized that whatever special function they were holding that day would begin in a few seconds. I snapped three or four more pictures of the sarcophagus and quickly walked back up the aisle and out the door. I'd been there for less than an hour, but I had accomplished my mission; I'd seen Frederick's sarcophagus, taken some pictures, and left my falcon bell.

The plaza in front was nearly empty as I strolled across it and went up the street to look for my car. Would it still be there? I was a little worried about that, so I walked as fast as I could to get back to it. It took me about fifteen minutes to reach the road I was sure it was on. My heart sank as I turned the corner. The blue Panda was nowhere to be seen. Could it really be gone? Did someone steal it? Or maybe I'd parked it illegally and the police had impounded it. If so, how would I ever figure out how to get it back? Maybe I should just call the car rental company and say I lost their car.

I felt panicky and broke into a cold sweat. But then I started wondering: a lot of these places look the same. Could this be the wrong street? I walked partway back to the cathedral, trying to slow down and think about the route I had taken. I'd been in such a rush earlier I didn't take my usual precautions of memorizing exactly where I had come from. Then it struck me: I had made a left turn and taken a jog one block over before turning right again. I hadn't done that coming back. So I walked my route again, slowly and deliberately, and this time I found my car, sitting just where I'd left it. The relief was instant and palpable. I felt like falling down on my knees in front of it, hugging it passionately and kissing its shiny blue hood.

So, problem number one was solved. But my next dilemma loomed before me: how to get out of Palermo. It was getting late, and I was sure that whatever kind of rush hour they have was probably already starting. I was hoping at least to get out of the city and back on the main highway before dark. I didn't know which road would be the best to take, but I knew the compass direction that would lead me to the main highway. I drove about a hundred yards down one road before realizing it was a one-way street going in the wrong direction. I was so close to the crossroad, I decided to push on in the same direction and turn onto the other road. Before I got there, a policeman appeared on foot and instantly raised his arm and blew his whistle.

For the barest fraction of a second, the whole scenario ran through my head — the cop screaming at me in Italian; me not understanding a word of what he was saying; the cop dragging me to the police station while my car was impounded. Of course, it may not have happened anything like that. Maybe we would've had a good laugh about it together. Maybe he would've turned out to be an excellent speaker of English. Hell, maybe he would've helped me get out of there, providing a police escort of little black-and-white Vespa scooters with screaming *hee-haw-hee-haw* sirens and flashing red lights to guide me to the city limits. I didn't wait to find out. Like an unconscious reflex, I made the quickest three-point turnabout I've ever seen and went racing away as the policeman ran as fast as he could behind me. For a minute I felt like I was in Mr. Toad's Wild Ride at Disneyland. As I reached the corner I looked in my rear-view mirror and saw him standing back there, gasping for air, occasionally giving a few shrill blasts on his police whistle.

I turned right and went tearing along for a couple of blocks then turned right again. I knew I'd have to go back in a direction that would take me near the spot where I ditched the policeman, but on the other side. I took a deep breath, let it out, and then turned right again. As I got close to the area where he had been, the road dropped lower and suddenly I saw what looked like a police roadblock up ahead. I felt sick. Was this all for my benefit? Had he radioed ahead and set up a trap for me? I glanced around, considering my options. I had none. I was on a one-way street with a high wall to my right and cars packing up behind me. There was nothing I could do but brazen it out.

I drove up to the policewoman standing by the barricade — and she waved me through. I started laughing hysterically. They were just trying to direct traffic to improve the flow. I was home free. Nothing could stop me now. And then I reached the end of the road, and it spilled into an area where several roads came together. And everything stopped. Like a swarm of tiny midges stuck eternally in a chunk of amber, hundreds of cars jammed together and all movement ceased.

As my shoulders locked up, I started digging through the glove compartment, searching for my ibuprofen. It was the most ghastly traffic jam I'd seen in my life. At one point, I moved a total of ten feet in forty-five minutes — I timed it. And everyone honked the horn constantly, as though that would somehow make things start moving again. Some people were yelling at other drivers and waving their hands wildly. And they kept pushing, pushing. Every time a one-inch space would develop, someone would force a vehicle into it. The scooters and motorcycles were the worst. They were everywhere and made it almost impossible for me to move my car, because I was afraid of crushing them. At first I tried to be polite, so people took advantage of me. Then I got tough: screaming at the other drivers in mock Italian and shaking my fist — trying my best to channel the spirit of a New York cab driver. But somehow it's hard to be macho when you're driving a tiny blue car called a Panda.

I started to wonder about this traffic jam. Was it like this in Palermo every day? I looked at the cars around me. They all had little nicks and scratches and scrapes and dents: even the expensive ones like Mercedes Benzes and Jaguars. Then I wondered what would happen if I had a little fender-bender right here. I reached for my ibuprofen again.

About two hours later, when I was finally nearing the end of the tangle, an ambulance pushed slowly through with its siren screaming. For one brief instant I had the wicked thought of driving my Panda right up against the back of the ambulance and following it through as it cut a narrow swath through the traffic, but a motorcycle beat me to it.

Slowly. Ever so slowly and gradually, things started opening up. I was moving again — five kilometers per hour; ten kilometers per hour — and, according to my compass, I was headed in the right direction. I started looking around, soaking in the ambiance of the streets of Palermo — the fruit markets, the street vendors, a fish market with a swordfish lying on a bed of ice in front. I thought back on the days in my early twenties when I worked on a swordfish boat off the coast of Southern California, throwing harpoons at those spectacular fish, but the cars in front suddenly stopped, jerking me from my reverie as I slammed on the brakes to avoid a rear-end collision. But I was over the worst of it. I had survived the traffic of Palermo and lived to tell about it.

As I got on the main highway heading back toward Messina, I knew just what I was going to do. I was like a rental horse that had just turned back in the direction of its stable. I would gallop all the way home — back to that sweet little room on the fifth floor of the hotel overlooking the ferry terminal in Reggio di Calabria. That's where I wanted to be; that's the only place I wanted to sleep that night. I pressed hard on the gas pedal and flew on through the darkness toward Messina, a three-hour drive away.

❦

I HAVE FAIRLY poor night vision, especially when my eyes are fatigued, and I get confused easily when I'm tired. This is a bad combination when you're entering a busy, bustling, congested city like Messina in the dark. Try as I might to go the right way, I missed the road to the ferry terminal and instead turned left, heading along a very busy road, several lanes wide, with a divider in the middle. OK. I knew I just needed somehow to do a U-turn or turn left on a street and then make my way back to the main road and turn in the right direction, going back the way I'd come. But left turns were illegal at every break in the divider I saw. I thought for a minute about making a right turn and then coming back to make a left turn on the road I was on, but that too seemed impossible. I'd never be able to get across the road in all this traffic.

As I looked toward the next break in the road divider, I saw that the traffic coming the other way had a sparse patch a little bit ahead. If I could just slow down a little . . . time it just perfectly so a gap in the traffic would form just as I went past the divider . . .

The car behind me got right on my tail, flashing its lights and honking, but the Panda wouldn't budge. I was doing it my way now, and I didn't care what anyone thought about it. I got to the break in the divider at the perfect instant and did a hard left, making a squealing U-turn across the traffic, almost going on two wheels as I completed the turn. I peeled away as fast as the Panda would take me, racing back to the ferry terminal. I was Mr. Toad again, and it felt good.

That night, walking into the hotel, I felt like a conquering hero. The concierge and the others at the hotel seemed genuinely pleased to see me again. They served me a great meal and plied me with plenty of red wine. I knew I had crossed a mountain in my journey that day. A great weight had come off my shoulders. I could take things more easily now. I'd make my way north the next day — maybe stay the night in Pompeii — and then spend three or four days in Rome, wrapping up the loose ends of my journey. I couldn't wait.

20

THE HAWKS OF
HERCULANEUM

I LEFT THE hotel early, right after breakfast, and made my way back onto the autostrada. I knew I'd have a few rough spots to go through again on the way north — all those places a couple of days earlier where I was stuck in bumper-to-bumper traffic for miles going through highway construction areas. But it didn't matter. For once on this trip I would be traveling in the known universe, passing through an area with which I was already familiar. And the weather was good this time, bright and sunny with a fresh breeze.

As I drove north on this day, the anniversary of Frederick II's death, I thought about him, especially his final couple of years when so many things fell apart, including his health. He had spent virtually his entire reign involved in the endless struggle between the Guelph faction, who supported the power of the Pope, and the Ghibellines, who supported the Holy Roman Emperor. In June 1247 the Lombard Guelph–leaning city of Parma expelled the Imperial representatives — a direct affront to the Emperor's power — so Frederick laid siege to the city and built a complete wooden town outside its walls, which he called Vittoria (Victory). He kept his Imperial treasury and his menagerie at Vittoria and stayed there for months as the residents of Parma moved closer toward starvation.

But the people within the city's walls watched and waited, and one day the following February, after they saw Frederick and his entourage ride off on a hawking excursion far from camp, they seized the initiative, spilling from Parma on horse and on foot, launching an all-out surprise attack on lightly defended Vittoria. They took everything — food, prisoners, Frederick's Imperial treasury — and set fire to Vittoria.

For Frederick it was a staggering disaster. Without the vast sum of money he had lost, it would be difficult to keep up the momentum in his struggle to rein in the rebellious cities in his realm.

Another disaster followed in February 1249, when his physician attempted to poison Frederick. The physician had been one of the people captured at Vittoria, and Frederick paid his ransom. But while he was being held, his Guelph captors persuaded him to attempt to kill the Emperor. As the story goes, one evening he offered Frederick a cup supposedly containing a tonic to improve his health. In reality, it held a deadly poison. Frederick somehow got wind of the plot and requested that some of the liquid be given to a condemned prisoner. The physician saw where that was going and deliberately dropped the cup. But enough of the poison remained that when it was given to the prisoner, it killed him instantly.

According to Matthew of Paris, Frederick wept when he discovered the plot. But worse was to follow. Some of the Emperor's advisers believed that Piero della Vigna — Frederick II's longtime adviser and chancellor — was implicated in the plot, although the actual charges brought against him had to do with embezzlement, not attempted assassination. For this, Piero della Vigna was blinded and thrown into prison. He subsequently dashed his brains out against a wall to commit suicide.

I'm not the first person to think Frederick might have been hasty in his judgment of Piero della Vigna. He was a remarkable man who had risen from the bottom of society — his parents were beggars — based on his abilities and vast talents. A poet, a man of letters, a statesman, he had set the tone of the Imperial documents for the realm. He had been a loyal aide to Frederick II for thirty years. He represented him before the Pope twice, he arranged a marriage between Frederick and Isabella of England, and he negotiated with the citizens of Padua to accept Imperial protection. I can't help thinking he was a victim of the Emperor's (perhaps understandable) paranoia and the slanders of other courtiers who were jealous of the success of a man from such humble origins. We may never know the truth.

One of Frederick's greatest tragedies was yet to occur. A few months later, in May 1249, his twenty-three-year-old son, Enzio, was captured by the Bolognese. Like all of the Hohenstaufens he was handsome, with long golden hair and a pleasant demeanor. He was an avid falconer like his father and had a great talent for singing and writing poetry. Despite all of the Emperor's threats and cajoling — at one point Frederick reportedly offered to encircle the entire city with silver coins to ransom his son — the noblemen of Bologna held fast. They took an oath never to release Enzio. So he sat in prison — bearing silent witness for the last twenty years of his life as Frederick II's enemies slowly destroyed the Hohenstaufen dynasty. It was said that in the mornings Enzio could be heard singing in his cell; in the evenings, he wept.

e⌒

THAT NIGHT, JUST before dark, I pulled into Pompeii — not the ancient Roman resort, destroyed by the eruption of Mount Vesuvius, but the neighboring modern town of the same name. I had recognized the profile of the great volcano, looming high above, as I approached the town on the autostrada.

I was quickly reminded it was almost Christmas. All over Pompeii life-sized Santa Claus figures with bags of toys slung on their backs were hung on lampposts and on the edges of balconies, as though they were climbing up to deliver presents. Pompeii was another tight little Italian town to drive in, but I felt like an old pro after Palermo. I quickly got through the traffic mess and headed up the hill, finally pulling into the first hotel I saw as darkness fell.

e⌒

FIRST THING IN the morning, I called the Vatican Library, hoping to get permission to look through some of the papers and manuscripts associated with Frederick II — especially the manuscript of *De Arte Venandi cum Avibus* the library held. It was a beautiful illuminated parchment manuscript, with rich, hand-colored illustrations of Frederick II and his falconers and numerous birds. His son Manfred — another avid Hohenstaufen falconer — had overseen the creation of this manuscript and written editorial comments in the work. I just wanted to see it. I didn't care about touching it or trying to read it. I would've been satisfied just to gaze upon it. This book is like the Holy Grail of falconry. I had been told by a couple of scholars that I would probably not be allowed to see the book, but I thought it was worth a try. I'd sent several e-mails and faxes to the library before leaving on my trip and didn't hear back. But this was the first time I called.

"Pronto," said the man answering the phone.

"Parla inglese?" I enquired.

"No," he said. "Five minutes . . . five minutes."

I called back in five minutes. "Pronto," the man said. Still no go. I waited fifteen minutes and tried again. Still no go. Then finally, thirty minutes later, I was put through to a woman who spoke English, but she told me she was the wrong person. I needed to speak with Sister Juscinta (at least, that's what the name sounded like), and she gave me another number. I called the number and a man answered: "Pronto."

"Parla inglese?" I asked.

"No."

"Sister Juscinta?" I asked.

"Call back."

"When?" I said. "Five minutes . . . ten minutes?"

"Call back," he said and hung up.

That was all the frustration I could stand at that moment, so I decided to get back on the road. I thought about exploring the ruins of Pompeii before I left the area. I'd heard about them since I was a child and always found the town's tragic story interesting. But Herculaneum was close by, too, and some friends had told me it was less touristy than Pompeii. This ancient Roman port town had also been submerged by the eruption of Mount Vesuvius in 79 A.D. But unlike Pompeii, which was largely covered by ash and burning pumice fragments, Herculaneum was buried by a river of volcanic mud, so it was excavated much later than its more famous sister city. The clincher for me was when I looked in my guidebook and read that birds of prey were being used in Herculaneum to chase pigeons away from the ruins. Apparently the acidity of the pigeon droppings can damage the ancient decorated surfaces in the ruins, so hawks were brought in to get the birds to move. That did it — another opportunity to meet some falconers.

I soon found that parking was a challenge in Ercolano, the modern-day city surrounding Herculaneum. The guidebook had said to go to a paid parking lot, where there was far less chance of having a car broken into or stolen. But the two lots I found were not only full — each one had three or four cars lined up with their drivers inside, waiting for an empty parking space to open up. I couldn't wait. I drove up and down the surrounding streets, and finally found a spot at the side of the road. As always, I wasn't sure if it was a legal parking space. It had a sign on a post beside it, which I couldn't read. I decided to take a chance and park there, hoping my luck would hold out. This would be my last day with the car. I planned to drop it off at the airport a few hours later and take a train into Rome. I'd be spending a couple of nights with Franco, a friend of Frikky's whom I had met in Scotland.

The weather had turned bad again, and I got caught in a cloudburst as I hurried down the road to the entrance of the ancient city. The woman at the ticket booth seemed surprised to see someone going into the site on such a miserable day — but at least she didn't try to sell me two tickets. I paused at the edge of the excavation, gazing down into the narrow stone streets of old Herculaneum more than thirty feet below me. It was remarkably well preserved, and I couldn't wait to get down there and start exploring. But first I had to make my way all the way to the end of the ruin and then to the other side to reach the stairs and go below. Near the souvenir shop I spotted a Plexiglas-enclosed gazebo with several raptors perched inside — a couple of Harris's hawks, a lugger falcon, and what looked like a peregrine but turned out to be a hybrid.

I saw a woman working in a booth nearby and inquired, largely through sign language, where the falconers were. She motioned that they were somewhere around but wasn't sure where. I decided to go below into Herculaneum and start looking around. And it was wonderful — amazingly well preserved after nearly two thousand years. I walked up and down the ancient streets — some of which were awash with rainwater, flowing like a shallow stream in places — and ducked into several of the dwellings, both to get out of the rain and to explore. Some places had spectacular murals and mosaics, nearly as vividly colored as they had been in Roman times.

When I walked back up the stairs, I saw two men standing near the hawk gazebo, both wearing vests with various falconry insignia. I introduced myself and said I was a falconer. Although they spoke no English, we had a great conversation for an hour or so just using my broken Italian (which was improving by the day), various kinds of sign language, and the Latin names of various raptors and prey species. The two men — named Gianclaudio and Mario — quickly came to understand how long I'd been a falconer, what kind of falcon I flew, how old he was, how much he weighed, and what he caught, and I found out the same information about them. It was difficult for me to imagine how they flew falcons in the middle of a city like this, but they assured me that their birds actually caught pigeons there. They would gladly have flown their birds for me, but the hard, steady rain made it impossible.

I finally bid farewell to Gianclaudio and Mario, promising to send them some pictures I'd taken of them with their hawks, and raced back to my car. Once again, my luck had held. The car was there and had not been broken into or mutilated in any way. By this time, I was eager to finish my journey to Rome. I resisted the impulse to visit Benevento, a provincial capital only thirty miles or so east of Naples — not just because I was running late, but because the city had such a sad significance for the Hohenstaufen dynasty. It was there, in 1266, that Frederick II's favorite son, Manfred of Sicily (who had been at his side at Castel Fiorentino when he died), was killed in battle with the Frenchman Charles of Anjou, to whom Pope Clement IV had given Manfred's kingdom. He was thirty-three years old.

Charles had marched southward in late 1265, crossing into the Kingdom of Sicily with thirty thousand men and after several clashes faced

Manfred's forces on February 26, 1266, at the Battle of Benevento. Fierce fighting raged through the morning. At first it looked as though Manfred would carry the day as the Saracen archers cut down the French infantry and his German soldiers launched a powerful countercharge. But the tide of battle eventually changed, and when Charles attacked both flanks of Manfred's army, many of his Italian nobles deserted him, leaving only Manfred and his most faithful followers to fight on. Refusing to surrender, Manfred charged headlong into the battle and was eventually cut down.

Many of the French knights were impressed by his gallantry in battle and requested that Manfred be buried with honor, but Charles refused to allow an excommunicated man to be interred in hallowed ground. (The Pope had excommunicated Manfred, as he'd done with Frederick.) Instead, the local people and a number of French soldiers buried him at nightfall beside the bridge of Benevento and together piled up large stones to create a cairn where he lay. The Pope thought even this was too good for Manfred. His envoy, the Archbishop of Cosenza, sent a group of men to exhume Manfred's body under cover of darkness, with their torches extinguished, and they threw his remains onto the banks of the River Verde.

The death of Manfred was not quite the end of the Hohenstaufens. The saddest part was yet to unfold. Frederick's fifteen-year-old grandson, Conradin, who lived in Germany, was urged by the beleaguered Ghibellines to recapture Sicily from Charles. Conradin rode triumphantly into Italy in 1267, thronged by cheering crowds everywhere he went — and suddenly it was like young Frederick all over again, the beautiful, fair-haired lad come to claim his birthright. Much of Sicily, Calabria, and Apulia began to rebel against Charles. That November, the Pope carried on the tradition and excommunicated Conradin.

Undeterred, young Conradin marched to Lucera to gather together the Saracen troops, loyal since Frederick II's time, then led a multinational army — Italian, Spanish, Roman, Arab, and German — against Charles and met him in battle on August 23, 1268, at Tagliacozzo, in the hills of central Italy. Conradin's army won the first assault, but then let their guard down. Charles's army counterattacked and won the day.

Conradin escaped from the field of battle but was later captured as he attempted to sail to the island of Sicily, and he was imprisoned in Naples. Charles then had him tried for treason and — to the great shock and dismay of many — had Conradin beheaded in a public square. He was sixteen years old.

The last remaining Hohenstaufen male was Enzio, still imprisoned in Bologona. As the story goes, he tried to escape, hidden in a barrel that a man was carrying out of the city, but someone spotted a tress of his distinctive golden hair protruding through a hole in the side, and he was found out. In 1272, four years after Conradin's execution, Enzio died in prison.

℮

MY DAYDREAMS ABOUT Frederick II and his luckless offspring were finally getting to me. It was such a sad tale with so many "if onlys" — the largest of which was, if only they'd had someone with Frederick's unique skills to run the show: to outthink the enemy at every turn. Maybe things would have turned out differently.

I finally stopped at one of the rest areas along the autostrada to eat and to take a break from the road. I'd been blasting along for hours, driving at near full speed in my tiny blue Panda. When I went back outside, I took time to repack all of my belongings — including everything in my glove compartment and the things scattered around in the car — redistributing them into a single small suitcase and a backpack. I wanted to be able to drop off my car and take everything out of the trunk quickly and easily. I knew I'd have only one more pit stop, at the last gas station I could find near the airport.

Everything went smoothly the rest of the way to Rome. I finally saw the place at the end of the autostrada where people handed in their tickets and paid their tolls. I knew I was rounding the turn into the home stretch, and it felt great. And there were convenient gas pumps right there. I pulled over to the pumps and got out to fill my tank. Unfortunately, they didn't have automatic payment gas pumps anywhere I traveled in Italy, so I had to go inside and give my credit card to the cashier. It took two or three minutes for her to process my payment, then I walked back to my car, which was parked on the far side of the pumps.

Just as I was getting into the car, I decided on a whim to get my camera out and take a picture of my loyal Panda before I turned it in at the car rental company. When I walked around back, my heart sank. Someone had pried up the trunk as I was inside paying my bill. I lifted up the trunk lid. My backpack was gone. I frantically ran to the front of the car and looked in the front seat, then in the back seat and on the floor. It was no good. The pack was definitely gone. I looked frantically around, this way and that, trying to see if any suspicious people were lurking nearby. There was no one. My backpack had disappeared without a trace. I felt sick. I walked inside to the cashier and tried to explain what happened. She stared at me blankly.

I was aghast as I walked outside. I'd put all of my important things in that backpack. I couldn't even remember everything that was in it. And they were all gone — all, that is, except my passport, my driver's license, and a bank ATM card, which I'd miraculously had the foresight to keep in a front zippered pocket on my shirt. Without those things, I'm sure I would've been hitchhiking to the embassy to beg for money.

My depressing journey on the train into central Rome, the hours spent searching for a police station and then sitting waiting to fill out a theft report, were nightmares I can barely stand retelling. I remember the policewoman taking down my story, then turning to the other police in the room and saying something in Italian, and all of them roaring with laughter — at me. And all the time I sat in a stupor, still not believing this had happened, after all the things I'd been through, after all the scary places I'd traveled through. I'd had my backpack taken at the eleventh hour by a silent, unseen thief — and I didn't even have a bump on the head to show for it. I felt like a complete fool.

Franco picked me up later that night in the street outside the main train station. The area where he lived was beautiful. And his flat was one of the most amazing homes I've ever seen. But I was blind to it. All I could think about was that damn backpack and everything I'd lost.

I spent a rough night in my tiny room, tossing and turning for hours as I kept remembering more and more of the things I'd lost in the robbery: my camera; my handwritten notes from the entire trip; more than two-hundred euros; my laptop computer. And my computer didn't just have all the pictures I'd taken in Italy — which would have been bad enough. I suddenly realized I hadn't backed up any of the pictures I'd taken in the past three or four months, except on an external hard drive, which had been stolen along with my computer. All the pictures I'd taken at the falconry meet in Kearney; the World Center for Birds of Prey in Boise; Macduff hunting in the field that season; my kids competing in soccer, basketball, and track and performing in concerts and musical plays; and even the taped interviews I'd done with Roger Upton, Umberto Caproni, John Loft, and the other falconers in Europe were irretrievably lost.

What was I thinking? How could I have been so stupid not to have made back-up copies on a computer or hard drive at home before I left? I put everything on the line for no good reason. My only excuse was that I'd been so completely driven for the previous few months. I had so many things on my plate that something had to give. After returning from Scotland, I never stopped running full speed ahead, working full-time at my day job, helping take care of my children, training (and then doctoring) my falcon, and struggling to put out my first issue as editor of the *NAFA Journal*. The latter was a huge amount of work and completely voluntary — something I was doing for the good of falconry. I had no previous experience in design, and I had to figure out how to do everything myself. I'm such a perfectionist I stayed up well past midnight, night after night after night, trying to create a publication that was up to my standards. I finished correcting the proofs, dropped them off at the printing press, and left straightaway for the falconry meet. A few days after I got home, I flew to Italy. I never had a chance to sit down and catch my breath.

I finally fell asleep just as it was getting light outside, and I slept for maybe an hour and a half. When I woke up, I tried my best to get myself in the morning mode, energized, ready to take on anything. But it was hard. I pulled my passport, a pen, and a few other papers out of my shirt pocket and started looking through them. I saw the notes I'd jotted on a piece of paper the morning before when I'd spoken to the people at the Vatican Library. I saw Sister Juscinta's phone number. Maybe I could still pull one good thing out of this trip. Maybe I could still get to see Frederick's manuscript.

I dialed the number and waited as the phone rang several times.

"Pronto," a man answered.

"Sister Juscinta?" I asked. He put me on hold, and the most awful music came on, something familiar yet somehow twisted. It was a piece of electronic music, probably played on a Moog synthesizer, but it was way too slow and off key — like Walter Carlos on Valium. The identity of the music suddenly dawned on me: "Be it ever so humble, there's no place like home."

I closed my eyes and suddenly felt like Dorothy in *The Wizard of Oz*. "There's no place like home … there's no place like home!" But when I opened my eyes, I was still in Rome.

A minute later, the phone clicked on again. "Sister Juscinta?" I said. A man's voice came on the phone: "Pronto … Pronto?" I hung up.

21

SEE ROME AND DIE

WALKING THROUGH THE streets of Rome that morning, I felt as bad as I've ever felt in my life. I don't know why that should be. The stolen items were only material things, after all. The camera equipment and computer could be replaced. The lost pictures, the notes I'd taken, and the taped interviews were a shame to lose, but still: it's not as though someone died or went to prison. Far worse things could have happened. But for me, I think this was the last straw — the final symbolic event that broke the protective wall of stoicism I'd built up for more than forty years. As I walked along, the skies overhead grew darker, threatening rain, and I felt myself descending, falling toward an inevitable crash. Where it would end I had no idea.

For the previous few months, I'd thought of nothing but Frederick II and his sons and his grandson and their whole sorry story. But on this morning I thought only about myself: how screwed up I was, how the one unifying theme of my entire life was loss. Things vanish. Nothing stays the same. All the people I'd known, all my friends and acquaintances, all the animals I'd gotten close to, even the places I'd roamed . . . all had disappeared without a trace. I'd had the curse of always being the new kid in class throughout my childhood, always leaving towns, provinces, states, countries — and it didn't get any better when I grew up. Everyone I knew as a teenager and young adult was gone. I always took it stoically. I moved on. I blocked it from my mind. But now it all came flooding back.

I realized I had no familiar landscape I could call my own. No home. The neighborhoods where my teenage friends had grown up had all changed. None of their families still lived there. They had sold off their houses long ago when real estate prices in Southern California skyrocketed. Some houses bought originally for $20,000 sold for up to half a million dollars. And the fields, hills, and woodlands I explored in my teens, riding my bike for miles and hiking overland to see the nests of eagles and hawks, are now all gone — lost to ravenous developers and the endless influx of new people searching for the good life and in the process destroying everything that was good about California.

Where is Mac now? Where is Hollis? Where are all those people I shared my youth with and who had meant so much to me? And where are all my hawks? And Rex? Of course, I know that most of the animals have died of old age by now, but why did they all have to vanish so completely and utterly like a shimmering mirage on a hot desert morning? At that moment, I wanted more than anything else in the world to know what happened to everyone and everything in my life. I wanted to see one of those follow-up scenes like they have at the end of some movies when they tell you what became of all the characters years later. I wanted to see a tally sheet with names, dates, and places.

I could feel the dam crumbling. I saw my father looming high above everything else — the drunken sailor, the ancient mariner who hung around my neck like a great albatross, always there, always hidden from view. But at least I knew where he was now. His ashes lay in a brown plastic box at my sister Maureen's house, as they had for the past ten years, waiting to be dispersed. I thought about him, about the strange series of coincidences that brought us back in touch with each other more than twenty years after he'd vanished from our lives — or more accurately, after we'd fled, racing away in the middle of the night and hiding out, never having a listed phone number; never doing anything that might attract undue attention, like receiving an award or being mentioned in the paper.

Years after we left him I began wondering about my dad. An absent parent creates an enormous gap in someone's life, even if that parent has many negative qualities. I felt I at least wanted to know if he were alive or dead. I called the information operator a few times and looked through some telephone directories at the library but didn't get anywhere. Then an odd thing happened. My girlfriend's mother was working with a man a few years younger than me who was also named Tim Gallagher, and, by coincidence, his wife was named Janet — the same name as my younger sister. One night they got a call from a man with a British accent. He said he was searching for his son, Tim Gallagher, and had found their number in a phone book. It was obviously my dad. He called back several times during the course of the next few weeks, even though the other Tim Gallagher assured him he was not his son. Then one night when Dad called, the man's wife, Janet, answered. That clinched it for my father. She must be his long-lost daughter. They felt sorry for him and had several long conversations with Dad before he finally stopped calling. This was the point at which I heard about it, and I told them to take down his phone number the next time he called. It didn't happen again for almost two years.

By then I was editing *WildBird*, a bird-watching magazine based in San Juan Capistrano. I called my father at lunchtime one day, and it was strange. It seemed like the most natural thing in the world to be talking with him, even though we'd been out of touch for more than two decades. I found out he had been living in Las Vegas for a few years, but before that we had lived almost parallel lives. He had rented an apartment in downtown Long Beach in the same neighborhood as the *Press-Telegram*, a daily newspaper where I worked for three years, and he often drank at a bar across the street named the Press Club. I'd been there many times myself, and I wondered if we had ever sat drinking at separate tables at the same time. I also found out later that we'd both been staying in London at exactly the same time in the 1980s. We knew because it was during the World Cup Soccer matches, and we both spent a lot of time in pubs watching the games.

He gave me his address at the end of the phone call, and I said I'd come and visit him sometime. I just didn't know when. But by the next weekend, I decided on an impulse to go. I didn't even call ahead. I figured I could stop at a phone booth somewhere along the way and let him know I was coming. But by the time I got to Las Vegas a few hours later, I still hadn't telephoned him. I finally just drove right to his apartment and knocked on the door. He looked so much older than he had the last time I'd seen him. He was almost seventy — but it was an old seventy. His life of hard drinking and chain smoking had finally caught up with him. He seemed almost mellow, a word I never before would have used to describe him.

I started visiting him from time to time, especially later, after I'd left my position at *WildBird* to be a freelance writer and nature photographer. At that time I would drive to the Canadian prairies and spend a few months each summer, camping out and photographing various birds and other wildlife and writing a photography column. I would always stop and spend a couple of days with my dad as I drove to and from Canada, because I went right through Las Vegas. We developed a closer relationship than we'd ever had before. When he had hip-replacement surgery later, I stayed at his apartment for a couple of weeks to take care of him. I introduced him to my German friends Tom and Hank, both of whom loved hearing his stories about World War II, even though in Tom's case, his father had fought on the other side. My sisters also got back in touch with Dad and visited him a few times.

I moved to upstate New York in 1990 to take a position at Cornell University as editor of the Lab of Ornithology's magazine, *Living Bird*, and within a year had gotten married and settled down. Rachel and I visited Dad once and had lunch with him when we were on our way to the Nevada desert on other business. The next time I saw him was in 1995, when he was on his deathbed. It was a ghastly time. A few months earlier, he and I had had a falling out. He had the attitude that he'd been a complete innocent in the breakup of our family and couldn't understand why we had left him. I used to just let it go and laugh it off, but finally one night on the phone I let him have it and told him what a terrible parent he had been and that he was lucky any of us would even talk to him. He didn't want to hear that, and it may have killed the relationship we'd been developing for the previous few years. He

stopped calling me, and on the few times I called him, he was standoffish and quickly got off the phone. But he stayed in close contact with
my sisters.

That September, my sister Janet was planning a long trip to Europe
with a friend, and she happened to mention it to Dad. He pleaded with
her to come and visit him first, which seemed unusual. He must have
known he was seriously ill and didn't have much time left. I'm sure he
thought this might be the last time he would ever see her.

I tried to call Dad a couple of weeks after Janet visited him, but there
was no answer on his phone. That didn't bother me at first. Sometimes
he would go away for two or three days. But after a week I got concerned.
I finally telephoned the police department in Las Vegas. They gave me
a list of hospitals in the area, and I called each one. At the very last
hospital, they found his name on the patient list. He'd had emergency
surgery a few days earlier and was recuperating. The receptionist put me
through to his doctor. He said my father had had surgery for bladder
cancer and that it would be a good idea to come as soon as possible to
see him. I made airline reservations to fly to Las Vegas the next day. I
planned to stay for five days.

Later that day, I reached my father on the phone in his hospital room.
His voice was slurred from medication. I told him I was planning to fly
there to see him. "Don't bother . . . don't bother," he said. I spoke for a
couple more minutes, but it was hard to reach through the fog of his
painkillers to communicate with him. I also called my sister Maureen,
who lived in San Diego. She planned to drive to Las Vegas, and my
mother was coming along to keep her company, although she had no
plans to visit my father.

Maureen and my mother picked me up at the Las Vegas airport the
next afternoon and drove me to the hospital. They had been there for
several hours, and Maureen had already spent quite a bit of time with
Dad, while my mother sat downstairs in the hospital lobby.

Dad was sleeping when Maureen and I entered his room, so we sat
together talking. Eventually he woke up, but he seemed far away, slipping
in and out of a Demerol-induced haze. He barely knew we were there.
A few times I noticed he would hold his hand a few inches in front of

his face and stare transfixed as he slowly turned it, examining it from different angles. I suddenly realized I'd seen my daughter Clara doing exactly the same thing when she was an infant and the total scope of her life extended only a few inches away from her eyes. Here was this thing, her hand, over which she had complete control. She could focus intently on it and turn it to reflect the light from changing angles. She seemed utterly fascinated. I'll bet my father did the same thing as a baby. And now that his life was receding and the focus of his world was shrinking, he was regressing back to that state.

I did manage to talk with him before we left the hospital that evening. He said he hoped none of us would ever have to go through anything like this. I remember staring at the tattoos on his forearms. They were so old they seemed formless: just blobs of red and dark blue. One had a couple of indecipherable words beneath it. I asked what it said, and he told me "Love Mother," something almost as mystifying as "Rosebud" in *Citizen Kane.*

Maureen, my mother, and I began a nightly ritual of going to a casino to eat dinner. We usually went to Caesar's Palace, which was surreal. They'd built a huge indoor shopping area that was supposed to resemble ancient Rome, with flagstone streets (lined with modern high-end retail stores), fountains, and statues. The simulated sky and clouds, painted on a ceiling high overhead, and the lighting made it seem like we were really outside. It had all the charm (and authenticity) of a Disneyland ride. I noticed a statue of a man holding a hawk on his fist. This was a complete anachronism. Falconry was not practiced in ancient Rome. The only Roman reference to falconry I've seen was a passage written by Pliny the Elder: "In that part of Thrace which lies above Amphipolis, men and hawks go in pursuit of prey as it were in a kind of partnership, for when the men drive the birds out of the woods and reed-beds the hawks bring them down as they fly; and after they have taken the game, the fowlers share it with them."

Before we left the casino one night, I saw a man who looked vaguely like my father. He stood near the entrance, inhaling so hard on a cigarette that the ash glowed like a hot ember of coal in the dim light. That's just how my father smoked.

I assumed when I saw Dad that first night he would get a little bit better each day — or at least more mentally aware and talkative. It didn't happen that way. The day I arrived was the high point. From there he descended into a darker and darker place and carried us along with him. He did ask about his cat from time to time, in his more lucid moments, and he wondered if he'd be able to keep her when he got out of the hospital. Ironically, she was the only reason he had stayed in America instead of flying back to England as soon as his illness was diagnosed. My father had always talked about returning there if he ever got cancer, because the doctors in Britain give heroin to terminally ill patients to ease their suffering. He often told me how he had talked with his sister on the phone at an English hospital just twenty minutes before she died of cancer and how peaceful she seemed. That's what he wanted. But because he had a shy, spooky cat, he didn't leave America. Instead he died slowly and painfully at a dingy hospital in Las Vegas.

I had a talk with his doctor the day I arrived. He was a thin young Pakistani man who had studied medicine in England and lived there for a time before immigrating to America. He laughed a lot as he spoke and told me how much he loved to play cricket. I asked him about my dad's prognosis, and it was grim. He might live for another two or three months, he told me. He'd be able to go home to his apartment but would require nursing care. When I asked about the cat, he smirked and shook his head. "Get rid of the cat," he said.

I think the cat became a kind of code for my dad. He knew they wouldn't let him keep his cat if he was near death. When we told him Maureen would be taking his cat home with her to San Diego, something changed inside him. He seemed to lose any interest in living any longer. He was obviously in great pain, but the doctors were holding back on the drugs because they might endanger his life. He eventually passed out and lay there for hours with his mouth agape. The other patient in his room looked the same. He hadn't moved at all since we'd started coming to Dad's room.

I finally had to take a break from the depressing atmosphere in the room, but there was no relief in the rest of the ward. As I strode down the gleaming linoleum hallway, I couldn't help glancing in other rooms.

Everyone looked the same: head back, eyes closed, mouth agape. I realized this was death row for the terminal cancer patients — the last stop before the morgue.

My sister and I and my mother decided to go to Dad's apartment and start cleaning it. It had become a mess in the weeks leading up to his surgery, and we wanted to tidy it up. Mostly, I think it was therapeutic for us, a way to escape for a few hours from the cancer ward and do something completely mindless but useful: scrubbing sinks, walls, and floors and vacuuming the carpet. And we were good at it.

As we sat taking a quick breather at one point, the cat finally emerged. We had no idea where she'd been hiding. She was already a spooky cat to begin with and would let only my father pet her, and then she had probably been traumatized by the frantic burst of activity when the paramedics came rushing in to help Dad. (He had called 911.) A neighbor left food for her each day, but no one had seen her since my dad went to the hospital. She didn't come near us, but at least she was walking around in the open and eating some food. At some point soon, we would have to get her into the pet carrier so Maureen could drive her home. I knew it wouldn't be easy.

That evening, everything came to a head. Suddenly the doctors were saying my father needed emergency surgery to remove a blood clot. He was in a deep sleep, so the surgeon, another Pakistani doctor, shook him and shouted, just inches from his face: "Mr. Gallagher ... Mr. Gallagher!" My dad woke with a start, a terror-stricken look on his face. "You have to go back into surgery," the man said, still shouting. "You have a blood clot, Mr. Gallagher."

"No ... no," my dad said. "No more."

"You must have the surgery," the doctor insisted.

"No ... no more ... please."

I stood up. "That's it. Leave him alone," I said.

After the doctors left, I sat beside my dad's bed and told him he didn't have to worry. They wouldn't be able to hurt him anymore. I'd take care of everything. I went to the nurse's station to find out what I had to do to stop them from taking extraordinary measures to keep him alive. It was all so horrible. He was caught up in a system that had nothing to do with preserving or improving life. It was just an insurance mill, where people were kept alive, no matter how poor the quality of their lives, so that insurance companies could be billed thousands and thousands of dollars for radical operations and hospital care just to prolong their suffering for a couple more months and reap the profits. It was all perfectly legal but no less despicable. The best thing for my father at this point would be to die peacefully in his sleep. He knew it. We all knew it — including the doctors.

I found out the hospital didn't have any kind of form for denying treatment. They gave me a yellow legal pad, and I wrote out a lengthy declaration in long hand telling the hospital not to take any additional measures to save his life, absolving the medical personnel from any responsibility for this decision. My sister and I both signed the paper and gave it to the head nurse, who made a copy for us. I asked her to make sure he got enough pain medication.

When we went back into my dad's room, he had pulled out all the tubes and sensors connected to his body, even his colostomy bag. He wanted to die right then. If he'd had enough strength, I'm sure he would've opened the hospital window and jumped out. The nurse dutifully hooked everything back up again, then left Maureen and me in the room with him. We talked to him for a while but he didn't answer. He seemed far away, drifting alone in his own private hell. Then he fell into a deep slumber, the rising and falling of his chest as he breathed the only sign of life. We finally stood up to leave. I stopped in the doorway and looked back at him.

"This is the last time we'll see him alive," I said.

"Really? Do you think so?" said Maureen.

I nodded, and we walked away.

When I got to the waiting room downstairs, I went to the pay telephone to call my wife. I didn't know what to say. I suddenly felt deep emotions welling up inside. I knew my whole façade would crumble if I spoke. When Rachel answered the phone, I didn't say anything for several seconds. I was trying desperately to maintain my composure. "Tell me about the kids," I said finally then stood there in silence as she spoke, leaning my head against the wall and feeling the coolness of the plaster creep gently into my skull.

I came back to the hospital early the next morning and all was still. I didn't see anyone at the nurse's station, so I walked straight into Dad's room. He looked exactly the same as he had the night before except that his chest was no longer rising and falling. I watched him for a few minutes to make sure. Then I put my hand on his hand, and he was cold to the touch. The nurse abruptly walked in, saw me, and burst into tears.

"You weren't supposed to see him like this," she said.

I hugged her. "It's OK . . . really," I said. "It's OK. Everything's fine."

Later that morning we had to make arrangements to have my father cremated. Everything was suddenly a big rush. The hospital wanted to know what to do with his body. The mortuary was bizarre — something straight out of *The Addams Family*. An obese man in a huge black suit greeted us as we went inside. He looked like Wolfman Jack, the famous disc jockey from the 1960s, only much bigger, with a black goatee and thick, jet-black hair slicked back. He had gold rings, some studded with diamonds, on each of his pudgy, pink fingers. We sat together at a round, faux-walnut table with a big glass ashtray in the middle, overflowing with cigarette butts, and he laid out our options. I chose the quickest, easiest arrangement. I was flying home the next day. He told us they would cremate him that afternoon, and we could pick up his ashes the next morning — and the whole thing would cost only $350 plus tax. We paid the money and left, and the three of us spent the rest of the day and the evening together.

First thing the next morning we returned to my dad's apartment. We wanted to finish our clean-up effort and pack his belongings, giving some things away to his neighbors. An elderly black woman asked me for a smoke, and I gave her a whole carton of Marlboros. "If you don't mind smoking cigarettes that belonged to a man who just died of cancer, you're welcome to these," I said. She shrugged and grabbed the box, rushing off to have a quiet smoke-fest somewhere. A short time later, a man in his midseventies with a Boston accent stopped by and asked what was happening. He'd seen me carrying a box to my sister's car. I told him my father had died and that I was gathering his personal effects. He blanched.

"Oh no . . . no," he said, shaking his head in disbelief. "He was a great guy . . . he would talk to me." He sighed deeply and his eyes misted. "He was great. He really was. I hope you know that."

"Yeah, I know," I said. "He was great."

The biggest task still lay ahead: getting Dad's cat ready for my sister to take home. I'd been dreading it for a couple of days. This was my last day in Las Vegas, and I knew no one else would be able to get her into the carrier. I was sure I'd get only one chance. If she got away and hid under the furniture again, we'd never get her out. I brought some fishy-smelling cat food to the apartment and opened the can. It was getting down to the last hour before I had to fly home, but she finally came out. She had been getting used to our presence while we were cleaning the apartment. I put the cat food into the carrier, and after a long wait she stepped partway inside and started licking it. I was bent over, ready to close the door in an instant if she stepped a couple of inches more inside. But suddenly she spooked, bursting from the cage. I sprang instantly and grabbed her — and she bit me hard, sinking her teeth deep into my right hand, piercing the center of my palm with a long fang and squeezing down. It must have struck a raw nerve. It was one of the most painful things I've ever experienced, far worse than anything a hawk has ever done to me, but I couldn't let go. I held firmly and put her back into the cage. Pushing against the door tightly with my knee, I released her and slipped my hands out before she could escape, then closed the latch.

My hand was bleeding profusely. We didn't have any first-aid equipment or enough time to buy some, because my plane would be leaving in less than an hour. I quickly washed the wound in the bathroom and swabbed it with tissue. I wrapped toilet paper around and around and around my hand, then clenched my fist, hoping to stanch the bleeding. My mother and Maureen dropped me at the airport ten minutes later and I raced inside, afraid I'd miss my plane.

I felt shell-shocked after the previous few days and was moving in a fog, oblivious of everything around me. As I rushed toward the ticket counter, I bumped shoulders with a middle-aged woman going the other way. I turned to apologize, and she slapped me hard in the face. "Sonofa-bitch like to a-knocked me down," she said in a thick Southern accent. I stood there stunned for a couple of seconds, then turned and continued on to the ticket counter, leaving a trail of tiny blood spots, dripping from my hand.

I was drenched in sweat when I finally got into my seat on the plane, and I started shivering. I felt alone and sick. After a mechanical delay, the plane finally took off, banking hard to the left as it gained altitude. I glanced out the window for one last look at Vegas and saw the faux-ancient edifice of the Luxor Casino looming large beneath me with its Sphinx and its glass pyramid, gleaming like a golden beacon in the mid-day sun.

℮

I CONTINUED WALKING through Rome, following the crowds flowing toward the bridge leading over the Tiber into the Vatican. It was a miraculous city with the most amazing ancient sites almost everywhere I turned. If only I'd been in the right mood to enjoy it. I finally reached Saint Peter's Basilica and got in line with all the other people waiting to go through the security checkpoint. It was at this very site, where the basilica now stands, that the apostle Peter met his martyrdom, executed by Nero's men during the persecutions following the Great Fire of Rome in 64 A.D. Peter declared he was unworthy of suffering the same kind of martyrdom as Christ, so he was crucified upside down. As the story goes, his followers buried him nearby in an area already used by pagans as a necropolis. A Christian burial ground grew up around his grave. The Emperor Constantine supposedly built Saint Peter's Basilica right over Peter's tomb to honor him. The basilica — which had become structurally unsafe — was completely rebuilt and expanded in the six-teenth century.

During excavations carried out beneath the Basilica in the 1940s and '50s, archaeologists found a pagan and a Christian graveyard and finally a semicircle of graves surrounding a central grave, which was covered with coins and various votives. The bones in the central grave were from a short, broad-shouldered man in his sixties who lived sometime in the early first century A.D. Many believe this to be the body of Saint Peter.

When I finally got through security, I walked along in the lower level below the basilica, past the sarcophagi of various popes, some who had lain there for centuries. I felt myself becoming more and more depressed. Some sarcophagi had a life-sized image of the pope interred within carved in effigy on the marble tops. They were not flattering depictions: withered little men with pointy hats and sour faces. I saw where Pope John Paul II lay, his sarcophagus adorned with numerous fresh-cut flowers. I wondered if he would still be getting fresh flowers eight centuries hence.

I finally went upstairs and entered the basilica, making my way toward the carved central door, which had been there in Frederick II's time. Then I saw it set into the floor, a large circular slab, more than eight feet across, made of red porphyry like Frederick's tomb. It was here that Charlemagne stood to be crowned — as did most other Holy Roman Emperors including Frederick II. Few noticed it now. Tourists with tiny pocket digital cameras streamed constantly across it, hurrying to snap pictures of various grand statues or the vast interior of the basilica, never stopping to look at the red circle beneath their feet.

I stood in the center of the circle and gazed at the interior of the great basilica, overwhelmed by its power and grandeur — amazed that humans could ever have built a place like this, so perfect, so colossal in every way. I closed my eyes and pictured Frederick as he rode along the Via Triumphalis, the ancient coronation road, thronged with the cheering citizens of Rome. He had stood on this very spot as Pope Honorius III placed a miter and crown upon his head and handed him a sword, which Frederick brandished symbolically three times. As he received the scepter and imperial orb, the choir burst into song, filling the basilica with their angelic chorus: "To Frederick ever glorious, of the Romans the unconquered Emperor, be Life and Victory." What a moment. What a spectacular triumph for a street urchin from Sicily.

As I stood there with closed eyes, I suddenly found myself sobbing uncontrollably, tears streaming down my face, and I couldn't stop. Was it for Frederick II or myself that I wept? I can't say. Thankfully, no one came up to me and asked what was wrong. They were as oblivious to my pain as any New York City crowd would have been, and I was glad.

When the flow of tears finally eased, I found a restroom and splashed water on my face. It felt good, completely refreshing.

I stepped outside, and the weather had improved markedly. The sun was out and a stiff breeze blew across Saint Peter's Square, where the ancient Egyptian obelisk — brought to Rome by Caligula — rose in the center. As the story goes, this obelisk was not toppled over as many others in Rome were, because people regarded it as the last witness to Saint Peter's martyrdom.

Oddly enough, I felt wonderful as I made my way back toward Franco's home. Somehow it seemed like a profound weight had passed from me, and I was eager to experience this glorious city.

I walked back across the bridge out of the Vatican, making my way through the throngs of people, most of them walking in the opposite direction toward Saint Peter's. I saw street performers — the same ones had been there earlier in the day, but I had barely noticed them then. They were amazing: several pretended to be statues, remaining perfectly still for hours as people walked by dropping coins in containers at their feet. One young woman dressed as the Statue of Liberty, with a long greenish gown, spiky headdress, and face painted metallic green to resemble weathered copper, stood on a box holding a torch aloft. She didn't move an inch either time I walked past. A man in white face paint dressed in a top hat and tails was bent over a make-believe silent-movie camera with a crank on the side. Once every twenty minutes or so he would turn the crank a few times and pan slowly with the camera as if he were shooting a movie, then freeze and become a statue again. They were all talented, but what a way to make a living.

As I crossed an alley along the main road, a motorcycle sped around the corner with its tires squealing and came right at me. I jumped out of the way just barely in time to avoid being splattered on the pavement. I suspect if this had happened earlier in the morning, during my depression, I might have just let him run me down. As it was, I just laughed. *See Rome and die*, I thought.

I decided to walk to the Pantheon, one of my favorite buildings in Rome. It's such a remarkable structure, and it was built twenty-seven years before the birth of Christ, during the reign of Augustus, Frederick

II's role model as emperor. It was seriously damaged a couple of times and had to be rebuilt, but the final structure has stood since the time of Hadrian in the first century A.D. The Pantheon was originally a temple to honor all of the Roman gods but has since become a Catholic church. According to legend, it was erected on the spot where, upon his death, Romulus, founder of Rome, was seized by an eagle and carried off into the skies to be with the gods. I like that image — the original sky burial. As I walked through the Pantheon on this bright chilly December day, it had never looked so good. I stood in the center for a while, soaking in its ancient ambiance as the light streamed down through the hole in the center of its massive dome.

From there I made my way back to Franco's home. He lives in the perfect place for a directionally challenged person like me — a five-minute stroll from the Pantheon, and just the other side of Santa Maria Supra Minerva, a beautiful old church built right over the spot where a Roman temple dedicated to the goddess Minerva once stood. I was fortunate to have the church as an orienting device. Any cab driver, almost anyone I asked directions of, knew where Minerva was. And as long as I could get to its front door, I could stroll through the church and come out the back door right into Franco's alley.

As I walked through the empty church, I stopped at the far end to look at a nearly forgotten statue by Michelangelo called *The Risen Christ*. (This is what I love about Rome: you can find these absolute treasures tucked away in churches all over the city.) It's the most original depiction of Christ I've ever seen and is more akin to Michelangelo's *David* than any other statue or painting of Jesus. There's nothing sorrowful about it. Christ stands proudly like an Olympic champion, holding his cross astride — tall and muscular, buck naked for all to see like a classic pagan god. For centuries, the Dominican friars have covered the statues' private parts with a gilded metal loincloth, which looks completely out of place and odd on the marble.

I finally stepped out the back door of the church and into the narrow alley. Franco lives in a five-hundred-year-old building only a few steps away. He had given me a set of keys to get through the main door at ground level and into his flat, several floors up. His home is exquisite, especially the furniture; most of it is hundreds of years old and from the Trentino region in northern Italy where he was born. He has various cabinets, chests of drawers, and a sideboard with elaborate patterns and even outdoor scenes inlaid in them, created by artisans using different shades of wood — museum pieces, all. Numerous rugs from the Caucasus lie on the floor or drape the walls. Franco's flat has wooden ceilings, about nine feet up, with great beams stretching across, supporting everything. I could have spent hours just exploring there. But really, all of Rome is a museum. Everywhere you look there are ruins. And almost anywhere workers dig, they find pieces of ancient statues and pillars. I suspect many homes in the area have ancient Roman artifacts. The entryway to Franco's building has a couple of nice small pillars that someone probably picked up for nothing decades if not centuries ago.

Franco wasn't home when I went inside, but his six-month-old boxer pup, Nina, ran over to greet me, jumping up and placing her huge paws against me about waist high so I would pet her. She was a nice dog but would never leave anyone alone. I finally went into my room to rest. I felt lazy and peaceful after my intense morning, and I wanted nothing more than to sleep.

22

HOMEWARD BOUND

I WOKE UP early the next morning. This would be my last full day in Italy, and I was finally going hawking. Frikky's friend Riccardo lived an hour's drive from Rome and was flying a tiercel peregrine. Another friend, Antonio, would meet us there, and we would spend the rest of the day flying peregrines at partridge and pheasant on an estate where Riccardo had leased hunting rights. But first I wanted to spend the early part of the morning with Franco, strolling through the streets of Rome not far from his flat. We took Nina with us and stopped at a coffee bar for espresso, which everyone in Italy uses to jumpstart the morning and to keep going all day long.

Franco is a tall man in his midsixties who has been retired for a few years. Though not a falconer, he often goes to Scotland to watch Frikky and the others hawk grouse in the early fall. He is an avid tennis player and plays at the same club as Frikky, which is where they met. He reminds me a little of Aldo Cella — the character in the old "Chill a Cella" wine commercials. Not that he looks like him but, like Aldo, women seem to flock to him. "Oh, Franco," they say and rush up to give him the obligatory hug and the kisses on both cheeks. Everyone seems to know him. And they all love Nina.

When Frikky finally arrived at midmorning, he had a difficult time making his way up the narrow alley to Franco's building in his big,

American SUV, a Jeep Grand Cherokee. Tiny Vespa scooters lined both sides of the alley, packed like colorful metal sardines, making the passage tighter still. We had to guide Frikky carefully, with only an inch to spare on each side of his Jeep. It was even harder a short time later when he had to back all the way out of the alley.

On the way to Riccardo's home, we drove through picturesque hills with cliffs and gorges pockmarked with deep caves. I asked Frikky if there were any subterranean dwellings in the area like the ones at Matera and Gravina in Puglia. He nodded and told me there was a complete Mithra temple nearby. "Mithra was a rival of Christianity in the early days," he said. It had a number of similarities with Christianity — such as a charismatic founder who was supposedly born of a virgin on December 25 — but it was several centuries older. The Mithra religion had been popular with Roman soldiers just as Christianity was later, which is why it spread so quickly, making its way along the military communication routes to the farthest boundaries of the empire.

The village where Riccardo lives is easily more than a thousand years old. High on a hill, surrounded by gorges, it has narrow cobbled streets and storybook houses made of stone. It was impossible to drive all the way to his house — the streets were far too narrow. We finally parked and walked the last couple of hundred feet. His home was beautiful — perhaps eight hundred years old or more with narrow stairs inside leading up to the tiny living quarters. He had wonderful little falconry sculptures here and there and paintings on the walls and a gun rack with classic side-by-side shotguns.

Riccardo has gray hair and is perhaps in his sixties but has a younger wife and school-aged children. After visiting for a while, we walked down the road to where he kept his tiercel peregrine. He proudly showed me the vintage 1970s Volkswagen van he uses to transport falcons to the field. I had to laugh. The Volkswagen van had been my vehicle of choice for hawking in the late 1960s and '70s, and I'd had three different ones over the years.

A treacherous cliff dropped away just past the little stone wall where we were standing. Up the gorge, I could see numerous holes and caves, accessible only by ropes. Riccardo pointed to a cave on a facing cliff and said that the Etruscans had raised pigeons in it thousands of years ago. He also told me that if people looked around below the cliff where we were standing they could still find small balls of lead from the Middle Ages when the townspeople had poured cauldrons full of sizzling molten metal down on attackers as they tried to scale the cliff to assault the village. It's a brutal history but fascinating. Other sections of the cliff have nesting falcons in spring, he said: a pair of peregrines and some lanner falcons.

After Riccardo put his tiercel in the van, we all climbed aboard and headed to his hawking area. He had paid for the right to fly his peregrine on a large estate where shotgunners also hunted, but it was well regulated so he wouldn't be in the field at the same time they were. The place was not ideal for flying peregrines and other large falcons but certainly acceptable. It had open fields, some of them agricultural, and some marshy areas, but also lots of brushy fencerows, stone walls, olive trees, and woodlands. It would be easy to lose sight of a falcon and also for the falcon's quarry to find a place to hide quickly. But we had the possibility of getting flights at pheasant, partridge, and ducks.

We were supposed to meet Riccardo's friend Antonio, who was bringing his peregrines, so we would have an opportunity to spend the entire afternoon hawking. As we stood beside a dirt road in the middle of a field, a man pulled up in a small car. It was the gamekeeper, who watched over everything in the estate. Frikky leaned toward me and whispered, "He's a Sardinian. They're very dangerous. They kidnap people and hold them for ransom."

I nodded. I love the way people in Italy still have such a strong allegiance to their city or region, just as Italians did in the Middle Ages. To this day, people from other parts of the country are often viewed as outsiders and mistrusted. The day I was robbed, I told Frikky and his friend Francesco about the theft, and they kept insisting it happened near Naples — and that the Neapolitans are wicked, dangerous people. I pointed out a couple of times that it actually took place right at the edge of Rome and even pointed out the location on a map, but they chose not to hear me. I later overheard Francesco telling someone else about what happened to me. Although he was speaking in Italian, I distinctly heard him mention Naples a couple of times.

Antonio finally showed up, driving an SUV with four peregrines in the back. He is much younger than Frikky and Riccardo, perhaps in his late thirties with dark hair, and works as a veterinarian treating horses. Antonio is an incredibly avid falconer and travels widely to fly at different quarries in a wide range of situations. He told me about a couple of trips he had taken to Mongolia, spending weeks trekking overland in a four-wheel-drive vehicle, flying his falcons at black grouse and other game. He happened to mention that his wife had just had a baby the night before.

"What are you doing here?" I asked.

He laughed. "My wife is wonderful," he said. "She knows I am only truly happy when I'm flying my falcons, so she insisted that I go hunting today." Antonio speaks English perfectly. When I told him I worked at Cornell University, he said he had been to a veterinary conference there years earlier. He mentioned he had eaten at a wonderful restaurant that had numerous game heads hanging on the walls. I laughed. Antlers is only a five-minute drive from my home, and my wife and I eat there frequently, I told him.

Antonio has two excellent pointers, and he let one go at the edge of a field. She was perfectly obedient, coursing back and forth as Antonio pointed to the areas he wanted her to check and coming back instantly when he whistled. At first she found nothing, but she finally lined up on a seemingly solid point. Antonio unhooded an intermewed female peregrine and held her into the wind. She circled up above him, reaching a pitch close to four hundred feet — not a great altitude but appropriate for this kind of broken country where quarry can reach cover quickly.

We moved in for the flush, but it was no good. The pheasant had probably run ahead of the point. Antonio called his bird down to the lure, and we went to another place up a hill, near a marsh. We were headed to an area with a ditch surrounded by shrubs that looked good for pheasants. On the way, we flushed a small flock of teal we hadn't seen, and we didn't get a chance to fly a falcon at them. A short time later, one of Antonio's dogs got a solid point along the ditch. He unhooded his favorite bird, L'Español, "The Spanish" — an intermewed peregrine from Spain. She went up well, and this time we flushed a big cock pheasant that burst from cover strongly, flying nearly forty feet in the air as he tried to make his escape. The peregrine stooped but instead of hitting the pheasant from above, she stooped down below it, swung up, and smashed into it on the uppercut, then rode it to the ground. She dispatched the pheasant quickly, and I knelt down near her to take a picture with the pointer sitting behind her. Of course, my good camera had been stolen, so I had to use a cheap disposable camera I'd bought at a tourist kiosk that morning on my walk with Franco. It was supposed to cost ten euros, but Franco had a talk with the shop owner in Italian, and the man ended up charging me half price. "I told him what happened to you," said Franco, "and I asked him to give you a special price . . . for the good name of Italia." Having been a professional photographer for many years, I was a little embarrassed to use the throwaway cardboard-box camera, but Riccardo and Antonio knew my situation.

It was starting to get late, but Riccardo was hoping to get a flight for his first-year tiercel peregrine. The bird had been ill with pneumonia and had nearly died, but Riccardo had managed to bring him around with heavy doses of antibiotics. He wasn't in top shape yet, but Riccardo was eager to give him a try at partridge. We made our way through some agricultural fields, and one of the dogs went on point. Riccardo quickly removed his bird's equipment, slipped off his hood, and released him. The bird didn't hesitate to start ringing up above us with the quick snappy flight of a tiercel, which I've always liked. When he got up about five hundred feet, we charged into the field and almost immediately flushed more than a dozen partridge. The tiercel stooped through them but didn't connect. Swinging up high, he went into another stoop, but we lost sight of him behind some trees.

We ran all the way there but didn't see him. As we walked along the row of trees and shrubs, we kept flushing more partridge, but there was no sign of Riccardo's peregrine. Riccardo pulled out his telemetry receiver and switched it on. All we got was static, not a trace of a signal. The bird's transmitter must have malfunctioned, so we were in the same shape we would have been in more than thirty years earlier when telemetry was in its infancy and few people had it. It was quickly getting dark. We all felt certain that his peregrine caught a partridge. He'd had such a good opportunity. We walked along the dirt path beside the trees. A couple of times, Antonio and I thought we heard a falcon's bell in the distance, but it was faint in the wind. It seemed to be coming from an olive orchard to the right. We finally spread out and started walking through the trees. Every so often we'd hear a bell again, sounding unbelievably close. We kept looking down, checking each bit of cover closely. Then Antonio spotted him above us, sitting on a tree. He'd probably been watching us the entire time. Riccardo called him down as the last rays of light receded, leaving us in near complete darkness.

Antonio and Riccardo had rubber boots and decided to go overland with their birds through a swampy area. They would swing back by to get Frikky and me. We were to walk farther along to where the path met a larger dirt road up ahead and wait for them there. It was amazingly dark by then, and we didn't have a flashlight.

"Maybe the Sardinians will come along and kidnap us," I said.

Frikky laughed. "I hope not," he said. "No one would pay my ransom."

℮

THAT NIGHT, FRIKKY was in a rush to get home because he was going to a Christmas party at the home of his doctor and was running late. I didn't have any money for a cab, but Frikky dropped me at a place where taxies gathered and paid the driver after giving him explicit instructions on where to take me — back to the Church of Santa Maria Supra Minerva. Of course, I would have to walk through the church to get to Franco's flat — there was no other way to get there besides walking all the way around through the labyrinth of tiny streets in the dark. I knew I'd get hopelessly lost if I tried that. I know my limitations. But my hiking boots were covered in thick mud from the fields where we'd been hawking. I finally took them off and carried them as I walked through the church in my stocking feet, pausing only to nod at Michelangelo's *Risen Christ* before ducking out the back door.

Franco blanched as I stepped inside his home, still clutching my muddy boots. "It's no problem," I said and quickly put the boots into a plastic grocery bag. He smiled and handed me a glass of wine. Together we sat drinking Apulian red wine in Frederick II's honor and watching soccer games on satellite television — not a bad way to spend my last night in Italy.

I left early the next morning, even though my flight wasn't taking off until the afternoon. I didn't want to leave anything to chance. I had to take a city train to a terminal and then catch another train to the airport, which was close to twenty miles away from central Rome. I didn't care if I had to sit around the airport for a few hours drinking rich Italian coffee. All I could think of was getting home. I knew I still had some potential problems ahead. I would be getting to JFK Airport fairly late. What if the last bus to LaGuardia (where I had to catch a connecting flight to Ithaca) had already departed? I supposed I could take a cab. But I didn't have any cash. What if my last remaining credit card didn't work in the ATM machine? And my American cell phone had been taken along with everything else, so I couldn't even call anyone when I got off the plane. It was almost enough to make me tense again — but not quite. I finally blew off my worries and got in line to check in my only remaining piece of luggage: a small, black, wheeled suitcase. I pulled a gaudy red, blue, and yellow plastic Old Navy bag from my suitcase to use for my carry-on luggage — which mostly consisted of my throwaway camera (I didn't want it to be zapped by the checked-baggage x-ray machine, which ruins conventional photographic film). I also put an Italian travel guidebook in the bag so on my plane ride to New York I could read about everything I'd missed seeing in Italy.

I had a *Twilight Zone* moment a short time after the plane took off. I was trying to figure out how to use the movie screen on the back of the seat in front of me. Each passenger had a personal movie player with a half-dozen different movies from which to choose. A five-minute promotional blurb for Al Italia Airlines came up first, and I didn't know how to bypass it. As I was sitting there, only half watching the screen, I suddenly saw a page from the Vatican Library's manuscript of *De Arte Venandi cum Avibus* float onto the screen. It was unmistakable, showing a flock of geese flying past and the dark, oddly shaped stain that runs through the middle of many of the pages. So here it was, the book I never got to see in Rome, taunting me, luring me back again. Maybe if I went back again someday, Sister Juscinta would finally open up its secrets to me.

And then a quote from the book came up on the screen, translated into Italian: "Nostra intenzione è far conoscere, attraverso quest'opera dedicata alla caccia con gli uccelli, le cose che sono, come sono, e di ricondurle alla certezza di un'arte." — Federico II di Svevia.

And then a rough English translation appeared: "Our purpose is to present the facts as we find them. Up to the present time the subject of falconry has been devoid of both artistic and scientific treatment." — Frederick II of Swabia.

I have no idea what that quote has to do with Al Italia Airlines. It was one of those rare examples of synchronicity and seemed aimed only at me — at least that's how I chose to look at it — and it made me feel good.

$e\rightarrow$

HOW DID I know how this trip would end? How did I know that I would be the last one standing at the baggage carousel at JFK, long after the other passengers had picked up their suitcases and left for their various destinations? The airline had accomplished what the Italian thieves had failed to do — they had lost my final piece of luggage and left me with nothing. I ran to the Al Italia office, filled out the lost luggage paperwork, and then raced outside the terminal to try to catch the last shuttle to LaGuardia. Something finally went right. I climbed aboard the bus, which only had one other passenger, and made my way across town to catch my other flight.

It was pouring when I landed in Ithaca — which was strange for late December, but the winter had been unusually mild up to that point in the Northeast, as it had been in Europe. As with most of the planes landing at Ithaca Airport, this one parked well away from the terminal, and the passengers had to disembark on the tarmac and run more than a hundred feet through the rain to get inside. I was wearing only a thin fleece jacket. By the time I reached the terminal, I was drenched. I had nothing left but the clothes on my back and the plastic Old Navy bag clutched in my hand, but it felt good. Nothing could beat me now.

EPILOGUE

WHEN I RETURNED from Italy, the first thing I did was take Macduff out of his flight chamber and start working with him. He seemed ready and eager to get back into the field, and his leg looked perfect. Although only a couple of weeks remained in duck season, I set about trying to get him back into shape, flying him hard every morning. Ducks had been fairly scarce on the local ponds so far. The fall and winter had been unusually mild. Many ducks still lingered farther north and hadn't been pushed south by storms yet, but I'd seen several high-flying duck flocks moving into the area during the previous few days, so I felt hopeful.

Shortly before dusk on Christmas, I checked several local ponds and on one of them saw a small flock of mallards splash down and disappear in the reeds along the edge. I was so eager that I got up well before dawn the next morning. It was once again the anniversary of Frederick's birth. I had no idea how Macduff would do on his first flight at mallards after his injury. Would he completely turn his nose up at them when I flushed them? Would he make a halfhearted stoop but pull out at the last second? Or would he go all out as he'd always done before and slam into a duck? And if he did clobber a mallard, would he reinjure himself? That would be the worst possible outcome. A veterinarian had told me there could well be some scarification in the muscle tissue of his left leg, making it less flexible and increasing the chances that something like this could happen again. Another injury in that leg might well spell the end of his career as a hunter. But I had to try; I had to hunt with him again before giving up and perhaps putting him in a captive-breeding project.

As it turned out, that morning was anticlimactic. I released him at the edge of the field and, as he rang up, I made my way carefully to where I'd seen the ducks the night before. But there was nothing on the pond. The ducks had apparently slipped away in the night and gone somewhere else.

So I blew my chance of getting a spectacular flight on Frederick's birthday, but three days later, it was a different story. Macduff blasted off eagerly as soon as I took his hood off, and he mounted high above me into a leaden winter sky. Then something happened as he got over the pond: he suddenly tightened his circles and started powering up, going higher and higher and higher. This almost always means he has seen ducks. As I peeked over the dike of the pond, I saw at least two mallards on the northeast corner and there were probably more. I knew I probably couldn't get them to flush from where I crouched at the west side of the pond, so I sprinted all the way around the entire pond, running along a path through the woods to get there, completely hidden from Macduff for several minutes. He held steady. I spotted him right away, a tiny speck in a gray sky, as I came running out the other side of the woods. I waited a few seconds, catching my breath and watching as he wheeled around, moving into perfect position, and then I charged, throwing myself bodily into the pond with a great splash.

Six mallards exploded from the pond, and Macduff turned downward, streaking after them like a guided missile. He cut down a hen mallard and shot back into the sky, looking back over his shoulder at the duck as it tumbled to the ground, and then he plummeted down after it. I ran as fast I could, but when I got there everything was under control and the duck was dead. I sat beside Macduff in the grassy field, watching him gorge on the mallard. He'd earned the reward.

Many thoughts went through my mind as I sat there with Macduff. It had been such a long and in many ways harrowing year. I felt as though in the past twelve months I had relived my entire life with all of its pain and frustrations. I had scraped away the scar tissue that blanketed my mind for decades — helping me to cope but also cutting me off in so many ways from life. I realized I'd been sleepwalking for the past forty years, and now it had come to an end. It was not an easy process. There were times, especially during my journey through Italy, when I thought

I could not go on — when I was overwhelmed by the sense of loss that runs like an unbroken, melancholy thread through my life. But what I attempted was ultimately a good thing. I'd roiled up the demons lurking deep in my psyche and then cast them out, and I felt better. Now I see life with a new clarity.

I had many questions when I began my personal quest twelve months earlier, mostly pondering why falconry had taken over my life so completely at such an early age. I'd hoped to use falconry as a device for exploring my psyche, and in that I was successful. Going back to my earliest days in the sport, when my passion for falconry was at its highest intensity, blasted through the fog I'd built up and unleashed a flood of memories. People, places, and events came cascading out in brilliant detail. I realized that falconry did not create the person I am. I was already an intense kid. What it did was provide the perfect outlet for me. I could focus all my energies on a sport — an art, really — that was all encompassing, that would take years to perfect. And I had the ideal temperament for it. I've always had the kind of voice, way of moving, and attitude that seems to be soothing to animals, which made it easier for me to work successfully with wild raptors. (I like to think that if I had lived in Frederick II's court, he would have singled me out to develop as one of his falconers.) Without falconry, there's no telling what direction my life would have taken or where I would've ended up, but I fear it would not have been good. Falconry really did save my life.

I thought of Frederick II's words: a falconer "must be diligent and persevering, so much so that as old age approaches he will still pursue the sport out of pure love of it," persisting in its practice "so that he may bring the art itself nearer to perfection." And I knew I'd never give up the sport again, come what may.

I finally picked Macduff up from the duck kill and gently wiped the blood and feathers from his bill with my fingers. Then I took a long walk around the field with him as he sat on my fist, fluffed up and contented. I have no idea how long Macduff and I will be able to keep up our hunting, year after year. But I know we're a team, and our fates are inextricably linked. So, "Lay on, Macduff, and damned be he who first cries 'Hold. Enough!'"

ACKNOWLEDGMENTS

I OWE A deep debt of gratitude to dozens of people — too many to list here — who helped me over the years to develop as a falconer and a person. I especially thank Jeff Sipple, whom I've known since I was twelve years old, for his steadfast friendship and generosity through all the ups and downs of my life; and Hollis Roberts — probably the most brilliant falconer who no one's ever heard of — who was my closest hawking partner in my late teens and twenties. I thank Jimmie White for helping my family and me get through an extraordinarily difficult time and also for making his personal collection of classic falconry books available to me when I was young and eager to gain a deeper knowledge of the sport. And I'm eternally grateful to my mother, Daphne Gallagher, and my sisters, Maureen Coleman and Janet Gallagher, for always standing by me — no matter what I did, no matter how much I screwed up my life.

I thank all the people who helped me in various ways with my travels while I was writing this book, such as author Roger Upton — master storyteller and unofficial historian of British falconry — and his son, Mark, who took care of me during my stay in Caithness, Scotland, and made sure that I got to see the best of traditional grouse hawking. I thank my Italian friends, Umberto Caproni, Fulco Tosti, and Ferrante ("Frikky") Pratesi, who — in addition to providing me with a dream vacation hawking red grouse with them in the highlands of Scotland — gave me a chance to experience what it's like to live like a duke. I thank John Loft, author, scholar, and friend, for the many letters and e-mails we exchanged over the years and for arranging to meet me in northern England to go hawking. And I appreciate the hospitality and good humor of Nick Fox in the days I spent crow hawking with him in Northumberland. These are memories I will cherish for the rest of my life.

I thank all of the superb falconry authors throughout history who inspired me with their writings. Foremost will always be Frederick II of Hohenstaufen, who did more for falconry than anyone who ever lived and would surely be the patron saint of falconers if an excommunicated man could be a saint. (All of Frederick's quotes come from the 1943 reprint of his falconry book, translated by Casey A. Wood and F. Marjorie Fyfe and titled *The Art of Falconry; Being the De Arte Venandi cum Avibus of Frederick II of Hohenstaufen*, published by Stanford University Press.) Another favorite of mine is Edward Blair Michell, the nineteenth-century bare-knuckle boxing champion, rower, and all-around athlete who through his book, *The Art and Practice of Hawking*, sparked my interest in training merlins. (Michell's boxing quote comes from the Badminton Library volume, *Fencing, Boxing, and Wrestling*, by E. B. Michell and others, published by Longmans, Green, and Company of London in 1889.) And Ronald Stevens, who had few equals as a writer and falconer, helped me to succeed in both fields of endeavor through his excellent books — *The Taming of Genghis, Laggard*, and *Observations on Modern Falconry*. I'm indebted to author Jack Mavrogordato for the insights and advice he presented in *A Hawk for the Bush* and *A Falcon in the Field* — two of the best books ever written on the sport. And I thank Phillip Glasier for writing his excellent memoir, *As the Falcon Her Bells*, which I read several times as a teenager. (I was fortunate enough to meet both Jack Mavrogordato and Phillip Glasier at different times while attending American falconry meets.) I also appreciate my friend and fellow author Stephen Bodio, whose book *A Rage for Falcons* is one of the best works I've read on American falconry. But the two authors who fill me most with admiration and nostalgia are famed conservationists Frank and John Craighead, who inspired me as a boy with their *National Geographic* falconry articles and their book, *Hawks in the Hand*. The books written by these and other authors provided me with a solid intellectual basis in falconry and helped me succeed at an early age as a game hawker.

I also thank the authors of the many historical works on Frederick II that I read in the course of my research for this book. I particularly enjoyed Ernst Kantorowicz's 1931 tome, *Frederick the Second, 1194–1250* (published by Constable and Company Ltd. of London), which I first read in my midteens. (Most of the historical quotes from figures other than Frederick come from this book.) Kantorowicz's unabashed enthusiasm for Frederick — especially during the young emperor's boyhood and his ascent to power — make it a joy to read. But I also appreciate David Abufalia's fine work, *Frederick II: A Medieval Monarch*, which in many ways served as a useful antidote to Kantorowicz's sometimes rhapsodic, over-the-top accounts of Frederick. I loved reading Janet Ross's book, *The Land of Manfred, Prince of Tarentum and King of Sicily* (published by J. Murray of London in 1889), about her rambles in remote parts of southern Italy, which at the time, in the 1880s, had remained unchanged for centuries. The sad tale of the Hohenstaufens is a central thread running through the entire work. This is travel writing at its best and made me yearn to have experienced the peasant culture of Apulia in the late nineteenth century, long before radio, television, mass advertising, and consumerism changed and homogenized everything. I read many more books about Frederick II, but these are the ones that stand out to me and were the most useful in my research.

Although I was not able to read her books, which are only available in Italian, Daniela Boccassini of the University of British Columbia (author of *Il volo della mente: Falconeria e sofia nel mondo mediterraneo: Islam, Federico II, Dante*) kindly provided useful information and advice during a series of e-mail exchanges and telephone conversations.

Oscar Wilde's description of his visit to Frederick II's tomb came from *Selected Prose of Oscar Wilde*, edited by Jim Manis and published in 2006 by Pennsylvania State University Press, Hazelton, Pennsylvania. Pliny's quote about the falconers of Thrace came from *British Birds of Prey*, by William Kenneth Richmond, published by Lutterworth Press of London in 1959.

I am indebted to my literary agents, Maria Carvainis and Donna Bagdasarian, for their expert advice and encouragement through every phase of this project, and my booking agent, Jonathan Tunick, of Main

Stage Productions, who always sends me to such interesting places to speak.

And I thank everyone at Houghton Mifflin who helped make *Falcon Fever* a success, especially lead editor Lisa White, who worked with me on the project from the beginning, and manuscript editor Lisa Glover, who took *Falcon Fever* from a messy manuscript to a finely polished book. Thanks also to publicist Taryn Roeder, for promoting the book and arranging my tours, reviews, and interviews.

Above all, I thank my wife, Rachel Dickinson — a fellow author, who took time away from her own writing to read early drafts of *Falcon Fever* and provided invaluable advice and encouragement throughout the project. And I thank my children, Railey, Clara, Jack, and Gwendolyn, for putting up with all of my travels to faraway places and my state of distraction for months on end as I worked on this book. Without their support, none of this would have been possible.